INTERNATIONAL BAC

WAYS OF KNOWING
An introduction to

THEORY OF KNOWLEDGE

SECOND EDITION

Michael Woolman

Introduction

First published in 1999 by IBID Press, Victoria,

Completely revised 2006

Published by IBID Press, Victoria.

Library Catalogue:

Woolman M

1. Ways of knowing, An introduction to Theory of Knowledge

2. International Baccalaureate. Series Title: International Baccalaureate in Detail

ISBN: 1 876659 07 6

IBID Press thank the following owners of copyright for permission to reproduce their work: Aidan Seery, Kirti Joshi, David Pritchard, Tina Hickey & the United Nations.
The Book of Virtues by William J. Bennett. Reprinted with the permission of Simon & Schuster from *The Book of Virtues* by William J. Bennett. Copyright © 1993 by William J. Bennett.
An Intelligent Person's Guide to Ethics by Mary Warnock. Duckworth 1998. Reprinted with the permission of Gerald Duckworth from *An Intelligent Person's Guide to Ethics* by Mary Warnock. Copyright © 1998 Mary Warnock.
The Principles of Newspeak from *Nineteen eighty four* by George Orwell, copyright 1949 by Harcourt Inc. and renewed 1977 by Sonia Brownell Orwell, reprinted by permission of the publisher.
Is Economics a Science? by Arthur Williamson and *Is Economics a Science?* a reply by Seamus Hogan, published in *Chem NZ*, Number 47, May 1992, © 1992 the journal of the New Zealand Institute of Chemistry.

Diagrams by Mirko Cirrito.

Cover design by Adcore.

Published by IBID Press, 36 Quail Crescent, Melton, 3337, Australia.

Printed in China by Everbest Printing Co. Ltd.

To Maja

"All science is either physics or stamp collecting."

Ernest Rutherford

(Who was of course a physicist)

"... As imagination bodies forth

The form of things unknown, the poet's pen

Turns them to shapes, and gives to airy nothing

A local habitation and a name."

William Shakespeare

(Who was of course a genius)

PREFACE TO THE ORIGINAL EDITION

Theory of Knowledge teachers are professional questioners. They ask questions to stimulate their students to explore ideas, to promote thought and to encourage awareness of what it is to know. In order to begin to answer many of these questions students need a core of knowledge about knowledge. This book has been put together to provide that core. In it I have summarised fundamental Theory of Knowledge concepts and presented them simply and precisely. With this basic core of knowledge available to their students Theory of Knowledge teachers can continue to ask their questions confident of their students' awareness of the issues and concepts embedded in the questions.

The content and structure of the book comes from the International Baccalaureate Theory of Knowledge Programme; from my contact with the many experts that induct international school teachers into that programme; from my experience as a Theory of Knowledge examiner and from my years as a teacher at Munich International School. I owe a particular debt of gratitude to Mary Enda Tookey not only for a fine course I once attended in New Mexico but also for the stimulating journal Forum which she so skillfully edited and which is an inspiration to Theory of Knowledge teachers throughout the world. My debts to her, and to the other International Baccalaureate Theory of Knowledge teachers and examiners, are immense. If, however, in attempting to reduce Theory of Knowledge to its debatable basics I have distorted or omitted significant ideas, the fault is entirely mine.

My thanks go to the Board of Directors of Munich International School and the Head of School, Dr. Ray Taylor, not only for the sabbatical they granted me to complete this book but also for their encouragement. I am grateful too to my colleagues at school: Aidan Seery, David Pritchard and Kirti Joshi who contributed; Jean-Marie Briginshaw who nagged me to ensure I kept my English simple and ESL-friendly; Anna Wietrzychowska for meticulously reading the drafts, and Helen Thomas for her patient support in the library.

Finally I thank Maja and all my ToK students over the last several years. Maja is real, real smiles and scowls. She was in my class. She isn't exactly as I have portrayed her but whenever I was writing and unsure exactly how to proceed I thought of her and her alert presence in class and wrote as I would speak to her. I hope this book will make Theory of Knowledge as accessible and enjoyable to all students who use it as it was, I hope, for Maja.

REVISED EDITION

Thank you to all those students and teachers who have commented on the First Edition. Your comments and advice have, I hope, led to improvements. And as many of you ask, yes, Maja is real and flourishing. This edition includes, amongst many other changes, extra material on Faith as a Way of Knowing. For advice on that I especially thank Dr. Aidan Seery of the Education Department at Trinity College Dublin. Despite the fact that she frequently finds my ways of knowing a little weird, I also thank my partner, Ann Hickey, for her encouragement and support.

Michael Woolman,

Coudrée, France 2006.

CONTENTS

AN INTRODUCTION...

NOT TO THIS BOOK BUT TO THEORY OF KNOWLEDGE

By the time you leave high school to go to college you have acquired a lot of formal knowledge, a lot of 'academic' knowledge. You have studied your own language and learned how to use it effectively. You have probably also studied a second modern language, a subject from the natural sciences (biology, chemistry, physics, environmental systems), some mathematics, a subject or two selected from the arts (perhaps music, literature, drama or art), some subject from the human sciences (psychology, or economics, maybe) and almost certainly you have been introduced to history, in some form or other, and aspects of geography or earth science.

May I introduce my good friend, Theory of Knowledge, You may not realise it but my good friend here has two very distinctive features...

Each of these different subjects, or disciplines, you have studied, is special in its own way. What you have learned in science is a different kind of knowledge from the knowledge you have learned in history. And what you have learned in history is a different kind of knowledge from the knowledge you have learned in mathematics. 'Of course it is', I can hear you impatiently saying, 'in science we learn about the physical world; in history we learn about the past; in maths we learn about abstract space and quantity. Of course these subjects are different'. And you are right. These disciplines have their own subject matter, their own content, with which you are already very familiar.

These subjects are different in other ways too. They are different in the way their knowledge is created. The way in which scientists advance the boundaries of scientific knowledge is different from the way historians add to their historical knowledge. And mathematicians have quite a distinct way of creating mathematical knowledge. This means also that the nature of the knowledge itself, not only its content, varies from discipline to discipline. The kind of knowledge you have acquired from studying science is a different kind of knowledge from the knowledge you have acquired in math or history. Theory of Knowledge examines these differences. It examines each of these disciplines, science, history and math, and looks at the 'truth' that underpins their concepts and at their tests for validity. **That is the first distinctive feature of Theory of Knowledge to which you should be introduced: Theory of Knowledge examines the nature of knowledge in each of the disciplines.** Each discipline is not, of course, entirely independent. History uses science and mathematics, science uses mathematics and history. Theory of Knowledge explores not only what is distinctive about each academic discipline but also what it has in common with other disciplines.

Of course you have learned many other things in your life, both in and out of school, in addition to the formal knowledge of the school disciplines. You have acquired a set of values which decide, for instance, how you treat other people, where you go for your holidays, what books you read, how you decorate your bedroom walls, what tattoos you have and where you have them, what your study habits are, how you will vote at the next election, and under what circumstances, if any, you are prepared to lie or to kick your grandmother to death. Theory of Knowledge explores the nature of the knowledge on which your values and beliefs are based.

That brings us to **the second distinctive feature of Theory of Knowledge to which you should be introduced: Theory of Knowledge explains how we know what we know, our ways-of-knowing.** Before you look at the nature of science, or math or history we need to begin to understand the different ways-of-knowing we have acquired since we were born, and just as significantly the ways-of-knowing the human race has acquired, since, or even before, we first started to use our brains. We know certain things because our senses perceive them. Other things we know because we reason them out. Some things we know through our intuition, or through our beliefs. We know things in a variety of ways. Being aware of these ways-of-knowing is part of Theory of Knowledge. When we begin to understand how we know something we are on the way to understanding the value of what we know.

Theory of Knowledge also invites you to think critically about both the different forms of knowledge and different ways-of-knowing. You are invited to evaluate the relevance and significance of different disciplines and relate them to your values and your own ways of knowing, thinking, learning and creating. Different disciplines demand different ways of thinking. Because of this, Theory of Knowledge will help you with your other studies: if you know what a subject is really about, as distinct from knowing something within that subject, then your understanding of that subject, and how to study it, will be widened. You will begin to understand why certain subjects are, for you, 'easier' than others, and this understanding will help you improve your performance in both those subjects you find challenging, and those you learn with ease.

Theory of Knowledge is not an abstract, academic subject, although understanding parts of it certainly requires abstract thought. Theory of Knowledge is a practical subject that helps you understand yourself and the subjects you are studying, or may study, in the future. It helps you to begin to understand not only the nature of different disciplines and how you respond to each one, but also your own way of thinking and learning and your own value system.

You know (although I'm not sure How I know) I might be able to make use of this creature, it's just a matter of getting to know.....

A NOTE FOR THE USER

This book is based on six premises about understanding Theory of Knowledge. These premises in turn suggest ways to use this book.

1.   That Theory of Knowledge is most effectively understood through the existing knowledge of the learner.
        When a new idea or concept is introduced the examples and illustrations to illuminate that idea should be provided by the learners. They must relate the new concepts to their own experience, turning their knowledge into an explicit understanding of the concepts which underpin Theory of Knowledge.

2.   That discussion is a key activity.
        Through discussion, knowledge, that is knowledge of language, of truth, of mathematics, of knowledge itself, becomes meaningful. Theory of Knowledge classes are occasions when students and teachers spend time talking and listening together and discussing the issues that are currently concerning them.

3.   That Theory of Knowledge classes should explore a wide variety of cultural perspectives.
        Using their explicit experience, students are able to explore different cultures within the group.

4.   That Theory of Knowledge is intellectually demanding and stimulating.
        To be increasingly aware of the way we adjust our ways of knowing to the knowledge we acquire is intellectually demanding. Approached as an interactive, experiential, discussion-based subject it is also intellectually stimulating.

5.   That Theory of Knowledge needs a framework within which it can be understood.
        Theory of Knowledge is not a linear subject, but students and teachers need a framework within which to structure their exploration of the subject. This structure needs to be flexible, but clearly visible.

6.   That Theory of Knowledge is something with which you involve yourself.
        Theory of Knowledge is something you do. One of the main aims of Theory of Knowledge is to engage students in thinking about the bases of the different kinds of knowledge and to question these bases, using their own experience and learning. For this reason each chapter is preceded by a list of suggestions of things to do before you read the chapter. The chapters also all end with suggestions for further things to do.

But you said use it, so I used it to light a fire. Theory of Knowledge is really helpful.

These suggestions are the most important part of the book. Some activities may best be undertaken individually, others may be group activities. Some may require written responses, others oral. Whether individual or group, written or oral, Theory of Knowledge requires the involvement of the learners, who must actively relate the material to their own experiences and ways of knowing and question, question, question. Don't just read this book, use it.

PROLOGUE

MAJA'S WAYS OF KNOWING

Maja is a 17 year old IB Diploma student. Here is a list of twelve things she claims to know. She claims to know a lot more than these twelve things of course, but these twelve 'things' represent knowledge she has acquired in different ways: knowledge which shows some of her different *ways-of-knowing*.

1. She knows a candle flame will be extinguished if she covers the candle with a glass jar.

2. She knows if the sum of two of the internal angles of a triangle equals 110° then the third internal angle will be 70°.

3. She knows that the construction of the Great Wall of China began in about 210 BC.

4. She knows the Olympic Games were held in Athens in 2004.

5. She knows how to ride a bicycle.

6. She knows it is wrong to steal.

7. She knows the manufacture of land mines should cease.

8. She knows the moods of her friend Aravapo.

9. She knows how it feels to be in love.

10. She knows how her friend, who has just failed his driving test, feels.

11. She knows when she dies she is going to heaven.

12. She knows how to breathe.

Each of these things she knows in a different way. But what does it mean to say she 'knows in a different way'?

Look again at the list of things she claims to know and, as you do, decide if you agree with the short description of the way-of-knowing that follows each claim. Decide also what the attributed way-of-knowing means: what does it mean for instance to have knowledge which *is empirical*, or *intuitive* or based on her *faith*?

Introduction

1. **She knows a candle flame will be extinguished if she covers the candle with a glass jar.**
She knows this because she saw it happen. She knows it *empirically*. Empirically means by observation, by the use of her senses. In the science laboratory she covered a burning candle with a glass jar and *saw* its flame go out.

2. **She knows if the sum of two internal angles of a triangle equal 110° then the third internal angle will be 70°.**
She knows this *logically*. If the sum of two internal angles of a triangle is 110° and she knows that the sum of all the internal angles of a triangle is 180°, then logically she knows that if she subtracts 110 from 180 she will get 70, the size of the remaining angle.

3. **She knows the construction of the Great Wall of China began in 210 BC.**
She knows this by *authority*. She read about the construction in a history textbook which was written by an authority on Chinese History. (Where and how 'Authority' gets its knowledge is, of course, what much of Theory of Knowledge is about.)

4. **She knows that the Olympic games were held in Athens in 2004.**
She knows this by *memory*. She can remember the Olympic Games of 2004 and knows that they took place in Athens, the capital city of Greece.

5. **She knows how to ride a bicycle.**
She knows this through *practice*. When she was a child she was given a bicycle and learned how to ride it by practising with it.

6. **She knows it is wrong to steal.**
She knows this because her *conscience* tells her it is wrong to steal. From an early age she has been aware of her conscience guiding her behaviour.

7. **She knows the manufacture of land mines should cease.**
She knows this because of her *moral belief*. She is aware land mines kill people and she believes killing people is evil and therefore the manufacture of land mines should cease.

8. **She knows her friend Aravapo.**
She knows him by *acquaintance*. She and Aravapo have been friends since they started school together in kindergarten and Maja has grown up with him and understands his family background, character, values, beliefs and attitudes.

9. **She knows how it feels to be in love.**
She is in love with Aravapo's friend Leo who also loves her. She has examined her own feelings about Leo and knows that she is what is known as 'in love' with him. She knows this by *introspection*. She also knows she loves her mother and father and her sister because of the deep affection she has for them.

10. **She knows how Aravapo, who has just failed his driving test, feels.**
She knows this by *empathy*. Although Maja herself has not taken the driving test she is able to put herself in Arapavo's situation and know how he feels.

11. **She knows when she dies she is going to heaven.**

She knows this by *faith*. Her faith in god tells her that she will go to heaven when she dies.

12. **She knows how to breathe.**

She knows by *instinct*. From the moment she was born she began to breathe and has continued to breathe ever since. Although occasionally aware of her breathing, most of the time she simply breathes without thinking at all that she is, continually, breathing.

THE BEWITCHMENT OF THE WORD 'KNOWS'.

As you will read (in chapter 5) language can bewitch your understanding: it can lead you to believe you understand or 'know' something when perhaps you haven't understood it or only partially know it. Here is an example of that bewitchment of understanding.

When Maja claims to 'know' something, the meaning of 'know' is bewitching. When Maja says she 'knows' there are 180° in a triangle that 'knows' is quite a different kind of 'knows' to the 'knows' she has when she empathises with Aravapo when he has failed his driving test. Her knowing has moved from the impersonal, rational knowledge of mathematics to the personal, emotional knowledge of empathising. Because we have used the same word, 'knowledge' we can be bewitched into thinking it has the same meaning. Maja in fact has acquired knowledge, 'knows', in a variety of ways. These 'knows' or ways-of-knowing, to use a Theory of Knowledge term, can be very different. Since the days of Ancient Greece, academic thinkers[1] have been fascinated by both ways of knowing and the nature of the knowledge that these ways of knowing create. It is quite clear, for instance, that mathematical knowledge is based on reason and that faith-based knowledge is not.

Maja's 'ways-of-knowing' are not equally convincing. Most of us would accept the validity of her logic and empiricism knowledge as being rational, based on a reasoning we all understand and accept. Some of her other ways-of-knowing produce knowledge we might be tempted to be a little cautious about accepting as rational. Maja herself may be just as certain that when she dies she is going to heaven as she is that the internal angles of a triangle when added together equal 180 degrees. She 'knows' she is going to heaven because she holds certain values; values based on her emotional response to her experience of being alive and living with other human beings. These values are just as convincing to her as those empirical or logical truths which we all can accept as valid.

In Theory of Knowledge we attempt to understand these different ways-of-knowing and to evaluate them to help us become critical thinkers. Critical, that is, not in a negative sense, but in seeing the knowledge presented to us for what it is. If we understand the nature and source of the knowledge we are presented with, we are able to evaluate and respond to it in the light of our evaluation. Maja's emotional empathetic way of knowing may be quite different from her logical, rational way of knowing but the knowledge created by her ways-of-knowing are equally important.

We also attempt to understand how appropriate a particular way-of-knowing is for each of the subjects we study. How do we 'know' in science? In history? In economics? In psychology? In literature? In art? And in addition to these 'academic' subjects what ways-of-knowing underpin

---

1. The study of the varieties, grounds and validity of knowledge is called *epistemology*, (from the Greek word *episteme*). Epistemology is a branch of philosophy and the philosophers who study it are *epistemologists*.

what we call ethics or morals? What kind of knowledge is ethical knowledge? Can faith or empathy or instinct really provide us with knowledge? Are logic and empiricism the only acceptable ways-of-knowing in our academically oriented world?

For two and a half thousand years epistemologists have attempted to answer questions similar to these. Plato in the 5th Century BC produced a precise definition of a way-of-knowing. It is a definition that many subsequent philosophers have admired, and still continue to admire. But it is limited. It applies only to those ways of knowing based on reason. Plato's definition of knowledge, Propositional Knowledge, describes the high status knowledge we are introduced to in schools and universities. In the next chapter we will look at what Plato means by Propositional Knowledge, his Knowledge by Description.

Now *you have read the Prologue and met Maja, consider or undertake the following:*

1. *Look again at the twelve ways Maja 'knows'. List twelve things you know in the ways Maja knows. Discuss the lists you have made, matching the appropriateness of the 'knowledge' you have chosen with the way-of-knowing to which it belongs.*

2. *Are there any ways-of-knowing that you see as obviously missing from the list?*

3. *The 'official 'ToK programme divides ways of knowing into four categories: perception, reason, emotion and language. How easy is it to fit Maja's ways of knowing into these categories?*

4. *Is it understandable that some people value certain of these ways-of-knowing, and the knowledge created by these ways of knowing, more than they do others? Attempt to make a league table of the knowledge created by Maja's ways of knowing, starting with the knowledge you consider would be most universally accepted as the most important. How valid is the idea implied in this exercise, that there is a hierarchy of knowledge?*

SECTION ONE
WAYS-OF-KNOWING

PERCEPTION

1

CHAPTER CONTENTS

- Sensation
- Perception
- The word 'perception'
- Some complications
- 'Empirical' knowledge
- The Allegory of the Cave

SECTION ONE:
WAYS OF KNOWING

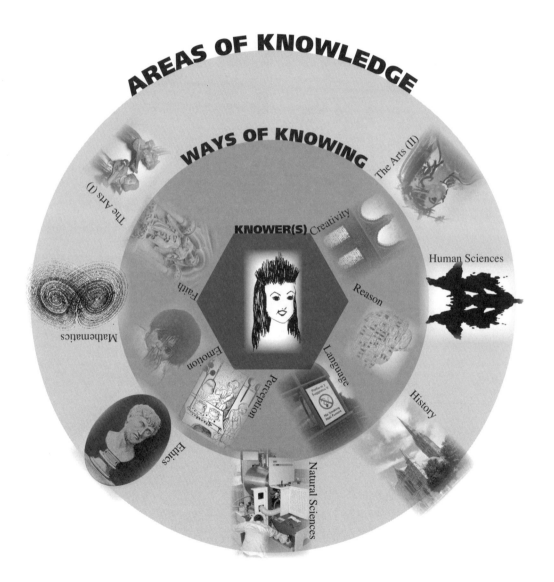

1.0 PERCEPTION

A SENSATIONAL WAY OF KNOWING

Before *you read Chapter 1 ...*

consider possible responses to these:

1. Think of specific ways in which you have used your senses today to give you knowledge of what is going on in the world around you. Did the senses alone give you the knowledge?

2. Magicians entertain by deceiving us. Describe a magic 'trick' you have seen and attempt to explain how it was done and how you were deceived.

3. What possible reasons could there be for 'clubs' to keep the lights low and the volume of the music high?

4. Attempt to imagine how a dog would perceive the room you are in now.

5. 'I see' often means 'I understand'. Why don't we say 'I taste' or 'I smell' instead?

'Disco-gym'

SENSATIONS

At any one moment our senses are gathering vast amounts of information. As you read this, your senses, as well as telling you what you are reading and where you are reading it, are telling you who else is in the room, what colour the walls are, the temperature, the brightness of the light that is enabling you to see the page, the clock in the corner is ticking, the shoe is pinching your big toe, the collar is touching your neck, and if you are unlucky, the taste of what you had for breakfast. And a myriad of other things you can list for yourself if you pause and let yourself be aware of these sensations.

SENSE THRESHOLD

What we can actually sense depends on what psychologists call our sense threshold. Different animals have different thresholds. A tracker dog's sense of smell is quite different from a human's sense of smell and there is even a great difference between the senses of smell amongst humans. In a crowded room with lots of people speaking I find it very difficult to focus on the one or two people I may be having a conversation with. What I have to do is attempt to filter out all that background noise and concentrate on what is being said in my small group. This is known as 'signal detection' and when I do this I am trying to minimize all the sounds other than those coming from my group. I am deliberately trying to filter the sensations I am receiving.

Maja knows a candle flame will be extinguished if she covers the burning candle with a glass jar. She knows this because she has used one of her senses, sight, and seen it happen. The most obvious way Maja, and the rest of us, know anything is through our senses. Our senses connect us to our environment through touch, taste, sight smell and sound.

BEWARE BEWITCHMENT

Language in general and words in particular 'bewitch our intelligence' (you can read more about that in Chapter 5) as easily as our senses are bewitched by our perception. 'Perception' is certainly one of those bewitching words.

In the statement 'Our sense perception enables us to relate the world', 'perception' would seem to be a straightforward process. What is out there we see or smell and therefore interpret the world around us.

'Perception' in everyday language means something a little different. It means 'opinion judged on your experience'. If you are asked the question 'What is your perception of Maja?' You are being asked for much more than a physical description of Maja. You are being asked 'What, in the light of your experience, is Maja like?'

Often the phrase 'My perception of the situation was ...' is used. The implication here is that there is possibly another interpretation of the situation. 'Perception' here means 'my interpretation'

Our brains, the physical organs through which we 'know' everything, are insulated from the 'real world' by our skulls, strong walls of bone. We can receive knowledge into our brains only through the connections that link the brain to the 'real world'.

These connections are linked to:

- our eyes, which respond to wavelengths of electromagnetic radiation or 'light';

- our ears, which respond to changes in air pressure or 'sound';

- our noses and tongues which respond to chemicals or 'smell' and 'taste';

- our skin, which senses change in temperature and humidity or 'tactility'.

The sensations of light, sound, smell, taste and tactility are turned into nerve impulses, or messages. These impulses, or messages, are the only information the brain receives. The brain itself has no direct contact with the outside world. Using the impulses our brains create the 'real world' inside our skulls.

'PERCEPTION'

'Perception' is one of those words which is worth thinking about.

In the statement 'Our sense perception enables us to appreciate the world' 'perception' would seem to be a straightforward process. What is out there we see or smell and the perception of what we see and smell is reasonably objective.

'Perception' in everyday language means something a little different. It means 'opinion judged on your experience'. If you are asked the question 'What is your perception of Maja?' You are being asked for much more than a physical description of Maja. You are being asked 'What, in the light of your experience, is Maja like?'

Often the phrase 'My perception of the situation was ...' is used. The implication here is that there is possibly another interpretation of the situation. 'Perception' here means 'my interpretation'.

SEE

SMELL

SAY

TOUCH

HEAR

A simple analogy is that of an insulated underground bunker following a nuclear explosion. Any people in the bunker (the brain) can receive information only through any sensors they may have available to them. They may have temperature and radioactivity sensors and video-cameras monitoring the outside world, but they do not have direct access to it. The information they have is only that which the sensors give them, plus their experience in interpreting that information.

PERCEPTION

But, 'knowing' through our senses isn't only being aware of the sensations bombarding us. Our brains don't just receive signals, they interpret them, placing the signals in the context of everything they already know. Our brains do this automatically. They can't do otherwise.

On the following pages you will find a list of some of the 'information' the brain uses when interpreting the sense signals it receives. You can probably think of other experiences to add to this list. You will certainly be able to provide examples from your own experience to add to those given.

Because our brains continually interpret the sense data they receive, some psychologists and philosophers claim that the old adage:

> seeing is Believing .....

> > should really be .....

> > > Believing is Seeing

EMPIRICAL KNOWLEDGE

Knowledge that we obtain through our senses is called empirical knowledge.

The word *empiric* comes from the name of Sextus Empiricus, a philosopher and physician who lived and worked in Alexandria and later Athens in the 3rd century AD. Little is known about him but one of his main works *Against the Professors* is an early Theory of Knowledge treatise in which he examines the nature of knowledge in the arts and sciences. In this work he defined the two main principles of what is now known as empiricism:

One: All knowledge is based on experience, especially the experience of the senses.

Two: The knowledge we acquire through experience is the basis of understanding, which is the making of that experience meaningful to us.

Hard line empiricists claim that all knowledge must be based on 'the test of experience'. They reject all other ways of knowing. It is not always clear what is meant by 'the test of experience'. A common understanding of the word is 'based on observation and experiment', the former of which is completely sense dependent.

PERCEPTION: SOME COMPLICATIONS

Beware of what your senses tell you. Or, more accurately, beware of how your brain filters what your senses tell you. Often your brain uses information it already has to interpret what you see and feel and hear and touch and smell. This interpretation can easily distort the 'reality'. Here are some of the ways your brain may filter information from your senses.

1. *Through your past experience.*
Your past experience can often condition you to expect things and we often see or hear what we expect rather than what really happens.
What does your past experience tell you is going to happen when you are watching a movie and you hear low, slow, quiet music from the soundtrack?

2. *Through social and cultural conditioning.*
Our prejudices and assumptions often lead us to false conclusions.
What would you immediately think if a new male teacher came into the room this morning with an unshaven face, three earrings in each ear and wearing a T-shirt on which was written: Shit Happens?

3. *Through spatial familiarity.*
Our brain appears to need to want us to see patterns or shapes with which we are already familiar.
Most people who look at this two pronged trident try in vain to interpret it as a three dimensional object.

4. *Through our biological limitations.*
Our perception is limited by our biology. Humans can only perceive what their senses and nervous systems allow them to perceive. Some of us can certainly see further and hear more clearly than others, but none of us can see as clearly at night as an owl or hear as keenly as an elephant.
What would your 'real' world be if you had the sight of an eagle, the hearing of a dog or the taste buds of a cow?

5. *Through our existing learning structures.*
The way we perceive the world is influenced by an important part of our conceptual structure: how we use our brains to solve problems or create new knowledge for ourselves. If you are learning a foreign language, you try to use the conceptual structure you have learned from the other languages you already know. If the structure of those languages is different from those you already know you may have difficulties. If, for instance your known languages are all based on sentence structures that need verbs, and the new language sentences do not need verbs, you may have initial difficulties learning the language.

6. *Through seeing what is not there.*
We cannot explain what happens when we are faced with optical illusions. If something is not there, how can we see it?
How can you 'see' plaster mouldings around windows which turn out, on close inspection to be painted on a flat surface? These are at Jaiper in India.

7.   *Through our dependence on language.*
The labels we use for ideas and objects (our language) influence the way we think (or don't think) about those ideas and objects. Advertisers are very aware of the power of 'language' to influence our perception of products.
What does the word 'colonial' mean to you?

8.   *Through filtering.*
Our senses receive much more information than we are capable of processing. At any one time, we filter out much of the information we are receiving and accept only that which is understandable or of interest. Sometimes we don't even notice things we don't understand. If you visit Russia without knowing any Russian, you will not even notice many street signs or directions or advertisements which you cannot understand.

9.   *Through self perception.*
Finally, we have a perception of ourselves. It is different, probably, from the perception others have of us. But it seems likely that how we think of ourselves will influence our perception of ourselves in relationship to others.
I, Michael Woolman, regard myself as a kindly, benevolent man with the best interests of my students at heart. How does this influence my perception of you, as students?

PLATO'S ILLUSTRATION OF THE PERCEPTION'S FILTERS

The great Greek philosopher Plato, as we shall see, was a pioneer of Theory of Knowledge. He also did pioneering work on understanding sensation and perception. Here is his famous *Allegory of the Cave*. (From Chapter 7 of *The Republic*).

'I want you to go on to picture the enlightenment or ignorance of our human condition somewhat as follows. Imagine an underground chamber like a cave, with a long entrance open to the daylight and as wide as the cave. In this chamber are men who have been prisoners there since they were children, their legs and necks being so fastened that they can only look straight ahead of them and cannot turn their heads.

Some way off, behind and higher up, a fire is burning, and between the fire and the prisoners and above them runs a road, in front of which a curtain-wall has been built like the screen at puppet shows between the operators and their audience, above which they show their puppets.'

'I see.'

'Imagine further that there are men carrying all sorts of gear along behind the curtain-wall, projecting above it and including figures of men and animals made of wood and stone and all sorts of other materials, and that some of these men, as you would expect, are talking and some not.'

'An odd picture and an odd sort of prisoner.'

'They are drawn from life,' I replied. 'For, tell me, do you think our prisoners could see anything of themselves or their fellows except the shadows thrown by the fire on the wall of the cave opposite them?'

'How could they see anything else if they were prevented from moving their heads all their lives?'

'And would they see anything more of the objects carried along the road?'
Of course not.'

'Then if they were able to talk to each other, would they not assume that the shadows they saw were the real things?'

'Inevitably.'

'And if the wall of their prison opposite them reflected sound, don't you think that they would suppose, whenever one of the passers-by on the road spoke, that the voice belonged to the shadow passing before them?'

'They would be bound to think so.'

'And so in every way they would believe that the shadows of the objects we mentioned were the whole truth.'

'Yes, inevitably.'

'Then think what would naturally happen to them if they were released from their bonds and cured of their delusions. Suppose one of them were let loose, and suddenly compelled to stand up and turn his head and look and walk towards the fire; all these actions would be painful and he would be too dazzled to see properly the objects of which he used to see the shadows. What do you think he would say if he was told that what he used to see was so much empty nonsense and that he was now nearer reality and seeing more correctly, because he was turned towards objects that were more real, and if on top of that he were compelled to say what each of the passing objects was when it was pointed out to him? Don't you think he would be at a loss, and think that what he used to see was far truer than the objects now being pointed out to him?'

'Yes, far truer.'

'And if he were made to look directly at the light of the fire, it would hurt his eyes and he would run back and retreat to the things which he could see properly, which he would think really clearer than the things being shown him.'

'Yes.'

'And if,' I went on, 'he were forcibly dragged up the steep and rugged ascent and not let go till he had been dragged out into the sunlight, the process would be a painful one, to which he would much object, and when he emerged into the light his eyes would be so dazzled by the glare of it that he wouldn't be able to see a single one of the things he was now told were real.'

'Certainly not at first,' he agreed.

'Because, of course, he would need to grow accustomed to the light before he could see things in the upper world outside the cave. First he would find it easiest to look at shadows, next at the reflections of men and other objects in water, and later on at the objects themselves. After that he would find it easier to observe the heavenly bodies and the sky itself at night, and to look at the light of the moon and stars rather than at the sun and its light by day.'

'Of course.'

'The thing he would be able to do last would be to look directly at the sun itself, and gaze at it without using reflections in water or any other medium, but as it is in itself.'

'That must come last.'

'Later on he would come to the conclusion that it is the sun that produces the changing seasons and years and controls everything in the visible world, and is in a sense responsible for everything that he and his fellow-prisoners used to see.'

'That is the conclusion which he would obviously reach.'

'And when he thought of his first home and what passed for wisdom there, and of his fellow-prisoners, don't you think he would congratulate himself on his good fortune and be sorry for them?'

'Very much so.'

'There was probably a certain amount of honour and glory to be won among the prisoners, and prizes for keen sightedness for those best able to remember the order of sequence among the passing shadows and so be best able to divine their future appearances. Will our released prisoner hanker after these prizes or envy this power or honour? Won't he be more likely to feel, as Homer says, that he would far rather be "a serf in the house of some landless man", or indeed anything else in the world, than hold the opinions and live the life that they do?'

'Yes,' he replied, he would prefer anything to a life like theirs.'

'Then what do you think would happen,' I asked, 'if he went back to sit in his old seat in the cave? Wouldn't his eyes be blinded by the darkness, because he had come in suddenly out of the sunlight?'

'Certainly.'

'And if he had to discriminate between the shadows, in competition with the other prisoners, while he was still blinded and before his eyes got used to the darkness - a process that would take some time - wouldn't he be likely to make a fool of himself? And they would say that his visit to the upper world had ruined his sight, and that the ascent was not worth even attempting. And if anyone tried to release them and lead them up, they would kill him if they could lay hands on him.'

'They certainly would.'

PERCEPTION

SOME PERCEPTIVE COMMENTS ABOUT PERCEPTION

A.   *A fool sees not the same tree as a wise man sees.*

William Blake

B.   *People only see what they are prepared to see.*

Ralph Waldo Emerson

C.   *Were the eye not attuned to the Sun, the Sun could never be seen by it.*

Göethe

D.   *What can give us surer knowledge than our senses?*
With what else can we distinguish the true from the false?

Lucretius

E.   *A rock pile ceases to be a rock pile the moment a single man contemplates it, bearing within him the image of a cathedral.*

Saint-Exupery

F.   *All seeing is seeing-as ... There is no 'innocent eye'. Nietzsche called this the 'fallacy of the immaculate conception'. In order for you to receive something you must add to your sense datum; you must furnish an element of projection.*

R Abel

G.   *It seems that the human mind has first to construct forms, independently, before it can find them in things. Knowledge cannot spring from experience alone, but only from the comparisons of the inventions of the intellect with observed fact.*

Albert Einstein

H.   *Observers are not led by the same physical evidence to the same picture of the universe unless their linguistic backgrounds are similar or can in some way be calibrated.*

Benjamin Whorf

I.   *The subtlest and most pervasive of influences are those which create and maintain stereotypes. We are told about the world before we see it. We imagine most things before we experience them.*

Walter Lippman

J.   *The human brain craves understanding. It cannot understand without simplifying; that is without reducing things to a common element. However, all simplifications are arbitrary and lead us to drift insensibly away from reality.*

Lecomte du Nouy

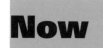

you have read Chapter 1...

consider or undertake the following:

1. What do YOU think the hard line Empiricists meant when they claimed that knowledge must be based on 'the test of experience'?

2. How appropriate do you find the analogy of the insulated bunker (page 19)? Can you think of a more suitable analogy?

3. Discuss each of the 9 'filters' described on page 21 and think of examples, from your own experience for each filter.

4. Read the *Allegory of the Cave* and discuss its relevance to the problems of perception. How could the allegory be made more meaningful to 21st century students?

5. Which of the comments on perception (page 25) seem most appropriate for you? Are there any with which you would disagree?

6. Knowledge, not eyes, it has been said, is the true organ of sight. Can knowing something help you to literally see things clearly?

7. Does technology's ability to enhance our sense perception change the reality of our world?

8. Are you morally obliged to be aware of your own perceptual filters?

SECTION ONE
WAYS-OF-KNOWING

JUSTIFIED TRUE BELIEF

2.1

CHAPTER CONTENTS

- Test for justified true belief
- Belief: necessity for knowing
- Truth: a working definition
- Justification: logic, empiricism, memory and authority
- A definition of knowledge

2.1 JUSTIFIED TRUE BELIEF

Before *you read Chapter 2.1 ...*

consider possible responses to these:

1. What are you claiming when you claim to know something? Does it vary according to the thing you are claiming to know or is it the same for each thing?

2. Under what circumstances could you justifiably claim your watch keeps perfect time?

3. Can you believe something without knowing it?

4. Can you know something without believing it?

Plato

2.1 JUSTIFIED TRUE BELIEF

Almost two and a half thousand years ago a wealthy and aristocratic Athenian, Plato, founded, in his city state, the Academy. This Academy became a centre for mathematical, philosophical and scientific research. It was, in fact if not in name, the first university. Plato and his students at the Academy, like professors and students in universities today, were concerned not only with the advancement of knowledge but also with being sure their knowledge really was valid; that it was something of which they could all be absolutely certain. For them the only way-of-knowing was a way-of-knowing that led to certainty, that led to certain knowledge. For them intuition or faith or empathy did not generate certainty. For the students at the Academy in general, and for Plato in particular, the only way-of-knowing that had certainty was a way-of-knowing which produced knowledge which could be both described and effectively and accurately communicated to others. They further agreed, not only must the knowledge be describable and communicable, it must also be absolutely convincing to any reasonable person.

This way-of-knowing, Plato's way-of-knowing, is often called *knowledge-by-description*. Another name for it is *propositional knowledge*. ('Propositional' here has nothing to do with sexual activity. This is not Plato describing sure-fire approaches to sexual propositioning, however knowledgeable he might have been about them). A proposition, here, is a formal statement of convincing knowledge. Knowledge by description also known as *knowing that* .... ('that' being the prelude to a specific statement, a statement that communicates a convincing piece of knowledge).

The way-of-knowing which produces knowledge-by-description, propositional knowledge, or knowing that ..... is regarded by many philosophers, because of its rational base, as the only acceptable way-of-knowing. For Plato the only real knowledge was knowledge you could be certain about and the certainty of which his academic colleagues would agree to accept.

In their search for certainty Plato, and his fellow academicians, asked themselves this question:

How can I be sure I know something?

They came up with an answer that is even now, almost two and a half thousand years later, still regarded as good an answer as you can get.

Let's look at this answer.

According to Plato and his colleagues, for you to be sure you know something, for you to have certain knowledge, knowledge-by-description, you have to subject a statement of what you know to three tests.

The first test is you must believe the statement.

The second test is your belief has to be true.

The third test is your true belief must be justified.

These may seem a strange trio of tests. The second test alone might seem to be sufficient if 'true' was defined carefully, and what is 'belief' doing there? And if a statement is true, why do you have to justify it? Isn't justification implied in truth?

THE THREE THINKERS
SOCRATES, PLATO AND ARISTOTLE

Socrates (469-399 BC) befriended and inspired Plato (428-347 BC) who in turn befriended and inspired Aristotle (388-322 BC).

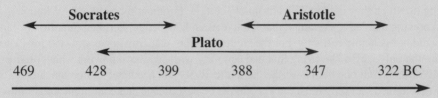

Socrates is well known for his use of questioning in teaching, which has become known as the Socratic Method. He asked his students or followers for definitions of concepts (usually moral concepts). If their answers exposed uncertainty or ambiguity of thought he encouraged them to deepen their enquiry by thinking again about the answer. He maintained that all wrong doing was based on ignorance, that no-one really wanted anything bad to happen and that it was more improper to act unjustly that it was to be the victim of injustice. Not surprisingly this doctrine did not go down well with the rulers of Athens who charged him, among other things, with the 'corruption of youth'. He was found guilty, sentenced to death and condemned to die at his own hands by drinking hemlock, a poison prepared from the herb of the same name. Despite offers from his friends to help him escape to exile, he took the poison.

Socrates wrote nothing himself but we know about him and his ideas through his disciple, **Plato**. In 387 BC Plato founded the Academy, which specialised in the study of mathematics and logic. Plato's own philosophical thought, which covered metaphysics, ethics and politics, was presented in written Dialogues, in which Socrates questions his students, whose answers are usually confused and contradictory. His most celebrated dialogue is *The Republic*, in which he develops the idea of a political paradise, ruled by philosopher-kings who have studied the 'form of Good' and have total control. Most of Plato's ideas about knowledge and knowing are contained in his Gorgias Dialogues, a sample of which you can see on page 89.

Aristotle was a student at the Academy but then moved on to the island of Lesbos where he studied biology. After some time there he moved to Macedonia and became tutor to the child Alexander, (later, the Great). He returned to Athens in 335 BC and founded his own school, the Lyceum. Aristotle studied every field of known knowledge including logic, metaphysics, ethics, rhetoric, poetry, biology, physics and even psychology. Almost two thousand years after his death, during the Renaissance in Europe, he was known as The Philosopher. Today his works, especially the Organon (treatises on logic), Politics, Poetics and Ethics are still studied and valued.

Let's look closely at the tests described on page 29 and see precisely what Plato means by justified, true belief, as he called it.

Let us assume you know, for certain, your watch keeps time absolutely accurately. You can, indeed say with certainty "I know for sure that my watch keeps time accurately".

According to Plato and his Academy colleagues, for you to really know your watch keeps accurate time, and for you to be able to convince other reasonable people that your watch keeps accurate time you must apply these three tests to your claim: you must believe it does, your belief must be true and your true belief must be justified.

TEST ONE: YOU MUST BELIEVE YOUR STATEMENT

You must believe your watch keeps accurate time

BELIEF

At this point you may well be asking yourself what has 'belief' got to do with knowing. You may know someone who believes the world would be a much better place if we all ate a kilo of cheese every day. Belief, you can claim, is an attitude of mind. Beliefs can be true or false, inspiring or ludicrous. So why has Plato got it into his mind to be concerned with belief as his first test for true knowledge?

Well, consider for a moment the statement 'I know that my watch keeps accurate time but I don't believe it'. This statement clearly does not make sense: it contradicts the meaning of the word 'know'. If you know something you must believe it. If you have no belief at all that your watch keeps accurate time then you cannot know that it does. Belief is an attitude of mind, but we need it before we can claim to know anything.

Many people, when they first come across this idea, find it rather strange that you must have belief before you can know something. But pause for a moment and work it out for yourself. Can you think of anything you can claim with certainty you know, and then claim you don't believe it? Plato was absolutely clear: for a statement to contain knowledge it has to be believed.

It might help you to understand this idea if you substituted the word 'conviction' for belief. Conviction is perhaps a more neutral word, without the emotional or religious overtones of belief, but it can mean something very similar. If you claim: I know my watch keeps perfect time but I'm not convinced it does, then the contradiction of your claim is made very clear. Likewise you couldn't claim to know you were sitting on a chair and yet not be convinced you were sitting on a chair or that you know your teacher thinks you are brilliant even though you are convinced that she thinks you are not.

But belief in itself is not enough. It is necessary to believe in the knowledge but that is not, in itself, sufficient. In philosophers' terms belief is a necessary condition for knowing but it is not a sufficient reason. Belief, as a way of knowing, is a much discussed concept. You can read more about it in Chapter 3.

Now let's look at test number two.

TEST TWO: YOUR BELIEF HAS TO BE TRUE.

Your watch must keep time accurately. If it loses five minutes every day then you cannot know that it keeps time accurately. Your belief has to be true.

TRUTH

Now, what does 'true' mean? Much has been said and written about the nature of truth. It is one of those words which bewitch the human intelligence. Philosophers cannot agree exactly, or even roughly, on what truth is. There are those who believe there is a single, absolute, objective truth. These are called, for obvious reasons, *absolutists*. And there are those who are utterly convinced that everything is subject to human interpretation. These are called *relativists*, as they regard everything as being relative to human understanding. For the purpose of our understanding of Plato's Justified True Belief we must be careful not to allow ourselves to be bewitched. Plato was an absolutist. Accept for a moment a simple three pronged, absolutist definition: truth is public, truth is independent of anyone's belief and truth is eternal. (See the box for a summary of what these things imply.)

THREE CHARACTERISTICS OF TRUTH

1
TRUTH IS PUBLIC

Truth is the same for everyone.

If p is true it is true for everyone.

If p is false it is false for everyone.

2
TRUTH IS INDEPENDENT OF ANYONE'S BELIEF

p may be false even if everyone believes it to be true

p may be true if nobody believes it to be true

3
TRUTH IS ETERNAL

A true statement is true, was true, and always will be true.

You can find more about Truth later but for the moment let's not be distracted from our consideration of Justified True Belief.

Now back to Plato's tests for his way-of-knowing, his knowledge by description.

TEST THREE: YOUR TRUE BELIEF MUST BE JUSTIFIED

You must have justification for your statement that your watch keeps time accurately.

JUSTIFICATION

What kind of evidence or good reason will give justification?

It is probably easy to justify your statement about the accuracy of your watch: you check it at eight o'clock in the morning when you listen to the news on the radio and it is always accurate to within one second; you use your watch to tell you when to go and catch the bus and it has always got you to the bus on time; you have had it for two years and the only time it wasn't accurate was when the battery needed changing and you changed the battery only three months ago. So logically and empirically you can be justified in stating that you know your watch keeps time accurately.

How do you justify other things you know to be true? Justification, for our purposes in defining knowledge-by-description, can be achieved in four ways: by logic, by empirical evidence, by memory and by authority. Let us briefly look at each of these ways of justifying.

GOOD REASON FOR JUSTIFICATION 1: LOGIC

The first source of evidence or good reason for your being justified in your belief is logic. Logic is the basis of much of our knowledge. As a ToK student you need to understand certain things about logic before, for instance, you can appreciate the differences between scientific knowledge and historical knowledge. In order not to get distracted from Justified True Belief let's think of it as simply *correct, universally accepted, reasoning*.

If you were at school last Friday at 3 p.m. you could not *logically* have been at home. I am speaking literally here, not metaphorically. I would like to think that you felt at home at school but feeling at home is not the same as being at home.

If you use a standard base 10 numerical system you know, *logically*, that $3 + 7 = 10$.

If I am visiting Tokyo and the Tokyo I am visiting is the capital of Japan then, *logically*, I know I am visiting the capital of Japan.

All logic, of course, is not as simple as this. There are two main divisions of logic, deductive logic and inductive logic. You can read more about deductive and inductive logic later. Logic, in whatever form, is an important justification for true belief.

Some philosophers, called Rationalists, claim that knowledge can only be obtained by logical deduction.

RATIONALISM

Rationalism is the doctrine or theory that reason rather than experience is the foundation for certainty in knowledge. Rationalists argue that experience cannot be trusted and can, therefore, give no sound reason for knowledge. If we can know anything at all they claim it is because we have reflected rationally upon it. This 'rational knowledge' is called *a priori* knowledge, knowledge which is created by reasoning and reasoning only. The Latin phrase *a priori* literally means 'from what is before' so rationalist knowledge is knowledge which comes 'from what is before' in our rational minds. Rationalists develop knowledge from what they claim are self evident facts, which are *a priori*, and which we know by rationalising. Mathematical axioms are good examples of *a priori* knowledge. You can read more about *a priori* knowledge in Chapter 8.

GOOD REASON FOR JUSTIFICATION 2: EMPIRICAL EVIDENCE

The second source of evidence or good reason for your being justified in your belief is what is called the empirical evidence of your own senses.

What your senses perceive, your sense perception, is one of the main sources of your knowledge of the world. Your five main senses are, of course, sight, touch, taste, smell and hearing.

You are justified in saying that some roses are red because you have seen a red rose.

You are justified in saying that concrete is hard because you have felt it.

You are justified in saying that sea water is salty because you have tasted it.

You are justified in liking the smell of roses because you have smelt them.

You are justified in recognising the sound of a helicopter cruising above because you have heard it.

But beware of sense perception. Everything is not what it appears to be. Generally you can rely on your senses but they can be beguiled; they can be fooled. You can never be absolutely sure your emotions are not involved in your perceiving. We will return to this problem later. The justification given previously for your belief in the accuracy of your watch is empirical evidence; evidence you have obtained by your experience with the watch.

GOOD REASON FOR JUSTIFICATION 3: MEMORY

The third source of evidence for your being justified in your belief is memory. Now memory is notoriously fickle (Where exactly were you last Friday at 3 p.m.?) Descartes, of whom more later, claimed that memory has been breathed into us by a malicious demon. But approached with care, memory is generally reliable. Can you remember the plot of the last novel you read? Or the last grade you got in History? Or the shape of the African continent as it is shown in a standard Mercator projection? Or the time of your bus home after school? Memory may be fickle and influenced by emotion but, used with care, it can be used as justification for belief although many philosophers would dispute this.

GOOD REASON FOR JUSTIFICATION 4: AUTHORITY

The fourth and final source of evidence which we will consider for your being justified in your belief, is authority. You know the mean distance from the earth to the sun is 150,000,000 kilometres because you have been told this by someone who is an authority on that subject and whom you have good reason to trust. You visit your doctor if you are ill because your doctor is an authority on illness and you have reason to trust him. Of course we must be very careful who we accept as an authority, but in our everyday lives we can accept that authorities do exist and that we can trust them.

BACK TO JUSTIFIED TRUE BELIEF

So, for you statement to qualify as knowledge-acceptable-to-Plato you must believe your watch is accurate, your watch in truth must be accurate and you must be justified in believing it is accurate.

Then you can say, "I know my watch keeps time accurately" and know you know that your watch does indeed keep time accurately. Applying Plato's three tests has given you a certain piece of knowledge-by-description that is describable, communicable and acceptable to other people.

You might think that the example of the watch is rather mundane and so it is. So, try substituting a rather more controversial and personal statement which might be relevant to some of you using this book.

I know that at the end of my twelfth grade I will obtain an IB diploma with at least forty points.

TEST ONE: BELIEF

Do you *believe* that at the end of your twelfth grade you will obtain an IB diploma with at least forty points. If you don't believe this then you cannot know it. It would be ridiculous to claim you know you are going to get a diploma with more than forty points if you really don't believe you are going to.

TEST TWO: TRUTH

Is it *true* that at the end of my twelfth grade I will obtain an IB diploma with at least forty points? Can you be sure of this? Is there any possible doubt you will get such a Diploma? Is it possible to know the truth about the future?

TEST THREE: JUSTIFICATION

Is your belief that you will get a diploma with forty points *justified*? Now, here we have to weigh the evidence. What are your predicted grades? Have you completed all the necessary course work? Are you a conscientious and talented student? Can you really justify the notion that you will get a diploma with at least forty points?

To what conclusions do these three tests lead you? Do you now know, with Plato's way-of-knowing, that at the end of the twelfth grade you will get an IB Diploma with at least forty points? Be sure now. Test the statement step by step. If you do not believe your claim, if your claim is not true, and if your claim is not justified then you do not have knowledge which measures up to Plato's way-of-knowing.

So now you have a neat little formula which you can use to test the different kinds of knowledge you meet in the various disciplines you study.

JUSTIFIED TRUE BELIEF

Or Propositional Knowledge or knowledge that …

Must be justified by empirical evidence or logic or memory or authority

Must be true

Must be believed

Only four, rational ways-of-knowing are used in the tests for justified true belief. But other ways-of-knowing are just as important to all of us. As ways-of-knowing acquaintance, belief, faith, introspection, empathy and conscience may have an emotional basis but they may also have more influence on decisions than logic, empiricism, memory and authority. Emotions may not generate justified true belief but they are important ways-of-knowing.

'KNOWLEDGE'

Recent ToK examination questions included 'What criteria do you use to distinguish between knowledge and opinion?' and 'Discuss the importance of reason and emotion in distinguishing between belief and knowledge?' The implication in these questions seems to be that 'knowledge' is the clear certain thing that Plato wants it to be and that it does not include the knowledge by acquaintance that Maja has of her friend. Or does it? The ambiguity is there for you to explore. As with many words, you have to examine 'knowledge' in context to attempt to understand its meaning. If in doubt make clear your understanding of the word, based not on a dictionary definition but on your awareness of it in the ToK context. *Knowledge* is one of those words that bewitch our intelligences and in *Theory of Knowledge* it is particularly important that you are aware of the spell '*knowledge*' casts. For Plato and his associates 'knowledge' was only that clear, certain and communicable understanding provided by justified true belief. But as you know there are other kinds of knowledge; knowledge by acquaintance and faith, for example that would not pass Plato's rigorous scrutiny. We still call what we know in these ways 'knowledge'.

KNOWLEDGE OR OPINION?

BRITISH PARLIAMENT

FREUD'S 'COUCH'

SPACE

DARWIN'S TORTOISE

you have read 2:1 …

consider or undertake the following:

1. How do YOU decide if you accept something as knowledge?

2.

   i.   Select examples of one specific thing you have learned in
        A. history
        B. science
        C. mathematics

   ii. Turn each piece of knowledge into a statement that can be tested by
        the three tests for Justified True Belief.

   iii. Subject your statements to the three tests.

   iv. On the evidence of your tests examine the validity of Justified True,
        Belief.

3. What, for you, is an acceptable definition of the word *knowledge*?

4. Are the four types of justification, logic, empiricism, memory and authority
mentioned in this section equally reliable? Put them in a hierarchy and
attempt to justify your hierarchy.

5. What are you claiming to know when you claim to 'know' a piece of music?

6. What is the difference between someone saying 'I am certain' and 'It is
certain'.

SECTION ONE
WAYS-OF-KNOWING

TRUTH

2.2

CHAPTER CONTENTS

- Plato's truth
- Absolute truth and relative truth
- Three Theories of Truth
  - Correspondence
  - Coherence
  - Pragmatism

Before *you read Chapter 2.2 ...*

consider possible responses to these:

1. What is the difference, for you, between *believing* something to be true and *knowing* something to be true? Is there anything that you believe, and others in your class believe also, but you don't *know*? Is there anything you all know you know to be true?

2. Can a statement be true for you and not true for someone else? If so, why?

3. Under what circumstances could you claim it is true that your watch keeps time perfectly?

4. Can you know something to be true when it has not yet been proven true?

2.2 TRUTH

We have seen that, according to Plato, anything less than Justified True Belief cannot be knowledge. To help you understand Justified True Belief I gave you a simple definition of truth. Truth for Plato, has three characteristics: it is public, it is independent and it is eternal. Let's just look again at those three characteristics of Plato's truth.

CHARACTERISTIC OF PLATO'S TRUTH 1: TRUTH IS PUBLIC

Truth is public. Truth is true for everybody. You cannot say 'What is true for me is true for me and what is true for you is true for you'. No matter how strongly you believe your watch keeps time perfectly if it does not keep time perfectly your belief is not true: you cannot, truthfully, claim your watch keeps time perfectly. You could, truthfully claim that your belief is that it keeps time perfectly. But that is a different truth. That is a truth about your belief. There are two truths here.

1.   Your watch keeps time perfectly
2.   Your belief that your watch keeps time perfectly.

Both of these statements are true both for you and everyone else.

CHARACTERISTIC OF PLATO'S TRUTH 2: TRUTH IS INDEPENDENT

Truth is independent of anyone's beliefs. The truth of the statement 'Your watch keeps time perfectly' is independent of whether you think it is true or not. You could persuade all your friends that your watch keeps time perfectly; indeed you could persuade the entire world your watch keeps time perfectly but that doesn't mean your watch keeps time perfectly. The statement can be false even though everyone you know, indeed everyone in the world, believes it to be true.

THE INQUIRY OF TRUTH: THE SOVEREIGN GOOD OF ALL HUMAN NATURES

Francis Bacon (1561-1626) English philosopher and politician was a pioneer ToK man. He wrote two great philosophical treatises, *The Advancement of Learning* and *Novum Organum*. (Aristotle, you may recall, wrote the original *Organum*). The second is a classification of what he sees as the relationship between the main three areas of knowledge - history, poetry and philosophy - to the three mental faculties, memory, imagination and reason. His most popular work is a collection of essays. In his essay *Of Truth* he writes 'The inquiry of truth which is the lovemaking or wooing of it; the knowledge of truth, which is the praise of it; and the belief of truth, which is the enjoying of it, is the sovereign good of all human natures'.

CHARACTERISTIC OF PLATO'S TRUTH 3: TRUTH IS ETERNAL

Truth is eternal. Now here we have a slight problem with your watch. It might be that as your watch gets older it no longer keeps time perfectly (if it ever did). But the current proposition *Your watch keeps time perfectly* (if it does) is true for now and will be true 'for now' forever. If your watch changes, the truth that it once kept perfect time will not change. Truth is not a watch.

This simple, many would say too simple, definition of truth is a very limited definition. Much philosophical thinking has taken place since Plato's day and this straightforward definition of truth is now considered a little naïve.

Philosophers, however, still agree (in as far as they ever agree on anything) on three things connected with belief and truth.

They believe:

1. that beliefs are true when they agree with reality; when they reflect things as they really are. If your watch keeps time perfectly then your belief that it keeps perfect time is true;
2. that beliefs are false, not true, when they are not in agreement with reality. If your watch does not keep time perfectly then your belief that it does is false.
3. that there is a difference between true beliefs and false beliefs. Your watch either keeps time perfectly or it does not.

But that is where their agreement ends. What they don't agree about is what makes true beliefs true and false beliefs false. They do not agree on what it means to say something is true or something is false. To continue with the watch example their problem is not *Is it true your watch keeps time perfectly? (*That is a verifiable empirical problem) but *what does it mean to say that it is true your watch keeps time perfectly? (*And that is a philosophical problem.)

ABSOLUTE TRUTH AND RELATIVE TRUTH

Plato saw truth as absolute. He was quite clear on this: you must be absolutely certain before you claim to know the truth. Truth for him, and many later philosophers, is a straightforward, simple matter: plain objective fact, transparent and open, empirically and logically proven. It describes objective and rational reality.

Other philosophers claim there is not such thing as absolute truth. All truth is relative, they argue. For them nothing is plain or objective. There is no one truth. There is no one reality. Reality is different for each of us, people and different groups of people, have different understandings of reality. Truth for you is different from truth for me. The greatest relativist of them all, Nietzsche, wrote 'There are no facts, only interpretations'.

ABSOLUTE TRUTH

This seems the common sense approach. Truth is what really is out there. Reality is objective. It does not depend on what we think it to be. The room you are sitting in now either has a door or doesn't have a door. The sun is shining outside or it is not shining. You went to school this morning on foot, in a car or on the train, or by some other method of transport or a combination of all those methods. The book in which this piece was originally written was *Ways of Knowing*.

RELATIVE TRUTH

Relativists argue that everything is subject to human interpretation. We are forced, whether we want to or not, to see the world from our own partial and therefore restricted perspective. Simply put, your understanding of the door in the room you are now in is different from the perspective (of the door) of the other users of the room. Maja, who is sitting opposite you in the room, sees the door quite differently or perhaps she doesn't even see the door at all because of where she is sitting. And you might be able to see outside the window, while she has her back to the window. So Maja's interpretation of reality, her perspective on reality, is quite different from yours.

That example is about a physical perspective. Consider an ethical example: Maja has asked you to help her with her final ToK essay, the one which she has to sign as being all her own work. How much help can you give? She says you can give unlimited help because in the end it is she who writes the essay and it will be her work. Is there a clear cut line between her work and what she makes of your work? Where is the truth?

RELATIVIST TOOLS: LANGUAGE, CULTURE AND EXPERIENCE.

Relativists insist there are many different ways of understanding the world and none of them really reflect the Way Things Really Are. We understand the world, they claim, by inquiring into it and reaching an understanding of it. That understanding we arrive at is our belief of how things really are, our truth. There are many different ways of making that inquiry and the tools we use influence the 'truth' we arrive at. The tools we use to make our inquiry, our language, our culture and our experience, they argue, make truth relative. Absolute truth is unattainable.

An amusing example of the relativity of truth is described in the much anthologised verse.

SIX WISE MEN OF HINDUSTAN
There were six men of Hindustan,
to learning much inclined,
Who went to see an elephant,
though all of them were blind,
That each by observation
might satisfy his mind.

The first approached the elephant,
and happening to fall
Against his broad and sturdy side,
at once began to bawl,
"This mystery of an elephant
is very like a wall."

The second, feeling of the tusk,
cried, "Ho, what have we here,
So very round and smooth and sharp?
To me 'tis mighty clear,
This wonder of an elephant
is very like a spear."

The third approached the elephant,
and happening to take
The squirming trunk within his hands,
thus boldly up and spake,
"I see," quoth he,
"the elephant is very like a snake."

The fourth reached out an eager hand,
and felt above the knee,
"What this most wondrous beast
is like is very plain" said he,
"Tis clear enough the elephant
is very like a tree."

The fifth who chanced to touch the ear
said, "E'en the blindest man
Can tell what this resembles most;
deny the fact who can;
This marvel of an elephant
is very like a fan."

The sixth no sooner had begun
about the beast to grope,
Than seizing on the swinging tail
that fell within his scope;
"I see," said he, "the elephant
is very like a rope."

So six blind men of Hindustan
disputed loud and long,
Each in his own opinion
exceeding stiff and strong;
Though each was partly in the right,
they all were in the wrong!

So, What is Truth?

So we have a philosophical debate about the nature of truth.

The debate has probably been running since the early hunter gatherers sat around the fire roasting the mastodon of the day and trying to agree who actually struck the blow that killed the beast that now fills their bellies. Greek, Chinese, Indian, and Arab thinkers, hungry or well fed, continued to debate the matter over the centuries. Then came the twenty-first century, not a mastodon in sight, but many heavy Theories of Truth roam the philosophical plains of the world's academies.

The Correspondence Theory of Truth, the Semantic Theory, the Deflationary Theory, the Coherence Theory and the Pragmatic Theory (to name but five) are out there to be hunted down and savoured. Let's look at three of these beasts, the Correspondence Theory, the Coherence Theory and the Pragmatic Theory.

The Correspondence Theory

Plato and his Athenian friends were the first to formulate this theory and it is still the most easily understood and accepted theory of truth.

Truth, according to this theory, *is what propositions have when they correspond to reality.* (Note it is the proposition that is true, not the reality).

Put simply: For any proposition (p) p is true if, and only if, p corresponds to the facts.

So here is a proposition: *Astana is the capital city of Kazakhstan.*

Then, yes, you have it, this proposition is only true if Astana is the capital city of Kazakhstan.

A closer to home example (unless you live in Astana) is a proposition based on my belief that all my ToK students arrive punctually for class.

Here is the proposition: *my ToK students arrive punctually for class.*

That is true if, and only if, my ToK students really do arrive punctually for class. If I am in the classroom just before the class is due to start and I see them all arrive punctually, the truth of my proposition, according to the Correspondence Theory, is established. The proposition is true because it corresponds to the facts.

THE COHERENCE THEORY

The Correspondence Theory claims you have truth when a proposition corresponds to reality. The Coherence Theories (there are a lot of them) claim *you have truth when a proposition is compatible with other propositions you accept as established truth*. When all your established truths cohere, when no truth contradicts another truth, then you have it.

Here is an example. Maja's mother wakes her up an hour earlier than normal and tells her not to use the bathroom she generally uses because there is a python in there which has come in during the night through the toilet waste pipe and she (the mother) is waiting for the health authorities to send someone to take it away. Using the Coherence Theory (probably without consciously knowing she is) Maja assesses the proposition *There is a python in the bathroom that has come in through the toilet waste pipe*. She does this by rapidly reviewing what other beliefs she accepts as true which cohere, or not, with the proposition. These might include:

- Pythons can't enter bathrooms through waste pipes.
- The area she lives in is not an area where pythons live.
- There is not a zoo or snake park near her from which it could have escaped.
- Her mother would be panicking it there really was a python in the apartment.

And most of all
- Her mother thinks she should get up earlier than she habitually does.

So her mother's proposition fails to cohere with many other things she has good reason to believe are true. So, knowing it is not April 1st, Maja somewhat bluntly tells her mother to shut the door and go away.

With the *My ToK students arrive punctually for class* proposition, what cohering propositions might allow me to accept this as true?

- My students are always conscientious and reliable.
- They love coming to the ToK class.
- The class is never the first class of the day, so there is not a problem with arriving late at school.
- They are reliably punctual for all other classes.
- They hand in their assignments on time.

(I think you could rename this theory the Ostrich's Head Theory of Truth. The truth you get when you bury your head in the sand and refuse see the truth).

Coherence theory, to summarise, states that a proposition is true if it is consistent with other established truths.

THE PRAGMATIC THEORY

The Pragmatic Theory of Truth is based on the ideas of American Philosopher, Charles Sanders Pierce (1839-1914). His Pragmatic Theory claims that a proposition is true if it is useful to believe. Beliefs that are most useful to us, beliefs that are the best justification for the things we do, beliefs that promote success, are truths. Truth is proved, or disproved, by our subjective experience.

Let's stay with Maja. She believes that there is a god keeping a watchful and caring eye on her, indeed on everyone. She also believes that she is surrounded by people who love her and care for her. So the pragmatists say her proposition *I am surrounded by people who love and care for me* is true if she finds it useful. Her belief justifies what she does and promotes success for her. Until such time as she finds, through her subjective experience, that the proposition is not useful, it will be true, for her.

Examine my proposition *My ToK students arrive punctually for class* through the lens of the Pragmatic Theory and what do you get? The Theory says the proposition is true if it is useful to believe. It is useful for me to believe because I want the students to be punctual. If they are not punctual, and I still believe they are, where does that leave the truth? Is it useful for the students to believe they arrive punctually even when they do not? The pragmatists would say, you have to be pragmatic. If it is useful to me to believe the truth that my students arrive on time, then I must pragmatically accept that they do arrive on time. If it is useful for the students to believe the truth is they arrive on time, then they arrive on time. Our beliefs promote success. Pierce would say they enable us to predict experience.

MIRAS INTERNATIONAL SCHOOL - KAZAKHSTAN

Now *you have read Chapter 2.2 …*

consider or undertake the following:

1. Think of a 'true fact' you have learnt in one of your math classes that you believe to be absolutely true and apply the tests of 'public, independent and eternal' to it. Now do the same for a 'fact' you have learned in history. Based on these two examples, are tests helpful in establishing truth?

2. Does the verse about the six blind men get to the heart of the relativity of truth? How convincing do you find the concept of relative truth? Can something be true for you and not true for someone else? Or are others simply having a perception problem?

3. Here is the final paragraph of the International Baccalaureate Organisation's mission statement:

These programmes encourage students across the world to become active, compassionate and lifelong learners who understand that other people, with their differences, can also be right. (©IBO)

What does that last word 'right' mean? Does it mean that 'other people' have true beliefs which may be different from your true beliefs? And does the statement mean that IB students must be sympathetic to those beliefs? Is the statement declaring there is no 'right' that is true?

4. Take the proposition '*It is true that ToK makes you a critical thinker*' and assess its truth in terms of the three Theories of Truth described.

5. Here is a truth continuum with absolute and relative poles:

Absolute ──────────────────────────────────▶ Relative

Where on the continuum does your concept of truth lie? Or is that a silly question? Does your concept of truth change according to the truth proposition being discussed? Can you think of a truth proposition which is absolute? Another which is relative? And another which is in the middle.

47

Want to know more?

You will find the following two books challenging but informative.

Truth: A Guide by Simon Blackburn (Oxford 2005) and

Truth and Truthfulness by Bernard Williams (Cambridge 2002).

Dirse

SCEPTICISM

2.3

CHAPTER CONTENTS

- Scepticism: a definition
- 'I think, therefore I am'
- Descartes First Meditation
- Bacon's Idols
- Frankfurt's Bullshit

Before *you read Chapter 2.3 ...*

consider possible responses to these:

1. Challenge yourself: make a statement about something of which you are absolutely convinced. Attempt to think of at least five ways in which you could be made to doubt your statement.

2. Most of us at some time during our lives discover that a belief we have is not 'real'. For instance many people believe that if they work hard they will be successful and even when they have worked hard all their lives and are still not successful they are reluctant to let go of this belief. Think of a belief you once had but now do not have and examine why you thought it was once true and now do not.

3. Think of any arguments you might use to persuade yourself that it is impossible to be really certain you know something.

4. In the last 24 hours have you doubted the reliability of any thing you have heard, or read, or been told? If you have, what has caused the doubt?

Header from a propaganda leaflet dropped on the English village of Halstead in August1940

2.3   SCEPTICISM

A WAY OF NOT KNOWING

Some philosophers, known as Sceptics, claim that not only should we not trust any knowledge we obtain through our senses but that it is impossible to be sure of anything. These Sceptics hold the view that certain - 'certain' here in the sense of 'undisputable' - knowledge may be sought but will never be found. Sceptics believe you can never be sure of anything.

Absolute Sceptics claim that we cannot know anything. Absolute Scepticism would seem to be impossible: if you don't know anything how can you know you don't know anything?

Relative Sceptics claim that, well, perhaps we can know something but we must be very, very careful in our claims to know.

Scepticism may seem very strange: it may be obvious to you that you do know certain things so why should anyone suggest or argue that you don't know these things?

Sceptics have three main arguments for their attitude.

1.   **Our senses often deceive us.**
     Sceptics argue we can never know for certain when we are being deceived by our senses and when we are not. So, if we can't be certain of our sense perception, we can't be certain of our knowledge of the external world that we receive through our senses.

2.   **We can never be sure if we are dreaming or not.**
     Sceptics maintain that we can never be sure whether at any moment we are dreaming or not. If, they claim, you can't be sure you're dreaming then you can't be sure you are experiencing reality either.
     Perhaps after all you are not reading these words, you are dreaming that you are reading these words. If we don't know whether we are dreaming or not, how can we be sure of anything?

3.   **Our thoughts are an unreliable interpretation of reality.**
     Our thoughts are the only things we can really be sure of and our thoughts may be completely different from the reality they attempt to interpret.
     The most celebrated argument for Scepticism is to be found in Descartes' First Meditation *On Doubt & Certainty*. Like Plato, Descartes wanted to establish what it was possible to be sure of knowing. Before he could begin to undertake this task he believed it essential to free himself from all his existing beliefs because they might be incorrect, and he had no way of knowing whether they were correct or not. Once he had got rid of all his beliefs, he claimed, then he could start to build up a body of knowledge which was acceptable to him as certain. He came up with the idea that he should *pretend a cunning evil demon was trying to deceive him and all the information he was receiving through his senses was created by this evil demon only to deceive him. He would then be able to force himself not to believe the information because it was created by the evil demon.*
     After taking the Sceptical argument to its limit in the First Meditation he establishes, in his Second Meditation, that there is one certainty, the certainty he exists. He exists because he thinks. He argues that even if there is a demon trying to deceive him, he, Descartes, must exist, solely because he is able to think about the demon. His thinking alone was evidence

for his existence. His thinking doesn't have to be profound, it just has to be thinking. His body may be the creation of the demon, but his thoughts are not. His thoughts are independent of external things, independent of any sense experience. His thoughts must exist independently of anything the demon could create. Hence the famous 'Cogito, ergo sum', 'I think, therefore I am'.

[The *First Meditation* is a significant document in both the history of western philosophy and the history of knowledge so I have included in this section (below) an abridged version of it for you to read for yourself. In making this abridgment I have attempted to retain the mood and tone of the original.]

RENÉ DESCARTES (1596-1660)

The father of modern philosophy, René Descartes was born in central France in the town of Le Haye, which is now named Descartes in his honour. He studied at a Jesuit College but was so discontented with the philosophical ideas of the time that were taught there that he joined the army of the Duke of Bavaria and travelled widely across Europe. In Bavaria, in the winter of 1619, cooped up in his military billet, he conceived the idea of reconstructing the whole of philosophy anew, with mathematical reasoning as the model of all 'rational' knowledge.

After leaving the army he developed his philosophical ideas in Paris, and later, from 1628, in Holland. As well as developing philosophical 'rationalism' he was the founder of analytical geometry. His most celebrated work is a series of essays, the *Meditations,* published in 1641. The essays are written in the first person singular - I - and the reader is invited to identify with the 'I' and become personally involved in the arguments.

As well as being known as the creator of the phrase *Cogito, ergo sum*, Descartes is also popularly known for his Method of Cartesian Doubt: treat all your beliefs as if they were false. This, and only this, he argues, will enable you to discover from where sure, or certain, knowledge can be developed.

ON DOUBT & CERTAINTY
THE FIRST MEDITATION - RENÉ DESCARTES

A few years ago I thought about the number of things I now know are false which, when I was a child, I accepted as true. Then I thought of all the subsequent ideas I developed based on this false knowledge. And then I realised that if I was to establish any real truth for myself, I had to forget everything I ever knew and start learning all over again. This seemed an enormous task and I put the project off. But I feel I can put the project off no more, and at this moment, being quite alone, I am going to devote myself to getting rid of my false knowledge.

It would be impossible for me to go through each piece of knowledge individually so I will go straight to the basic principles on which my knowledge is based. What I have, up till now, accepted as true has come through my senses. But from time to time these senses have tricked me and once your senses have tricked you it is better not to trust them as much as you did before.

But there are things our senses tell us that are impossible not to believe. For example, I am here, sitting by a fire, wearing a thick dressing gown, with this piece of paper in my hand.

How could I not believe these hands and this body are mine? I could of course be mad and believe as mad people do that they are kings when they are beggars or that they are pumpkins or made of glass. But such people are mad and I would be thought mad too if I took any example from them.

That's a brilliant idea! Because... I have when I am asleep the same experience as a mad person - sometimes I have even more bizarre experiences when I'm asleep as mad people do when they are awake. When I am lying undressed in my bed I sometimes dream that I am here, in my dressing gown, sitting by the fire. In my dream my eyes are wide open and I shake my head and it is not asleep and I stretch out my hand and I know exactly what I am doing. I remember other times when I have been tricked by similar thoughts when asleep. As I think about it more carefully, I see clearly that there are no ways of knowing whether you are asleep or awake.

Suppose then that I am dreaming and that these things - my eyes being open, my head moving and my outstretched hands - are not true. Perhaps I don't have a body or hands. But these dreams may be like paintings which depict imaginary things: eyes, head, hands. Then at least the colours will be real even if the painted objects are not.

By similar reasoning, even if the heads and hands are imaginary, the things from which they are made are real.

These imaginary things seem to include everything physical, and the things that belong to these physical objects: their shape, their number, their physical situation and the time in which they exist. So, reasonably, you claim that physics, astronomy, medicine and all subjects which depend on a study of physical objects, are doubtful. On the other hand arithmetic, geometry and other subjects of this kind, regardless of whether they exist in nature, contain something certain. When I am asleep or awake, two and three add up to five, and a square has four sides. It seems impossible that such truths could be false.

And yet, rooted in my mind is the idea that an all-knowing God made me what I am. How do I know he has fixed things so there is no earth or sky, at the same time making them seem real to me? In the same way as I know people are sometimes wrong when they are sure they are right, could I always add two and three inaccurately or mis-count the sides of a square? But if God is God, as alleged, he would not allow me to be tricked in this way. And if he doesn't allow me to be tricked all the time why should he allow me to be tricked some of the time? Some people maintain that God is inconsistent, making everything uncertain. Others unable to accept complete uncertainty, deny the existence of God. For the moment let us agree with them. According to them, I am in my present state by fate or chance and, therefore, it is more than likely I will be tricked all the time. I have no answer to this argument so, accepting I will be tricked all the time, I must treat all my former beliefs as cautiously as I would obvious untruths.

But I find it almost impossible to treat my former beliefs as untruths. It seems much more reasonable to believe them than to deny them. So I must try another method to convince myself that these former beliefs are utterly false and imaginary. I will pretend that not God but some utterly cunning evil demon has employed all his skill in order to deceive me. I shall force myself to think that the sky, the air, the earth, colours, shapes and sounds, all external things are dreams the demon has created to trap and deceive my judgement. I shall force myself to believe I have no hands or eyes or flesh or senses, but only that I falsely believe that I do have them. I will resolutely insist on this so this demon will not be able to impose any knowledge on me.

PRACTICAL SCEPTICISM 1: IDOLS

Scepticism, the claim that the certainty of knowing is impossible, is an intriguing idea that philosophers will no doubt continue to explore for many years. In practice there is a much milder form of scepticism which is more meaningful to us in our everyday lives. The word 'sceptical', in everyday usage, means being doubtful as to the truth of an assertion or fact. As knowers at the centre of that ToK diagram, we should be wary of accepting 'knowledge' that is presented to us.

The first objective of the ToK programme[1] states 'students should be able to …. analyse critically knowledge claims, their underlying assumptions and their implications'.

Francis Bacon (see page 41), although he was not a Sceptic, was very aware that we could easily be misled into accepting as knowledge ideas and concepts which came from errors in our thinking, our processing of knowledge. He called these errors 'idols' and divided them into four groups: Idols of the Tribe, of the Cave, of the Market Place and of the Theatre. The word 'idols' here means false notions, fallacies. It comes from the idea in the Bible that gods other than the Jewish or Christian God were false. These gods were often worshipped in the form of a statue or idol, hence Bacon's use of the word here. Here are some of Bacon's Idols.

IDOLS OF THE TRIBE

'Tribe' is a metaphor for the collective human experience. These 'idols' come from the way humans sometimes are misled by what they want to believe, want to think or want to happen. Here are some of them.

BELIEF:
a tendency to accept beliefs one has always accepted regardless of evidence to the contrary.

WISHFUL THINKING:
a tendency to accept what you want to accept and believe what you want to believe.

OVERGENERALIZATION:
a tendency to be influenced by first impressions to the extent that one assumes every case is the same.

IDOLS OF THE CAVE

'Cave' here is a metaphor for the way we are nurtured; for our upbringing and our education. These 'idols' spring from our individual mental and physical conditioning and may vary widely from person to person.

INSULARITY:
a tendency to over-emphasise the value of things that are important to us personally.

CONSERVATISM:
a tendency to admire the past at the expense of new ideas.

NOVELTY:
a tendency to admire anything new merely for the sake of its novelty.

AUTHORITY:
a tendency to accept what authority proposes without critical evaluation.

---

1. Page 4, *Theory of Knowledge*, International Baccalaureate, Geneva 2006.

INERTIA:

a tendency to ignore problems that require arduous thought.

IDOLS OF THE MARKET PLACE

'Market Place' here is a metaphor for language; the market place being where language is often rather loosely and misleadingly used.

MEANINGLESS WORDS:

the use of words in such a generalised way that they don't mean anything.

DOUBLE MEANING WORDS:

the use of words with more than one meaning without specifying which meaning is intended.

JARGON:

a tendency to use technical or polysyllabic words that are not understood by the hearer.

PRACTICAL SCEPTICISM 2: BULLSHIT

Bacon warns the knower that it is his or her duty to be wary of idols; idols arising from our personal conditioning. With these Baconion idols we deceive ourselves. Harry Frankfurt, a distinguished contemporary moral philosopher from Princeton University warns us to be wary of a different idol which is deliberately foisted upon us to deceive: bullshit. 'One of the most salient features of our culture is that there is so much bullshit', is the opening line of his short, best selling book 'On Bullshit'. [2]

Bullshit is information which is presented to promote a particular cause and to gain an advantage for the bullshitter. It needn't be false or true. The bullshitter's fakery is not in misrepresentation, but in concealing his indifference to the reality of what he says.

There is a lot of it out there, he says and it is dangerous, more dangerous than outright lying. Liars are aware when they are lying, so, to some extent they must be aware of the truth. The essence of bullshit, Frankfurt claims, is that it has no regard for the truth at all. The bullshitter opts out of truth completely. Even when the truth is known, bullshitters have no concern for it. Bullshitters are indifferent to 'how things really are'. And this, says Frankfurt, 'is a greater enemy of truth than lies are.' Frankfurt's distinction is clear: 'The liar still cares about the truth. The bullshitter is unburdened by such concerns.'

And where do we find it? 'The realms of advertising and of public relations, and nowadays, the closely related realm of politics, are replete with instances of bullshit so unmitigated that they can serve among the most indisputable and classic paradigms of the subject'. Turn on the TV or the radio, read the paper, surf the Internet, visit your local coffee shop, read the restaurant menu, and there it is.

Knowing that there is bullshit out there masquerading as knowledge is one thing, identifying it is another. A little practical scepticism can be quite useful but perhaps full blooded Cartesian Scepticism should not be entirely dismissed. How can we be sure Harry G. Frankfurt himself is not bullshitting?

---

2. *On Bullshit* Harry G. Frankfurt Princeton 2005

Now *you have read Chapter 2.3 …*

consider or undertake the following:

1. Re-read the three main claims of Sceptics that you can never be sure you know something and apply each of these claims to your own experience. Recall a time:

  a. when your senses deceived you;
  b. when dreaming you thought you were awake; and
  c. when your thoughts were an inaccurate interpretation of reality.

Could the Sceptics be right?

2. Read the abridged version of Descartes' *On Doubt & Certainty* (page 52) twice. The first time you read it savour the argument and style and make sure you understand his reasoning. The second time you read it consider, as you do so, the possibility that you are not reading it at all and your belief that you are reading it is false. What arguments can you give yourself to reinforce this belief?

3. Examine and discuss Bacon's Idols (page 54 on) in the light of your own experience of the thinking of people with whom you are familiar, your friends for instance, or members of your family. (Not yourself, of course, that might be too humiliating!). Having examined the list and related it to your awareness of the thinking processes of your friends, consider again the viability of Scepticism.

4. Frankfurt suggests that most of us are pretty good at spotting bullshit.

Produce an example of what you would consider bullshit and explain to your group why you think it is that. How sceptical are you in general about the information that is presented to you daily by the media?

Want to know more?

You might find the following books helpful.

Hospers John *An Introduction to Philosophical Analysis* 3rd edition, Prentice Hall 1988

Warburton Nigel *Philosophy The Classics* Routledge 1998

Harry G Frankfurt *On Bullshit* Princeton 2005

SECTION ONE
WAYS-OF-KNOWING

LOGIC

2.4

CHAPTER CONTENTS

Before

you read Chapter 2.4 ...

consider possible responses to these:

1. Define to yourself, or your friend, or a partner, or your class what you think it means to be logical. Do you consider yourself to be logical in terms of your own definition? Support you claim with examples of your decision making over the last six months.

2. How will you, or did you, decide which College or University to attend? To what extent was your decision logical (in terms of your definition above) and to what extent were you influenced by non-logical reasons? Were your non-logical reasons illogical?

3. When you play the board game *"Clue"* (also known as *"Cluedo"*) you use logic to solve a murder mystery. If it is possible, play the game and determine for yourself the logical processes necessary to solve the mystery. Many other indoor games use logic, chess for instance and bridge. Does the most logical player always win?

4. To what extent can logic be used by United Nations personnel attempting to negotiate peace between warring nations or factions?

5. Can logic create knowledge?

6. In his book, *The Essential Difference*, Simon Baron-Cohen argues strongly that females are, by nature, more empathetic than males, and males more logical than females.

Does your own experience lead you to agree or disagree with this argument? And is even asking the question sexist?

Charles Lutwidge Dodgson better known as Lewis Carroll.

Author of *Alice's Adventures in Wonderland* and *Symbolic Logic*.

2.4 LOGIC

WHAT IS LOGIC?

Logic is the branch of philosophy that explores the way we reason.

It attempts:

1. to define 'correct' reasoning;
2. to distinguish good arguments from bad ones;
3. to pick out flaws and weaknesses in reasoning and
4. to create rules which enable us to test whether our reasoning is coherent and consistent.

Natural and human scientists, mathematicians, historians and scholars from all disciplines, frequently use logic to present their arguments and to justify, in part, their claims to know. Before we examine how logic is used in each of the disciplines, we need to have some idea of what logic is. Researchers in the academic disciplines are, of course, not the only people who use it. Most of us make quite a lot of use of it in our everyday lives.

Suppose today is Thursday and you have some math homework that has to be handed in at the start of school on Monday. Suppose also that you are keen on math and want to do the homework well. You know also the assignment will take about two hours. Now, you ask yourself, when will be the best time to do it? You are going to be away for the weekend, from after school Friday until late Sunday afternoon playing in a basketball tournament. You know it will be impossible to do the homework while you are away, so that leaves you Thursday (today) evening or Sunday evening. You have already promised your friend to go out both Thursday and Sunday (because you won't be able to go out together on Friday or Saturday) so you decide you will get up early on Friday, before school to do it then. But, you realise, if you do get up early on Friday you will be too tired on Friday evening to play well in the opening round of the basketball tournament. So you decide there really is no alternative: the only time you have to do the homework well is early on Monday morning, so you decide that is when you will do it.

This is clearly an example of your reasoning, your logical thinking. You have a problem: when to do your homework. You ask yourself what are the possible solutions to the problem. You consider each solution and finally conclude that there is only one time to do the work and that is early on Monday morning. You define a problem, you consider solutions, and you come to a conclusion. Your reasoning has produced evidence for your conclusion. Logic determines whether your argument, your reasoning, is good or bad, whether it is logical.

Logicians divide their subject into two parts: deductive logic and inductive logic. In order to appreciate the way logic is used in the disciplines, it is necessary for you to clearly understand the difference between deductive and inductive logic.

DEDUCTIVE LOGIC

Deductive logic is concerned with the rules for determining when an argument is valid. It structures arguments in a formal way to help us understand, as clearly as possible, the reasoning behind the arguments. It does not concern itself with truth at all, only with the process of reasoning. Deductive logic produces knowledge based on reason rather than experience.

Chapter 2.4: Logic

Reduced to simple deductive logic your 'homework' argument goes like this:

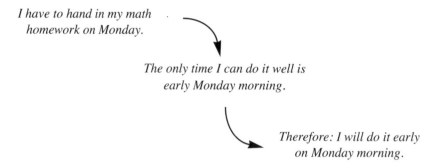

*I have to hand in my math
    homework on Monday.*

*The only time I can do it well is
    early Monday morning.*

*Therefore: I will do it early
    on Monday morning.*

(This simplified argument omits some implied premisses and conclusions which we will return to later.)

Consider this more straightforward argument:

*Maja is an 11th grade student at Munich International School.
All 11th grade students at MIS study taxidermy.
Therefore Maja studies taxidermy.*

This is a valid argument. If all the 11th grade students at MIS study taxidermy, and Maja is an 11th grade student at MIS then she must study taxidermy. Notice the argument does not have to be true to be valid. Nobody at MIS studies taxidermy but the argument is valid because the conclusions follow from the premisses. The premisses can be false but the argument is valid. Logic tests reasoning, not truth.

In the language of logic these three line arguments are called **syllogisms**. Each of the first two lines is called a premiss. The last line is called the conclusion. The three sentences together contain an argument. If the conclusion follows logically from the two premisses the argument is said to be valid. If the conclusion does not follow logically from the premisses it is invalid.

That is,

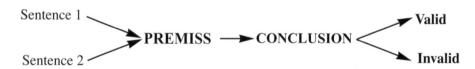

Sentence 1
Sentence 2
PREMISS → CONCLUSION
Valid
Invalid

Now consider this argument:

*If you study taxidermy you learn how to stuff dead animals.
Maja knows how to stuff dead animals.
Therefore Maja has studied taxidermy.*

This is an invalid argument because the conclusion does not follow from the premisses. Maja may know how to stuff dead animals without having studied taxidermy. We do not know if studying taxidermy is the only way to learn how to stuff animals. There may be other ways of learning, unlikely as that may seem. The first premiss does not say 'if you want to learn to stuff dead animals you must study taxidermy'.

Arguments like this are known as deductive arguments. Whether a deductive argument is valid or invalid depends on whether its form is valid. Here is a simple deductive argument that, despite its obvious lack of truth, is valid.

> *All 11th grade students are clever.*
> *Maja's dog is an 11th grade student.*
> *Therefore Maja's dog is clever.*

This is clearly a valid argument even though its premises (the second one certainly, the first you decide) are not true.

Of course most arguments are more complex than this. Very few 'real life' arguments can be reduced to two premises and a conclusion. Look again at your homework argument.

> *I have to hand in my math homework on Monday.*
> *The only time I can do it well is early Monday morning.*
> *Therefore: I will do it early on Monday morning.*

This is your argument reduced to its basic form. The full argument is much more complex. Some intermediate premisses and their conclusions have been omitted because it is assumed they are taken for granted or implied. Recall how your argument was developed. You know that the homework will take two hours and you want to do it well. An intermediate conclusion could be inserted between the first and second premiss.

> *I want to do my homework well.*
> *It will take me two hours to do it well.*
> *Therefore I must find two hours when I can do it.*

But that addition does not cover all your reasoning. You have not given the reasons why you cannot do it at other times.

> *From Friday after school until late Sunday afternoon I am away playing basketball.*
> *On Thursday evening and Sunday evening I have promised to go out.*
> *Therefore the only time left is early Friday or early Monday.*

Even this is not the full argument.

> *I want to play well in the basketball tournament.*
> *If I do my homework early on Friday I will be too tired to play well on Friday evening.*
> *Therefore I must not do it on Friday morning.*

The complete argument is now:

> premiss 1: *I have to hand in my math homework on Monday.*
> premiss 2: *I want to do my homework well.*
> premiss 3: *It will take me two hours to do it well.*

INTERMEDIATE CONCLUSION ONE:
Therefore I must find two hours when I can do it.

premiss 4: *From Friday after school until late Sunday afternoon I am away playing basketball.*

premiss 5: *On Thursday evening and Sunday evening I have promised to go out.*

INTERMEDIATE CONCLUSION TWO:

Therefore the only time left is early Friday or early Monday.

premiss 6: *I want to play well in the basketball tournament.*

premiss 7: *If I do my homework early on Friday I will be too tired to play well on Friday evening.*

INTERMEDIATE CONCLUSION THREE:

Therefore I must not do it on Friday morning.

premiss 8: *The only time I can do it well is early Monday morning.*

CONCLUSION:

Therefore: I will do it early on Monday morning.

Unless an argument is fully stated in this way, and often arguments in 'real life' are not fully stated, we have to guess what is assumed for the conclusion.

SYMBOLIC LOGIC

Logic, the systematic study of the patterns of an argument, is a sophisticated and complex subject. Logicians have devised ways of using symbols to depict arguments thus distancing themselves from the potentially ambiguous language of premisses and conclusions. Aristotle started this use of symbols when he laid down the rules for the use of syllogisms. (Syllogism is the word used by logicians to describe the argument in which a conclusion is based on two premisses). In the 19th Century, Gottllob Frege (1848-1925) a German mathematician devised the first complete system of symbolic logic, which included symbols for 'all' and 'some'.

Look again at the syllogism about Maja's dog.

> *All 11th grade students are clever.*
> *Maja's dog is an 11th grade student.*
> *Therefore Maja's dog is clever.*

This is what logicians call a 'categorical syllogism'. The premisses show that one set of things (a category, hence 'categorical'), in this case Maja's dog, is either included or excluded from another set of things, here 11th grade students. To distance themselves from emotive words like 'dog' and 'clever' logicians substitute symbols for verbal categories.

> All A is B   (All 11th grade students are clever)
> All C is A   (Maja's dog is an 11th grade student)
> All C is B   (Therefore Maja's dog is clever)

No matter the linguistic content of the syllogism, any argument in the same form is valid. Any differences may invalidate the conclusion.

Consider this argument, one you may be familiar with:

> *Lazy students never do their homework.*
> *Paulo never does his homework.*
> *Therefore Paulo is lazy.*

Represented in symbols this becomes:

> All A is B   (Lazy students never do their homework)
> All C is B   (Paulo never does his homework)
> All C is A   (Paulo is lazy)

The symbols clearly show the argument is invalid. Poor Paulo slaved away, night after night, earning money to go to college and then nursing his elderly mother. And his teacher thought he was lazy.

 'DO' SOME LOGIC: SYLLOGISMS

A. Examine the following arguments by:
- a.   Identifying the premiss and
- b.   Identifying the conclusion then
- c.   Add a premiss that will make the argument clear and finally
- d.   With your additional premiss turn the argument into a valid syllogism.

1.   That is not a tree because it doesn't have a trunk.

2.   Birds are not mammals because mammals don't lay eggs.

3.   All basketball players are tall so Karl is tall.

4.   The student did not do the homework therefore he is not conscientious.

5.   She passed the exam therefore she must have studied.

B.   Examine the following syllogisms and decide whether they are valid or invalid.

1.   All drug addicts are pathetic.
All drug addicts are unhappy people.
Therefore all unhappy people are drug addicts.

2.   Some animals are wild animals.
All dogs are animals.
Therefore some dogs are wild animals.

3.   All birds have feathers.
All Bombay Ducks have feathers.
Therefore all Bombay Ducks are birds.

4.   All electronic devices break down.
       My computer has broken down.
       Therefore my computer is an electronic device.

5.   All students enjoy weekends.
       Weekends are for relaxing.
       Therefore all students relax at the weekend.

III.   Represent the above five syllogisms in symbolic terms (See page 63).
       Does using symbols help you understand the validity or invalidity of the arguments?

INDUCTIVE LOGIC

GENERALISATIONS, CAUSES AND ANALOGIES

Inductive logic is the reasoning we use when we make generalisations or analogies. We use our experience, our empirical knowledge, and make inferences from that experience. Inductive knowledge therefore is fundamentally different from the pure reason of deductive logic which is independent of any empiricism (see Empiricism, page 20). When we use inductive logic the reliability of the empirical evidence on which we base our conclusions determines the soundness or otherwise of the argument.

INDUCTIVE LOGIC 1: GENERALISATIONS

If you were asked the following question how would you respond?

Will your next English class be interesting?

You would presumably base your answer on your experience of previous English classes. You would generalise from your experience. If your English classes have always been interesting (and for the sake of this example let us presume they have) it would be normal, rational and obvious for you to say, 'Yes, my next English class will be interesting'. When you make a generalisation like this from your experience, you are using inductive logic.

Inductive logic is not concerned with the absolute certainty of an argument. Its two main features are:

1.   it gives good reasons for supporting a conclusion but it does not guarantee that conclusion; and
2.   its conclusion contains information that is not in the argument.

You can see these features in the answer to the question about your English class.

Your reason might be:

1.   in the past my English classes have always been interesting (this is a good reason but not a guarantee) and
2.   therefore, it is likely my next English class will be interesting (this conclusion is not in the argument).

Of course, the 'it is likely' is important here. You cannot be certain your next English class will be interesting. Your teacher might not turn up, you might be given a surprise test which may not be at all interesting, and you may start a new text which you find totally boring. However if your experience to date indicates that you will find the class interesting, then it is likely the next class will probably be interesting too.

But can we cope with that 'it is likely'?

What makes your generalisation reliable?

Did you make your response on the basis of four previous classes?

Or forty? Or four hundred?

Have you had a sufficient number of classes on which to base your generalisation?

And are the classes you have had representative of the classes to come?

Can you be reasonably sure they will continue to be the same?

THREE TESTS FOR SOUNDNESS

Inductive reasoning conclusions based on generalisations must be treated with caution. There are three tests of the soundness of the generalisation which you should apply before you accept any knowledge based on generalisations, the tests of Sufficient Number, of Varying Circumstances and of the Search Exceptions. Take, for example, this generalisation:

In every country's capital city there is an international school.

TEST ONE: SUFFICIENT NUMBER
*   On what numerical information is this statement based?
*   Was it based on information from every country in the world?
*   Or was it based on information from most of the countries?
*   Is it a generalisation from a widely travelled educator who has visited many (how many is many?) countries and has found an international school in every capital?
*   Or is it a generalisation from a researcher who has researched 20% percent of the world's capital cities and found they all have international schools and therefore inferred that every capital city has an international school.
*   What numerical information would be acceptable as sound evidence for generalisations?

TEST TWO: VARYING CIRCUMSTANCES
Is the generalisation based on evidence from all parts of the world or is it localised? It might be that the generalisation was made based on the experience of someone living in Japan, who, aware of international schools in the capitals of all the countries near to Japan presumed that every capital city had an international school. Or it may be that the generalisation was made by business people who regularly visit the financial centres of the world and were aware that many of the expatriates with whom they work send their children to international schools. These people are not deliberately given uncertain information but the circumstances on which they base their generalisations are limited.

TEST THREE: EXCEPTIONS
Has a thorough and reliable search for exceptions been made? In the case of international schools in capital cities this would seem to be the most obvious test to start with. Look first at those capitals which are less likely to have an international school than the big international centres.

It might be that after applying these three tests to the generalisation you might change it to read:
   In almost every country's capital city there is an international school.

In this form the statement may be more acceptable as inductive logic.

INDUCTIVE LOGIC 2: ANALOGY

When we reason (or induct) by analogy we compare two things which are similar in some ways and then infer that they are similar in other ways too. For example scientists working with laboratory animals are reasoning by analogy when they apply the knowledge they discover about animal physiology to human physiology. They are inferring that because animal and human physiology is similar, the knowledge they create through animal experimentation will be relevant to humans.

You have probably come across analogies in tests you have done at school. Part of the American College Entrance Scholastic Aptitude Test (SAT) tests your thinking skills and vocabulary through analogies. You are given a pair of words and then have to select, from a given list, words which are similar in their relationship to the given pair.

Consider this example:

ACRE: LAND
   a.   distance: space
   b.   kinsfolk: family
   c.   gallon: liquid
   d.   degree: thermometer
   e.   year: birthday

You must first decide on the relationship between ACRE and LAND and then decide if any of the other pairs have the same relationship. The answer here is fairly obvious. In the same way an acre is a measure of land a gallon is a measure of liquid. (This is obvious if you know what a gallon is but many people living outside America measure liquid in litres. This question has a clear cultural bias of which the testmaker may not have been aware).

Areas of knowledge using analogies are ethics (in which a given situation may be compared to another for which a clear moral principle has been established), economics and history.

FALLACIES

FALLACIES: INVALID FORMS OF REASONING.
The word 'fallacy' is often used in everyday language to describe any kind of misinformation or error of thinking. We hear people say 'It's a fallacy that drinking coffee in the evening stops you sleeping' or 'It's a fallacy that it is always raining in Seattle'. What is meant here is simply that these commonly held views are not true. In logic the word 'fallacy' has a much more precise meaning. It means an argument that uses an invalid form of reasoning. Logicians divide these invalid arguments into two categories:

1.   formal fallacies and

2.   informal fallacies.

FORMAL FALLACIES

A formal fallacy is the invalid reasoning found in syllogisms. The syllogism concerning Paolo's laziness (page 62) is a good example.

Here is another:

> *All weight lifters drink a lot of milk.*
> *My neighbour drinks a lot of milk.*
> *Therefore my neighbour is a weight lifter.*

This is a formal fallacy because the logical structure of the argument is invalid. It doesn't follow that my neighbour is a weight lifter because he drinks a lot of milk. The first premiss doesn't state that everyone who drinks a lot of milk is a weight lifter, merely that all weight lifters drink a lot of milk, which is quite different.

INFORMAL FALLACIES

You are almost certainly familiar with informal fallacies, although you may not be familiar with them under that name. Logicians have compiled lists of these informal fallacies, some of which they have dignified by labelling them with Latin names. There is, for instance, the *Ad Hominum* fallacy. *Ad Hominum* means 'to the person' and the *Ad Hominum* fallacy is an argument which transfers attention from the argument itself to the person making the argument. 'I know that no-one as intelligent as you could possibly believe what you have just said. You can't really expect me to believe that you think ....', is a clear example of an *Ad Hominum* fallacy. The arguer's intelligence is nothing to do with the argument and to mention it is not only invalid in terms of countering the argument but is also rather devious. (It often works though. In this case it might work because it flatters the arguer. It is much more effective than saying 'Only somebody stupid could have put forward that argument.' Although that too is an *Ad Hominum* argument.)

One of the most frequently used informal fallacies is the:

EVERY-ONE-DOES-IT FALLACY

(in Latin the *Ad Populum* fallacy), an argument to justify bad behaviour.

You come late to class and justify your lateness by saying 'But everybody comes late to class ...'. Of course the argument is invalid, even if everyone did come late to class that is not a reason why you should. You are responsible for getting yourself punctually to class, not everybody else. Of course not everybody does come late to class, one or two people might, but not everybody. Your argument here is fallacious on two counts.

Another well known and well used informal fallacy is the

APPEAL-TO-AUTHORITY FALLACY

This invalid argument is often introduced by the phrase 'Research has shown ...' claim that is worthless unless backed up with specific references, which it seldom is.

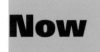 **HAVE FUN WITH FALLACIES...**

Identify the fallacious reasoning in each of the following statements and invent an appropriate name for each fallacy.

1. Did you see that truck driver overtaking dangerously? Truck drivers are such lousy drivers.

2. There is nothing wrong with downloading your essays from the Internet. Everybody I know seems to do it.

3. Those environmentalists are all so extreme. How can you believe any of them?

4. With lips like that she must be sexy.

5. There is no doubt about it. I know it always rains in Wicklow because every time I go there it rains.

6. There's no way I can cope unless I have a really up-to-date computer. I'll just fail the exam if I don't have one.

7. There's no doubt that the Dodgers will win because their coach says they will and if their coach says they will win, they will.

8. The horses I backed yesterday and the day before that didn't win, so the one I back today will be sure to win.

9. Because most people think the death penalty should be reintroduced then it is right that it should be.

10. Nobody with the slightest intelligence could possibly have believed what you have just told me.

11. People are like watches, to make sure they give their best, you have to keep them fully wound up.

12. We've won the first four matches of the season so we have as good as won the cup.

13. The principal didn't care if Shula missed her lunch break, therefore she doesn't care if we skip classes.

14. Students who study hard get good grades, so if you want me to study hard you should give me good grades.

15. There is no evidence to prove him guilty. Therefore he's innocent.

CAN LOGIC CREATE KNOWLEDGE?

The answer to this question, according to Dr Aidan Seery, the author of *The Limits of Logic* is a firm 'no'. Consider his arguments carefully and then

    a.   decide if you agree with his conclusions and
    b.   decide if your argument is logical.

THE LIMITS OF LOGIC,
(OR WOULD MR. SPOCK HAVE ENJOYED MEETING EUCLID?)

Despite the fact that this question explores the nature of logic so embedded in the notion of Mr. Spock, this is a question that few Trekkies have asked. To answer they would have to look briefly at the history of logic.

The ability to reason is often cited as the distinguishing characteristic of the human species. Logic began with attempts to bring some rules to this ability. The Greeks discovered common patterns that underpin reasoning. These patterns they defined with 'laws'. These laws, or arguments, were formulated by Aristotle in the realm of real language and by Euclid in geometry. Over two thousand years after Euclid the great German philosopher Kant (1724-1803) used Euclid's geometry to defend his revolutionary theory about the nature of mind and reasoning. Many thinkers of Kant's time dismissed the thought there might be many different kinds of points and lines in the one reality. '*Nichts sein soll was nicht sein darf*' as the German phrase says. Euclid was seen not only as the epitome of logical thought but also as being the source of the only and final description of true nature and reality.

The beginning of the demise of Euclidean geometry and with it the greatly influential theory of reasoning of Kant can be traced to a Jesuit mathematician named Saccheri, who predates Kant by several years. Saccheri, ironically, set himself the task of freeing Euclid, once and for all, from any doubt of flaw. To do this he made use of one of Aristotle's rules of logic: if you assume the opposite of a rule, and work with it, you should encounter a contradiction. This is sound logic! So Saccheri systematically worked out Euclid's propositions, one after another, while assuming that one of them was false. (The one he chose to assume was false was the fifth postulate: parallel lines only meet at infinity). He was rather disconcerted after thirty years when he had still not come across a clear contradiction. However, having decided he was almost sure of a contradiction, he decided to publish his results. The title of his book was understandably *Euclid Freed From Every Flaw*. He then died.

Sadly he died without being aware of his immense achievement. Contrary to proving geometry could not work without the five postulates of Euclid, he had developed what is now known as non-Euclidean geometry.

The story of Saccheri's disconcertment and his search for a preconceived conclusion suggests three things.

Firstly, and most importantly, the connection between logical structure and reality was questioned and this opened up the possibility of other forms of seeing and dealing with reality. The twentieth century debate on how to interpret the Quantum Mechanics pivoted on the adequacy of our logic to deal with the phenomena and theoretical constructs the physicists had developed.

Secondly, reasoning, while adhering to patterns that are as stable as rules does not guarantee the conclusion is understood. Saccheri did not understand where his conclusion was leading. If logic is only concerned with the structure of an argument, then it is clear that nothing can be learned from a conclusion. Thus logic does not lead to knowledge. I can produce a perfect line of argument that either Euclid or Spock would be proud of and nevertheless I may not understand the consequences of the conclusion.

Thirdly, even if the conclusion is reached by means of absolutely meticulous logical deduction, it can still be rejected because of deep prejudice. Saccheri not only did not realise the consequences of the argument he developed, he went further and claimed what he had discovered reinforced the thesis he had set out to prove: Euclid's geometry was free of flaws. Now it is one thing not to have understood the significance of an argument but it is more serious to then take the argument and use it in a way that twists the conclusion to one's own purpose. It is to be assumed that someone who spent thirty years attempting to prove Euclid was right was either fanatically devoted to him or passionately interested in the truth. After some research I believe the latter to be true. What can be deduced from the story is our prejudices and cultural imprisonment can dominate our thinking.

We have seen what logic is not: it is not a source of knowledge; it is not a picture of reality; it is not a defence against prejudice or cultural boundedness.

So what is it? The answer is embedded in the notion of Mr. Spock.

Observe him.

Firstly, he almost never takes the initiative: he is the watchdog over arguments that could be fallacious and therefore plays a reactive role. He points out irrelevant arguments but rarely adds a creative one.

Secondly, his picture of reality is very different from Aristotle's reality, or indeed from our own. His logic has nothing to do with a particular reality.

Thirdly, Spock is for the most part cultureless, or perhaps his culture is the culture of logic and thus not in conflict with it. (Even when the Enterprise seeks the supposedly dead Spock we get no sense of Vulcan culture). Thus Spock is fortunate (or unfortunate?) as his logic is not culturally distorted.

We have seen what logic is not. Let's end with what it is. In the form of a syllogism of course.

Logic enables us to recognise fallacies.

Fallacies occur in arguments that are at the centre of a theory of knowledge.

Therefore logic lies at the centre of knowledge.

And would Spock have enjoyed meeting Euclid? They would both have agreed on the need to avoid fallacious arguments but Euclid would not have understood Spock's concepts of space and reality. To what extent Euclid was something other than a logical egghead we cannot be sure. Does Mr. Spock enjoy meeting anyone? Certainly he would not have had much respect for Saccheri's misplaced search for truth.

MATRIX LOGIC

Many people use a matrix to help them make decisions. For instance they have $10 000 to spend on a car and can't decide which one to buy. They draw a matrix and list down one side of the matrix the cars available for $10000 and across the top of the matrix list their requirements. They decide which cars best fulfil each requirement and check the appropriate space. The car which has most checks is the one to buy. Logical, isn't it? Or is it? Which part of this process is logical and which isn't?

Some purely deductive logic problems can be solved simply by using a matrix.

I. HERE'S A SIMPLE EXAMPLE.
Before you look at the solution try solving it in a way that suits your style of problem solving.

Adam, Marco, Florian, Matteo and Kenji all have favourite subjects but no two have the same favourite. Using the following information determine which subject is the favourite of which student.

1.   Adam's favourite is not math.

2.   Marco dislikes math and English.

3.   One of the five really hates German.

4.   Florian's favourite is ToK.

5.   Matteo hates physics.

6.   Kenji's favourite subject is the one Matteo hates.

One way to solve the problem is to draw a matrix for the five students and the five subjects.

(Ignore the letters and numbers in the boxes until you read below).

	Maths	English	German	Physics	ToK
Adam	X1	Y5	X4	X2	X2
Marco	X1	X1	Y3	X2	X2
Florian	X7	X6	X4	X2	Y1
Matteo	Y7	X6	X4	X1	X2
Kenji	X7	X6	X4	Y1	X

To solve the problem.

1.   Find all the clues which give you a definite yes or no. (Marked X1 or Y1.)

2.   When you have marked Y you can put X in all the other boxes above and below. (X2)

3.   Look for any boxes that can now be filled. (Y3)

4.   The other boxes in this column can now be filled. (X4)

5.   Repeat 3. (Y5)

6.   Repeat 4. (X6)

7.   Repeat 3 horizontally. (Y7 X7).

Then you just read off the Y boxes:

> Adam-English,
> Marco-German,
> Florian-ToK,
> Matteo-Math and
> Kenji-Physics.

II. DESIGN YOUR OWN MATRIX TO SOLVE THIS PROBLEM:

Chris, Ankie, Tim, Lucca, Pamela and Maja decide to go out together for pizza. They soon find out they can't order a large pizza because each of them likes a different topping. They end up ordering six different pizzas: plain cheese; cheese and pepperoni; cheese, pepperoni and sausage; cheese and anchovies; The Works; and cheese and bacon. Using the following information, and a matrix, deduce who orders what.

Chris orders cheese and one topping that is not pepperoni. Ankie sits next to only one person and that person orders cheese and bacon. Tim hates any kind of fish.

The person who orders two items and cheese sits directly across from Lucca. Pamela orders The Works. Maja won't eat sausage or bacon. Lucca and Ankie sit next to one another. Tim and Ankie both order pepperoni.

III. NOW TRY USING MATRIX LOGIC TO SOLVE A REAL PROBLEM:

Consider that you have narrowed your choice of College or University to five possibilities, A, B, C, D, and E. and your concerns about selection to seven points: Cost, Situation, Quality of Tuition, Options within the academic program, Size of student population, Quality of accommodation and Opportunities for foreign exchange as part of the program. Draw a matrix and in each appropriate box grade each of the colleges or universities on a 1-9 scale. Now use your matrix to make a decision. How do you evaluate the information available in the completed matrix?

What does this problem tell you about the limits of logical thought?

SUDOKU

All you need to solve a Sudoku is logic and time. The rule is easy: Each column, each row and each box must contain each of the numbers 1 to 9.

Try this one. Maximum time allowed 15 minutes.

	4	5				8	1	
		7	5		9	4		
8								3
		8	3		4	7		
5								4
		6	9		5	2		
6								9
		9	7		3	6		
	2	4				5	3	

LOGIC: THREE PRACTICAL FOOTNOTES

FOOTNOTE 1

Professional logicians study only formal logic, working with rational, purely abstract patterns of arguing. Relating these abstract patterns of arguing to 'real' everyday arguments is not part of formal logic. These 'real' arguments involve many other issues and facts which are not part of logic. But logic, amongst other things can

- help to identify and clarify vague or ambiguous statements;
- indicate unstated assumptions or biases
- help us to identify unstated premisses; and
- make us aware of the strength and validity of analogies or comparisons.

FOOTNOTE 2

In order to understand the bases of knowledge in the traditional school subjects - natural science, math, history, economics and other 'human sciences'- we must consider the role logic plays in each of them. We need to be aware of the rigour of deductive logic and beware of its ability to produce valid arguments based on unreliable, or even downright impossible, premisses. We need to be aware of the 'probability' of inductive logic and beware of its not entirely logical rigour.

FOOTNOTE 3

In order to be clear thinkers ourselves we must be aware of how we ourselves use logic. We must be aware of how rigorous we are in applying logical thinking to our everyday decisions and how careful we are in forming and stating arguments, both when we speak and when we write. We are constantly being asked to believe things by ... politicians, newspaper articles and reports, television programs, our friends, salespeople, teachers. Of course we cannot respond to these requests to 'believe' with logic alone, but we ought to be aware which arguments are good and which are not.

Trains are usually assembled in 'marshalling yards' such as this one in Chicago.

Each set of 'points' represents a 'left/right' decision.

The whole is controlled using binary (two state) logic.

Now *you have read Chapter 2.4 ...*

consider or undertake the following:

1. Having read this introduction to logic and done the exercises in it, how do you rate yourself as a logical thinker?

2. Reread the definitions of Deductive Logic (page 59) and Inductive Logic (page 64). Make sure you really understand the difference.

How different are these definitions of logic from your everyday use of the word 'logic'?

3. Work through the matrix based logic exercises on page 71. How helpful could a matrix be in really helping you to choose a college or university?

4. Write a brief guide to the logic of Sudoku solving for someone who knows nothing about Sudoku.

5. Create two arguments for persuading someone you know to lend you money. Make the first argument entirely logical and free from any emotion and in the second allow yourself a little more freedom. Which argument would you use in practice?

6. Is it possible to study the logic of an argument regardless of its content?

7. Is logic used to create knowledge in all areas of knowledge?

Want to know more?

There are many books which explain logic in detail .

Logic by Robert Baum O.U.P 1995 is thorough and presents the reader with lots of opportunities to 'do' logic.

SECTION ONE
WAYS-OF-KNOWING

STATISTICS

2.5

CHAPTER CONTENTS

- Understand the reference
- Know how the numbers are generated
- Evaluate the validity of conclusions

Before *you read Chapter 2.5 ...*

consider possible responses to these statistically based 'facts':

1. Cigarette smoking causes cancer.

2. Speed kills.

3. We inherit our intelligence from our parents.

4. Exercise is good for you.

5. Twins run in families.

6. Average temperatures on Earth are rising.

Endangered?

2.5   AND, BY THE WAY, STATISTICS

A NUMERICAL WAY OF KNOWING

Maja, like you, is constantly bombarded with 'new' information. Much of this information - from the web, emails, television, newspapers, journals, radio, school text books, teachers – is statistical information.

Of course most of this statistical information is of no use and little interest to Maja - or you.

> ... the average length of palm fronds found on the remote pacific island of Tonuhatu is 2.417 metres according to research carried out...

But data obtained by serious surveys and research is the raw material from which much new knowledge is created. Statistical information is a reliable, rational basis for such knowledge. Statistics, after all is a branch of mathematics, and mathematics, with an exception or two, is a thoroughly reliable and rational area of knowledge. A number has a value we understand: meteorological figures can give us insight into a country's climate, population numbers tell us how big a city is. If we are told that 95% of the students in your class speak fluent Arabic then we certainly know something about your student population. Not so much, perhaps as we may think at first. What does 'fluent' mean in this context? What is meant by 'Arabic'? What is meant by 'your class'? But certainly we know something about them that is significant.

It is not my purpose here to give you a crash course in statistics. (If I did try to do that it would certainly be just that, and crash in the second paragraph.) Nor do I wish to repeat the populist folklore of statistics: that you need to be wary of them. Over fifty years ago a statistician, Huff, published an amusing but serious book *How to Lie with Statistics*. This immediately became a best seller and is still available in a bookshop near you.

As Theory of Knowledge students though you should be critical when presented with statistics. Be critical particularly of three things.

> Understand exactly what the statistic refers to.
> Know how the raw numbers were generated.
> Question the validity of the conclusions drawn from the statistics.

1. UNDERSTAND WHAT THE STATISTICS REFER TO

Some statistics mislead because using our 'common sense' we misinterpret them. I recently looked at the economic predictions for each of the countries of the world and was astonished to see the Gross Domestic Product (GDP) per head ($52 940) of Ireland indicating, so it seemed to me, that the citizens of Ireland had the third highest incomes in Europe. (Switzerland had $53 400 and Norway $70 400). Fortunately we had visiting us an Irish economist who pointed out that much of that GDP was created by foreign firms, so called multi-nationals, based in Ireland. A substantial proportion of the money they earn in Ireland is sent to shareholders elsewhere. The figure I really needed was the Mean Domestic Product (MDP) per head. This would give a more accurate indication of the mean income of the residents of Ireland. This MDP is much more difficult to calculate, and probably for that reason, was not given in the survey. The journal in which I read the information was certainly not attempting to deceive me. I was assuming something I should not have assumed: that GDP per head was equivalent to income per head. My knowledge problem was knowing - in this case not knowing - what was being measured.

Here is another example which is not quite so straightforward. You know that on the Internet you can find statistics which describe the climate of certain cities. Here, as an example, is the 'average' temperature for Beijing. What does 'average' here mean? Is it the average of the maximum and minimum temperatures based on daily readings throughout each month? Is it the average of a month's temperatures taken at a specific time each day? Is it the average maximum? Is it the average minimum? No doubt meteorologists know the answers to such questions, but if you don't, as a critical thinker, you need to be aware that you don't.

BEIJING

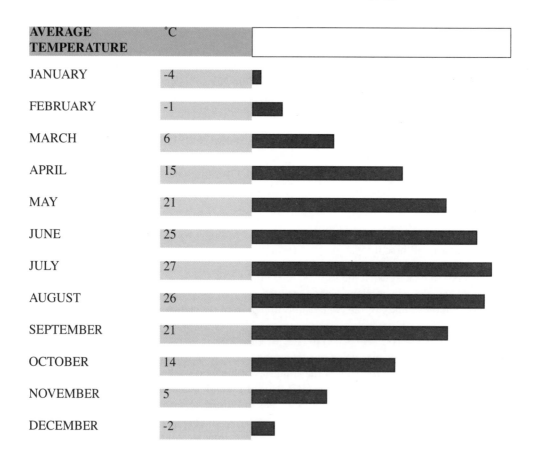

COUNTRY	LAT	LON	ELEV
CHINA	39.93 N	116.28 E	55 m

AVERAGE TEMPERATURE	°C
JANUARY	-4
FEBRUARY	-1
MARCH	6
APRIL	15
MAY	21
JUNE	25
JULY	27
AUGUST	26
SEPTEMBER	21
OCTOBER	14
NOVEMBER	5
DECEMBER	-2

2. KNOW HOW THE RAW NUMBERS WERE GENERATED

The important matter of the 'average' aside, there seems to be no reason to doubt the validity of these numbers describing the climate of Beijing. Presumably they are based on scientific measurements, using an accurate 'scientific' calibrated scale, made over an extended number of years. They reflect the physical reality of the temperatures in Beijing. 26°C is 26°C whether you are in Beijing or Azerbaijan.

Many statistics though are not based on such an accurately calibrated scale. You have almost certainly, sometime in your life, completed a survey questionnaire in which you were asked to rate things on a scale of 1 to 10, with 10 being the highest. For instance you may be asked to rate the meals served in your school cafeteria on a scale of 1 to 10. The information obtained by such a survey could be treated numerically, in much the same way as the temperatures in Beijing can be treated, they can be averaged and presented as hard information. But they don't have the integrity of the Beijing statistics. They have not been obtained using an accurate 'scientific' calibrated scale of measurement. They have been obtained by using an inaccurate, idiosyncratic 'human' scale of measurement, called opinion. This does not mean they are entirely without value, but their value is not the value of scientific measurement.

STANDARDISED TESTING

Another way that statistics of limited integrity can be generated is much more subtle.

Standardised Testing is a clear example of social scientists creating 'knowledge'. 'Standardised' means the scores are based on a 'standard' set by the designers of the test. The test designers first draft the tests and then 'test' them on a group of people as similar as possible to the group that will eventually be measured by the tests. This test group is called a 'sample population'. The test creators aim to produce a test, which, when taken by this sample population, will produce what is called 'a curve of normal distribution'.

A curve of normal distribution looks like this:

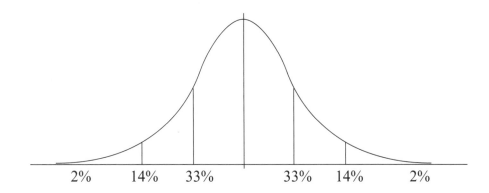

| 2% | 14% | 33% | | 33% | 14% | 2% |

A standardised test is designed so that the average score (from however many questions are asked) of the sample population will be at the top point of the curve, and the scores of an equal number of those tested will be on either side. Test designers adjust the difficulty of the questions until this curve of normal distribution is achieved. They may, for instance, take out the questions that too many people in the sample answer correctly and replace them with more 'discriminating' questions, that is, questions that fewer people can answer correctly. They then create the score by defining the central point as 100. If your score is exactly average you will have a score of 100. The 33% of the sample population who scored above the 100 are classified as scoring between 100 and 115, and the 33% below the 100 are classified as scoring between 85 and 99. The 14% above the 115 are classified as scoring 116 to 130 and the 14% below 85 are classified as scoring 70-85. Finally there are those who score below 70s and above 130s. Fine sub-divisions are of course possible, to get any score between, say, 65 and 135.

Standardised Test score range

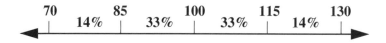

Standardised tests are easily misused. If you 'standardise' an English language test on a sample population of well educated children whose mother tongue is English and use the test on a group of non-English speaking poor immigrants the scores will be meaningless. All the ten year old children in St. Pauls, Wisconsin will have IQ scores above average if they are tested on a test standardised with a population sample of six year old children.

The first standardised test was developed in 1905 by the Frenchman Alfred Binet. He used it to help identify school students who needed extra help. The use of standardised tests spread quickly. The first mass use of these tests was in 1917 when the American Army gave them to 1.7 million recruits. In the 1950s and 1960s they were used in Britain to determine, at the age of eleven, the type (and quality) of education available to children. Those students who scored in the top 10% were guaranteed places in 'grammar' schools, which gave them access to universities and the professions. The remaining 90% left school at 15.

What you, as a critical thinker, must be aware of is the way these 'intelligence tests' are created. And how the numbers they create can be changed. Test designers could (and sometimes do) relabel the 33% on either side of the centre of the normal curve and then an IQ of 115 would become 130.

3. CHECK THE VALIDITY OF THE CONCLUSIONS DRAWN FROM THE STATISTICS

Mark Twain was clearly a critical thinker. He knew about the danger of drawing conclusions from statistics. I will leave it to him to humourously make the point.

Here an oft-quoted piece from his *Life on the Mississippi*. 'Cut-offs' are short channels formed when a river cuts through the neck of an oxbow.

Since my own day on the Mississippi, cut-offs have been made at Hurricane Island; at island 100; at Napoleon, Arkansas; at Walnut Bend; and at Council Bend. These shortened the river, in the aggregate, sixty-seven miles. In my own time a cut-off was made at American Bend, which shortened the river ten miles or more.

Therefore, the Mississippi between Cairo and New Orleans was twelve hundred and fifteen miles long one hundred and seventy-six years ago. It was eleven hundred and eighty after the cut-off of 1722. It was one thousand and forty after the American Bend cut-off. It has lost sixty-seven miles since. Consequently its length is only nine hundred and seventy-three miles at present.

Now, if I wanted to be one of those ponderous scientific people, and 'let on' to prove what had occurred in the remote past by what had occurred in a given time in the recent past, or what will occur in the far future by what has occurred in late years, what an opportunity is here! Geology never had such a chance, nor such exact data to argue from!

Nor 'development of species,' either! Glacial epochs are great things, but they are vague-- vague. Please observe: --

In the space of one hundred and seventy-six years the Lower Mississippi has shortened itself two hundred and forty-two miles. That is an average of a trifle over one mile and a third per year. Therefore, any calm person, who is not blind or idiotic, can see that in the Old Oolitic Silurian Period, just a million years ago next November, the Lower Mississippi River was upwards of one million three hundred thousand miles long, and stuck out over the Gulf of Mexico like a fishing-rod. And by the same token any person can see that seven hundred and forty-two years from now the Lower Mississippi will be only a mile and three-quarters long, and Cairo and New Orleans will have joined their streets together, and be plodding comfortably along under a single mayor and a mutual board of aldermen. There is something fascinating about science. One gets such wholesale returns of conjecture out of such a trifling investment of fact.

Now *you have read the Chapter 2.5 ...*

consider or undertake the following:

1. When is the best time to visit Beijing?

2. Do petrol prices rise at the weekend?

3. Bhutan has an 'index of national happiness'. How would you define this measure for your country?

4. Are you taller than your antecedent who celebrated the first AD/CE millennium?

5. Who has the best ever sporting statistics?

6. It is sometimes said that democracies do not make war on democracies. Is this true?

SECTION ONE
WAYS-OF-KNOWING

EMOTION

3

CHAPTER CONTENTS

Before

you read Chapter 3 ...

consider possible responses to these:

1. Psychologists claim to have identified 412 quite distinct human emotions. List what you think are the most obvious ten of these and consider in what ways you may have gained knowledge through them.

2. Can you have an emotion that can't be expressed in language?

3. Is there such a thing as 'collective emotion'? Have you ever experienced such a thing? Is racism a collective emotion?

4. How do you know the mood of a class when you enter it a little late?

5. How do you know what other people are thinking? How good are you at judging their thoughts and feelings? Can you, for instance, easily tell when someone (a) is despondent? (b) is pre-occupied? (c) is suspicious? or (d) wants to enter a conversation?

6. How good are you at not-believing what you don't want to believe? Have you ever continued to sincerely believe something when you know it couldn't possible be so?

7. Our conscience is, amongst other things, a collection of values which sometimes makes us feel guilty. What values are in your conscience? How did they get there?

8. Explain, to someone who has never ridden a bicycle, how to ride a bicycle. That is, share your knowledge of how to ride a bicycle with a non bicycle rider. He or she particularly needs to know how you keep your balance.

9. Does a doctor who has had a broken leg know more about broken legs than one who has not? Which of the two doctors would you go to if your leg was broken?

3.0 EMOTION

A PERSONAL WAY OF KNOWING

'WISSEN' AND 'KENNEN', 'KNOWING' AND 'KNOWING'

The German language has two words which both translate as 'to know'[1]. These two words 'wissen' and 'kennen' are widely used in everyday conversation and each has a distinct meaning. 'Kennen' means 'to be acquainted with' and 'wissen' means 'to have knowledge of'. The latter kind of knowledge, wissen-knowledge is the way-of-knowing described in Chapter 2 Reason: Plato's knowledge-by-description, his justified true belief.

Kennen-knowledge, the 'emotion' knowledge of the IB ToK diagram, is regarded by some philosophers as having rather dubious validity. It lacks the intellectual rigour of wissen-knowledge. It is a personal, often indefinable way-of-knowing which Plato would certainly not accept as 'knowledge'. It is knowledge we are acquainted with through our everyday experiences and our emotions, through our self awareness, instincts and intuition, subjectively through our environment and upbringing. It is 'direct and immediate', the knowledge which enables us to identify the smell of freshly baked bread and which prompts us to sympathise with a crying baby and empathise with someone who has just failed a driving test.

Bertrand Russell, a distinguished 20th century philosopher, used the phrase 'knowledge-by-acquaintance' to describe a specific kind of kennen-knowledge. The knowledge he stated 'a dog lover has of a dog.' Kennen-knowledge, although including Russell's intuitive knowledge-by-acquaintance, covers a much wider range of personal ways-of-knowing, including knowledge by empathy, by personal belief, conviction, introspection, intuition, and practice.

'Kennen' knowledge is, of course, a much less specific way of knowing than knowledge-by-description. Look again at the first part of the ways-of-knowing diagram.

KNOWLEDGE BY DESCRIPTION
LOGIC
EMPIRICISM
AUTHORITY
MEMORY

The first four ways of knowing, impersonal, objective ways-of-knowing, are open to testing by the 'justified true belief' formula. Maja's remaining ways-of-knowing (acquaintance, belief, faith, introspection, empathy, conscience, practice, instinct) are less rational, more personal ways-of-knowing. But that does not mean they are less important. Logic, empiricism, memory and authority are 'reason' Ways of Knowing within the IB ToK diagram. These remaining ways-of-knowing, placed within the same diagram, are 'emotion' Ways-of-Knowing. (I distort the grammar to fit the wording of the diagram). To understand the 'emotion' Ways-of-Knowing you have, first, to accept that emotion is a significant factor in our acquisition and understanding of knowledge. If you are a hard line rationalist you may find this difficult. Perhaps reading this chapter, and thinking about emotion as a way-of-knowing and its relevance to the creation of knowledge its different areas, may help you to think differently.

---

1. French and Spanish have similar words, *savoir/connaître* and *saber/conocer* respectively.

WHAT IS EMOTION?

Like the meaning of many words the meaning of *emotion* can bewitch our intelligences,

Dictionary definitions can be confusing but the fourth definition in the New Shorter Oxford English Dictionary is helpful for our purposes.

> *Any of the natural instinctive affections of the mind (e.g. love, horror, pity) which come and go according to one's personality, experiences, and bodily state; a mental feeling. Also mental feeling as distinguished from knowledge, and from will.*

Psychologists claim to have identified over 400 distinct emotions and have divided them up into eight main 'families'.

Anger: indignation, acrimony, exasperation ....etc.
Sadness: grief, dejection, gloom ....
Fear: consternation, edginess, dread ....
Enjoyment: joy, pride, ecstasy ....
Love: friendliness, trust, kindness ....
Surprise: astonishment, amazement ....
Disgust: scorn, distaste, revulsion ....
Shame: guilt, remorse, contrition ....

Paul Eckman, an American psychologist, claims that facial expressions indicating four of these (fear, sadness, anger and enjoyment) can be recognised by people of all cultures, from primitive Stone Age societies to sophisticated, educated city dwellers.

Notice I have not written 'emotional ways-of-knowing'. That would suggest the analysis and description of ways-of-knowing are themselves exclusively emotional. In the same way as empiricism and memory are never free of emotion, so these ways of knowing are not free from reason. But they lack the dominant rationality that would be acceptable to Plato and his justified true belief. Helping you to appreciate the strength of emotion and its validity as a way-of-knowing enables you to make effective comparisons between ways-of-knowing and areas of knowledge, a major objective of the ToK programme.

In the rest of this chapter I define seven different 'emotion' ways-of-knowing. Each of these seven ways can be described separately but, in practice, in dealing with our own emotions, they blend together. For the purpose of the ToK programme (the aims of which include developing an awareness of how knowledge is constructed and evaluated and connections between areas of knowledge) some of these 'emotion' ways-of-knowing are of more weight than others. One of the issues you should certainly address is what, for you, are the most relevant 'emotion' ways-of-knowing in each of the areas of knowledge.

3.1   ACQUAINTANCE

Maja knows the moods of her friend Janine because she is acquainted with them. She and Janine have been friends for several years and without thinking too much about them, Maja has grown familiar with her friend's moods: sometimes Janine is playful, sometimes cynical, sometimes happy, sometimes a little sad. Maja is acquainted with Janine in these moods and knows they are part of her personality, her being. Maja would find it difficult, if not impossible, to explain how she recognises Janine's moods, but she has no doubt that she can recognise them. Maja has knowledge of Janine's moods by acquaintance.

Experience is a major creator of knowledge by acquaintance. Experience includes "everything we do and everything that happens to us, it encompasses sensation and emotions and pains and aesthetic experiences and mystical transport" (Bertrand Russell).

Intuition is a form of knowledge by acquaintance. 'Intuition' means 'immediate apprehension without the intervention of reason or direct or immediate insights.' Maja, knows Janine likes her. She knows from the way Janine responds to her questions and answers. She knows from the way she looks at her. She knows from the way she smiles and the tone of voice she uses when speaking to her. Maja uses her experience of other people and the way they relate to her to understand and appreciate Janine's friendship. She doesn't attempt to explain this understanding. She simply accepts it.

Can you describe the feeling of sand under your feet? Or the smell of a dog kennel? Or how you can recognise your friends when you see them in the local shopping mall? These things you know by acquaintance.

3.2   EMPATHY

Maja, you may recall, knows how Aravapo feels after he has just failed his driving test. She knows this by empathy. She is able to empathise with Aravarpo, to understand his thoughts and feelings, his disappointment and sense of failure. What, you may ask, is *empathy* exactly and what is its value, its status, as a way-of-knowing, particularly as a way-of-knowing in the six areas of knowledge that are at the heart of Theory of Knowledge? Has it any value at all if it is the more or less instinctive reaction that it seems to be?

Empathy has been much discussed and analysed by psychologists. Here are some of the features which they have defined.

1.   Empathy is created and controlled in the brain by what are called *mirror neurons*. Mirror neurons are the brain cells that encourage people to copy other people's actions. Babies, for instance, imitate those around them and learn the emotional responses that create bonding. Mirror neurons become active when someone is watching some one else experience an emotion. They encourage the observer to feel the emotions, the sense of failure, disappointment, embarrassment and joy of the person they are observing.

2.   Empathy involves a leap of imagination into someone else's head.

3. Empathy is the ability of a person to spontaneously and naturally understand another person's thoughts and feelings. Strongly empathetic people don't just understand a small number of fairly obvious thoughts and feelings, like pain and sadness; they can understand a wide range of emotional conditions.

4. Empathic people respond to other people's tone of voice, scan their faces (especially the eyes) and the body postures to understand how they are feeling and what they are thinking.

5. Empathy makes real communication possible. It leads you to understand the person you are talking with, to check to see if they want to enter the dialogue, and what they think about the subject.

6. Empathy also motivates the empathetic person to find out and care about other people.

7. Empathy is used to build moral codes. We build moral codes from our feelings for others, as well as ourselves. And part of that feeling is compassion which is generated by empathy.

Psychologists claim there are two major components of empathy

The **thinking** component. Piaget, a famous 20th C Swiss psychologist called this 'responding non-egocentrically'. This component means setting aside your own perspective, your own thoughts and feelings and thinking of what another person's emotional state may be and inferring from their experience, what that emotional state is.

The **feeling** component. This is how the empathiser responds to that emotional state.

Empathy then defines how we relate to other people. It helps us understand other people's existence. In order to empathise we have to set aside our own world view, our perceptions, our knowledge, and our beliefs. It allows us to see the other side of an argument, another point of view, and another world picture. Empathy, it could be argued, is to the artist – the painter, the dancer, the poet, the novelist, the playwright – what empiricism is to the natural scientist: the basic tool with which they go about their businesses. How could the Greeks have written the great tragedies if they had not been empathetic? How could Shakespeare have written about jealousy and ambition and the problems of aging if he had not been able to project himself into the minds of his protagonists? How could Picasso have painted *Guernica* if he had not understood the effect of war on people's thoughts and feelings?

And for you, if you study literature or history or any of the human sciences, empathy must be at the core of your way-of-knowing. The very first examination assessment criteria for the Language A1 Commentary paper is

How well has the candidate understood the thoughts and feelings expressed in the text?

Those 'thoughts and feelings' are thoughts and feelings of a creative artist responding to a human dilemma; exploring through language an idea or an insight. Your task, reading literature, is to respond to those thoughts and feelings. Without empathy you would not be able to do that.

A TEST FOR EMPATHY

Psychologists have a variety of tests to measure empathy. In one of these 'Reading the mind in the eyes test' the testee is given 36 pictures of pairs of eyes and four adjectives and asked to choose which adjective best describes what the person is thinking:

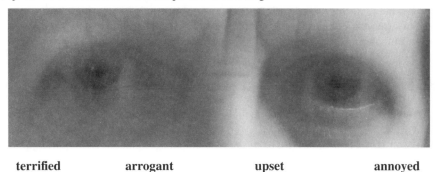

| terrified | arrogant | upset | annoyed |

3.3   BELIEF AND CONVICTION

From Plato's *Dialogue Gorgias*

Socrates:	You would agree there is such a thing as 'knowing'?
Gorgias:	Certainly.
Socrates:	And such a thing as 'believing'?
Gorgias:	Yes.
Socrates:	Well, do you think that knowing and believing are the same, or is there a difference between knowledge and belief?
Gorgias:	I should say there is a difference.
Socrates:	Quite right; and you can prove it like this. If you were asked whether there are such things as true and false beliefs, you would say there are, no doubt.
Gorgias:	Yes.
Socrates:	But are there such things as true and false knowledge?
Gorgias:	Certainly not.
Socrates:	Then knowledge and belief are clearly not the same thing.
Gorgias:	True.
Socrates:	Yet men who believe may be just as properly convinced as men who know?
Gorgias:	Yes.

This dialogue may seem to you to be stating that which doesn't need to be stated: something you know already and which is so uncontroversial it hardly needs to be discussed. The difference between believing something and knowing something is obvious. If you want to believe the sea is made of raspberry juice and all the fish that are swimming in it are juice drunk fairies, well go ahead and believe that. After all, what you believe is your business. People might be interested in hearing your arguments for believing the sea is raspberry juice but your claim is only that you believe it to be raspberry juice, not that it is raspberry juice. And providing you don't start collecting it and selling it as genuine raspberry juice, or expecting anyone else to think it is raspberry juice, why shouldn't you believe it? People on the whole are fairly tolerant and provided your belief doesn't harm you or them, why shouldn't you believe what you want to?

There is after all a big difference between belief and knowledge.

Or is there?

Are you quite sure where the boundary is between your knowing something and your believing something? For hundreds of years people knew the world was flat. And we know now that it is approximately spherical. Perhaps a lot of our knowledge is 'flat earth' knowledge and we are unaware of it. Perhaps there are many things we think we know but we only believe. Perhaps some of what we think is really important knowledge is belief.

There are two things about belief you should be quite clear about.

1.   What some people believe can be much more important to them than what they know.

For many ancient Greeks the belief that gods controlled their destiny was more important than anything else in determining their actions.

2.   Even though you think your beliefs are under your control and are a matter of choice, they are often not recognised as beliefs.

The Greeks didn't just believe the gods controlled them, they thought they knew, in the same way as people thought they knew the world was flat.

Beware then of underestimating the importance of belief as a way-of-knowing.

3.4   CONSCIENCE

Maja, like most of us, knows it is wrong to steal. Her conscience tells her it is wrong. Her conscience is her sense of right and wrong; it directs her ability to judge what she should do about moral issues. It tells her, amongst other things, it is wrong to spread malicious gossip. It tells her it is wrong to copy ToK essays from the Internet and pass them off as her own and it tells her it is wrong to 'borrow' from her small sister's money box. Her conscience tells her it is right to help old ladies cross the road, to support Amnesty International and to feel guilty because she lied to her parents about last Friday night.

Conscience has been described as a human 'faculty', in this case a special part of the mind which is responsible for moral decisions. Everyone, it is claimed, is endowed with this faculty, but of course not everyone is endowed to the same extent, which explains why moral behaviour varies from person to person.

Most of us do seem to have a conscience. Where does it come from and how do we know what it tells us to do? The values our conscience applies to make moral decisions almost certainly come from the environment in which we were nurtured. But these values are different from the conscience itself. Or are they? We must introspectively examine our conscience in order to make moral decisions and what can our conscience be except a collection of those values which determine our moral behaviour?

3.5   INTROSPECTION

Maja, remember is in love. She knows she is in love by introspection. Introspection is the examination of one's own mental and emotional processes. You are aware of what you feel, what you hope, what you think, what you believe, by examining your own mind and making yourself aware of what is there. These thoughts and feelings may be created and shaped by external contact but once you have them they are independent of things outside of you. The example of Maja's love is a good example of that independence. Love is an emotion based on the feelings she has for an external object. But is it only through her own introspection, an examination of her own emotional state that makes Maja aware that she is in love?

Perhaps a less emotional example might be helpful. Maja is a keen skier and she wants it to snow heavily on Friday so she can go skiing at the weekend. She wishes for snow. This is as certain a piece of knowledge for her as any piece of knowledge could be. You might claim again that the wish is focussed on an external event, in this case, heavy snow on Friday. But the heavy snow is not the state of wishing that she has. Her wish for snow she knows by introspection in a similar way to the way she knows she is in love.

There are problems, of course, with introspection. The main one seems to be that access to our own minds, which is what introspection is, gives us access to something which can be misleading. We have all seen people in love who don't realise they are in love or who try to repress the idea that they are in love; people who will not face up to the reality of what is in their minds. Haven't you ever taken pains to ensure that you did not accept some aspect of your thinking or feeling that you did not wish to acknowledge? Sigmund Freud warned us we are not the best judges of our own state of consciousness.

Another problem with introspection is that it is often difficult to describe the mental state which introspection presents. "Oh give me a break" is what we might mutter when we feel depressed or pressured or 'under the weather', without being able to say exactly why we need a break. It is not easy to put feelings into words. Introspection is considered by some philosophers to be a significant part of the way-of-knowing in those disciplines which examine human behaviour and institutions.

SIGMUND FREUD (1856-1939)

After graduating from medical school in 1882 Freud specialised in neurology and then psychopathology, the branch of psychology dealing with the abnormal workings of the mind. He developed and refined psychoanalysis as a revolutionary way of treating mentally disturbed patients. His major work *The Interpretation of Dreams* argued that dreams are disguised wish fulfilments, indications of suppressed desires and energies. His greatest achievement was to free the study of sexuality from the social controls that up to the late 19th century prevented any serious study of sex. Many psychiatrists now disagree with some of his ideas but his work had, and still has, a strong influence on many academic disciplines, including anthropology, sociology and criminology.

3.6   INSTINCT AND PRACTICE

Practice and instinct are certainly Ways-of-Knowing but neither fits comfortably under the heading of 'reason' or 'emotion'. Despite this they are both significant ways in which Maja knows what she knows.

INSTINCT

Instinct is certainly a way-of-knowing we all have. Animals, of course, survive by their instincts. Polar bears instinctively know to hibernate each winter. Swallows know they must fly north to avoid the southern winter. All mammal mothers know instinctively to protect their young. Humans also have instincts. These instincts make us act in certain ways without us having to consciously think about why. Most of these instincts are concerned with our physical survival. We know we must find shelter in a storm. We know we must eat to survive, and we know we must flee in the face of overwhelming danger. Instinct also drives us to mate. This instinctive knowledge is within us. It is innate. We are born with it. But that does not mean we cannot be aware of it and even, if necessary, overcome some of our instincts and act in ways contrary to what they tell us. Early humans, for instance, had to overcome their instinctive fear of huge animals, so they could approach them and kill them for food. People who enter hospitals and are operated upon have to overcome their instinctive fear of having their bodies cut open. It is possible to be aware of our instincts, to analyse them and the way they make us behave, and to overcome them. By becoming aware of our instincts, by becoming acquainted with them, we can begin to know them as something other than just unexplainable motivating forces.

PRACTICE

You probably know how to swim and you probably know how to ride a bike and you may know how to play the piano. You will not be surprised to know that this kind of knowledge is often called 'knowledge-how' to differentiate it from 'knowledge-that', propositional knowledge. You know how to do specific things because you have practised doing them and through practice you know how to do them. You probably know someone who plays the piano well. How do they know how to do this? They practised and practised and practised until they got it right. I cannot play the piano. If I asked one of my students who does know how to play the piano how they learned to play so well they would probably say 'I practised and practised and practised until I was able to play.' And this is what I would have to do if I wanted to play the piano, practise and practise and practise. Over and over again I would have to repeat the exercises until I was able to play automatically, like an accomplished pianist.

Much of Theory of Knowledge is concerned with justification for saying 'we know.' The scientific, empirical way-of-knowing and the logical, rational, reasoning way-of-knowing are easy to understand; they fit our western, 'justified true belief' model of knowledge. Maja's ways-of-knowing are many and varied, some considerably less rational than others, but nevertheless very important to her, as they are to many of us.

One way-of-knowing, faith, which you may have expected to be considered in this chapter on emotion as a way of knowing, is plainly absent. Because of its importance as a way-of-knowing to many people, and because of the controversies that it can and does cause, faith has been allocated a chapter of its own, beyond reason and emotion.

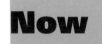

Now *you have read Chapter 3 ...*

consider the following:

1.

Here is a definition of *emotion* taken from the *New Shorter Oxford Dictionary:*

Any of the natural instinctive affections of the mind (e.g. love, horror, pity) which come and go according to one's personality, experiences, and bodily state; a mental feeling. Also mental feeling as distinguished from knowledge, and from will.

One of the things you must consider is your own definition of *emotion* in terms of knowledge. Do you consider *a mental feeling as distinguished from knowledge* as an adequate definition? What does that imply for the meaning of the word knowledge?

The NSOED has a definition of knowledge as

Intellectual perception of fact or truth; clear and certain understanding and awareness.

Is emotional knowledge simply a mental feeling? And what, in this context, is *will*?

2.

Which of the emotional Ways of Knowing can be taken seriously as leading to knowledge which you, personally, can accept as valid knowledge?'

3. Is emotion as a way-of-knowing independent of culture? Is there anything about it universal to all human cultures?

4. Experience creates knowledge by acquaintance. Is experience worthy of being a way-of-knowing in its own right or is it part of other ways-of-knowing?

5. Can you (a) understand and (b) agree with the statement on page 88 that empathy is to the artist what empiricism is to the scientist?

6. Read again the extract on page 89 from Plato's '*Dialogue Gorgias*'. Make sure you understand exactly what it is that Socrates here considers to be knowledge. Is such a definition of knowledge acceptable to you?

Want to know more?

You will find the following books informative and easy to read:

Emotional Intelligence by Daniel Goleman (Bloomsbury Paperbacks 1996) and

The Essential Difference by Simon Baron-Cohen (Penguin 2005).

SECTION ONE
WAYS-OF-KNOWING

FAITH

4

CHAPTER CONTENTS

- Faith and religiosity
- Justification of faith as a way-of-knowing: i. Historical ii. The nature of faith, revelation, meditation and holy writ. iii. Intellectual: Aquinas and Newman iv. 'Joy': C S Lewis
- Theories of Truth and Faith
- Postscripts: Intelligent Design or God of the Gaps? Music and faith. Faith and love.
- Five major religions

Before *you read Chapter 4 ...*

consider possible responses to these:

1. What do you consider 'faith'?

2. Should faith as a way-of-knowing be included in the chapter on emotion (or reason?) or is it quite a distinct way-of-knowing?

3. In what areas of knowledge is faith a necessary way-of-knowing?

4. How important is faith in your life?

5. Where does your faith - or lack of faith - come from?

4.0   FAITH

A SPIRITUAL WAY OF KNOWING

As you read earlier Maja knows when she dies she is going to heaven.

She knows this by *faith*. Her faith in God tells her that she will go to heaven when she dies. She is absolutely convinced there is a benign God who will give her life in heaven after death. She might also be convinced that God has also given her a conscience and a sense of morality; a sense of what is right and wrong, good or evil. Her belief that killing people is wrong is probably based on her belief in God.

But what exactly is faith and from where does Maja get it? And how does it fit into our Theory of Knowledge understanding of the ways-of-knowing. Does she know about her faith through sense perception? Through reason? Language? Emotion?

FAITH: DIVINE TRUTH AND REALITY

Before answering these questions we must be aware that 'faith' here is used in a specific way. In general, everyday usage *faith* means simple trust or confidence. I might once have said to Maja, 'I have every faith in you to get a good end of term grade'. What I meant was that I had confidence in her. I trusted her to do well. There was nothing mystical or spiritual about my faith in Maja's ability to do well. I was simply stating what I considered a practical likely outcome, justified by the fact I know how she has worked. I know she is reliable and capable. I was in fact being rational. Maja's faith in God is different. Her faith is a system of firmly held beliefs based on her personal, spiritual knowledge of 'divine truth and reality'. Her spiritual faith is different from my 'rational' faith, which predicts her success.

Whatever the origins of her faith or religiosity, for many people in the 21st century God gives meaning and purpose to life. For them God is the source of all good and the creator of the entire universe and all things within it. God, they argue, is deeply concerned about the condition of humanity in general and with the behaviour of individuals. God cannot be 'known', perceived or understood, in the way we know other things such as science or mathematics or art. He/she cannot be seen or heard and there is absolutely no physical proof of his/her existence. Knowledge of God's existence is, therefore, entirely different from any other kind of knowledge.

THE JUSTIFICATION OF FAITH

Faith, spiritual knowledge, is a way-of-knowing that affects our daily lives. As critical thinkers we should be aware of it and attempt to understand it. Let us look at arguments that, in ToK terms, can be used to justify faith as a way-of-knowing.

There are as many justifications for faith as there are religions but I have attempted to explore four.

1.   Historical justification.
2.   Justification through the nature of faith itself, meditation, revelation and holy writ.
3.   Intellectual justification.
4.   Justification by joy.

JUSTIFICATION 1: HISTORICAL

THE ORIGINS OF RELIGIOSITY I: EVOLUTIONARY ADVANTAGE

Richard Dawkins[1], a leading Darwinist, argues that religiosity - the inclination towards faith - is, in evolutionary terms, a cost rather than a benefit. 'Religious behaviour in bipedal apes' he wrote, 'occupies large quantities of time. It devours huge resources. A medieval cathedral consumed hundreds of man-centuries in its building. Sacred music and devotional paintings largely monopolised medieval and renaissance talent. Thousands, perhaps millions, of people have died, often accepting torture first, for loyalty to one religion against a scarcely distinguishable alternative. Devout people have died for their gods, killed for them, fasted for them, and endured whipping ..... for the sake of religion.'

If this is so why did religiosity arise? A distinguished American professor of biology and anthropology, David Sloan Wilson[2], has a suggestion: religiosity emerged as a useful human trait because it unified social groups. Hunters and gatherers could hunt and gather more effectively if they could cooperate. The more organised and cooperative the group the better they could hunt, the healthier they became and the more able they were to pass on their genes. Shared religious beliefs could provide cohesion and a moral code. A shared religion could be an evolutionary advantage.

THE ORIGINS OF RELIGIOSITY II: FINDING MEANING AND VALUE

This is another equally practical but less worldly justification for faith. Humans, it seems, started to worship God, to have faith, as soon as we learned to stand upright. This faith arose from our wonder and awe of the natural world we inhabit and an attempt to find meaning and value in our lives and our place in that world. And to help us find this meaning and value we created gods. Gods, and our faith in them, are probably the most powerful force in the history of the human race.

In the Palaeolithic period, when agriculture was developing, the cult of the Mother Goddess expressed a sense that the fertility that was transforming human life was sacred. Artists carved statues showing her naked and pregnant and these statues have been found all over Europe, the Middle East and India. The Great Mother remained important for several thousand years. She was called Inana in Sumeria, Ishtar in Babylon, Anat in Canaan, Isis in Egypt and Aphrodite in Greece. In each of these cultures she was worshipped and stories about her abounded. The stories were not taken literally but helped people to be aware of the sense of what they perceived as the unseen forces surrounding them and controlling their lives.

These 'unseen forces' are at the heart of faith. People wanted to get in touch with these forces, to work with them and to admire them. When we personalise these unseen forces and make them gods we are expressing our sense of affinity with them and the world they live in.

Throughout history we have experienced this dimension of life that goes beyond our everyday, pragmatic existence. However we choose to interpret it this 'transcendence', as it has been often called, is a fact of our historical development. Many societies have called this transcendence God and have been awed by the concept they have created. Jews, for instance, are not allowed to pronounce the sacred name of God, Muslims must not depict the divine visually.

---

1. Quoted in *The Story of God* by Robert Winston. Transworld Books. 2005.
2. ibid.

FAITH AT THE BEGINNING OF THE 21ST CENTURY

Since humans first appeared on earth they have had faith and have been seeking understanding of God, they have had an inclination to religiosity. Despite, or even because of the technological age in which we live, their search continues. Many find what they are looking for. A special report in a leading US weekly journal in 2005[3] made that quite clear. 67% of those polled by the journal believed, as does Maja, that when they died their soul would go straight to heaven. Some other statistics from the same poll: 79% described themselves as 'spiritual', 57% describing spirituality as 'very important' in their daily lives, 39% practised religion 'to forge a personal relationship with God', 64% engaged in religious or spiritual activities daily, 40% felt the strongest connection to God when they were praying alone and a huge 80% believed that God created the universe.

This poll was taken in the United States where religiosity is deeply rooted but the power of faith is not seen only in that country. The strength of the faith of many Muslims is seen in the minarets rising above the streets in many burgeoning cities of the Gulf region and all the other areas of the world where Muslims now live. The influence of the Buddhist, Hindu and Taoist faiths is embedded in the customs and life styles of people all over the world. Israel is a country whose existence is due to the spiritual faith of its citizens. Only in Western Europe does the influence of faith seem to be declining, as Christian churches lose their congregations, but even there millions of faithful followers attend rallies to receive the blessing of the Pope.

JUSTIFICATION 2: FAITH, MEDITATION, REVELATION AND THE SCRIPTURES

I. THE NATURE OF FAITH

For many devout people faith does not need justification. Faith is not justifiable by reason or emotion. Faith, like reason, is what it is, faith. As reason is reason so faith is faith. Any attempt to explain it in any other terms is to misunderstand the nature of faith as a way-of-knowing. History is full of attempts by philosophers and scholars to justify faith with reason but the conclusion is inevitable: there is no rational justification for faith. On the following pages I have summarised three attempts by distinguished scholars, St. Thomas Aquinas, Cardinal Henry Newman and C. S. Lewis to explain the origins of their faith. Read Newman particularly with sympathetic care and you will perhaps become aware of the uniqueness of faith as a way-of-knowing. Newman emphasises what he calls conscience and imagination and probability. The main problem for people searching to understand faith is the fundamental point on which all who do have faith agree: you can't understand it unless you have it and you can't have it unless you understand it.

II. REVELATION

Thomas Aquinas claimed there are two ways-of-knowing which lead to faith, reason and revelation. This latter he described as knowledge 'by descent, by the mode of revelation, of divine truth which exceeds human intellect, yet not as demonstrated to our sight, but as a communication delivered for our belief'.

Aquinas himself experienced a divine revelation during a church service. A prolific writer before his revelation he wrote nothing at all after it, explaining to a fellow churchman: 'All I have written seems to me like straw compared to what has now been revealed to me.' Four months after his revelation he died.

---

3. *Newsweek* September 5 2005

Revelation, the communication of knowledge by divine or supernatural means, has long been the source of knowledge about faith and matters of religion. Moses was made aware of the Torah by divine revelation and his receiving of the Ten Commandments is a familiar story.

The most famous revelation of all is certainly the revelation of the Koran to Mohammed. One night in the year 610 AD Mohammed awoke in terror and felt himself surrounded by a fearful divine presence. This divine presence, which he later described as an angel, commanded him to recite. Mohammed, not wishing to be taken for a 'reciter' (then a kind of soothsayer you visited if you wanted to recover a lost camel) protested and felt himself in such a fierce embrace he could not breathe. After three such embraces and commands to recite, words poured out of his mouth. These words, the first words of God to be given in Arabic, became the Koran, which means the recitation. The complete Koran was revealed to Mohammed bit by bit over the next 23 years. Listening carefully to the divine words he entered a trance and often sweated profusely. As he could neither read nor write he recited the revealed words aloud and his followers learned them by heart, or if they were one of the few who were literate, wrote them down.

III. MEDITATION

Meditation is used for a wide variety of purposes, some of which are secular but many of which claim to produce a mental and spiritual opening to the divine and to create the possibility of guidance from, and knowledge of, God and his will. Prayer, it has been said, is humans speaking to God, meditation, God speaking to humans.

Most religions have a tradition of using meditation to get close to God.
*   **Hindus** use a variety of meditative techniques including yoga, transcendental meditation and 'sound and light' meditation.
*   **Sikhism** encourages meditation on God's name.
*   For **Buddhists** meditation is the essential path to enlightenment. The Buddha himself achieved enlightenment while meditating under a tree.
*   Kabbalah and Hassidic **Jews** use ritual meditation and much of Jewish prayer is meditative.
*   **Christians** have a variety of meditative practices. Quakers worship in silence, waiting for the 'inner light' to guide their ministry. Monastic life often includes times for meditation focussed on the text of the scriptures.
*   Within **Islam**, meditation is normally associated with Sufism, a mystical tradition seeking knowledge of the divine through focussed contemplation.

IV. HOLY WRIT

A major source of spiritual knowledge is the holy or sacred writings of religious groups. These texts, usually of considerable antiquity, are the basis of many of the beliefs and practices of each of the religions. Some of these texts, the Koran, for example, were obtained by revelation. Mohammed (see above) had the Koran revealed to him over a period of 23 years, and Moses received the Torah from his God in a much shorter time. Amongst other sacred texts are the Bhagavad-Gita of the Hindus, the Buddhists' Tripitaka and the Sikhs' Adi Granth. Despite the age of these texts, people turn to them in times of crisis and speak confidently of what they mean, even though devout religious leaders may not always agree on what that meaning is.

Because of their origins in times when the ability to read and write was very rare, most sacred writings were designed to be listened to or chanted rather than read. The study of holy texts was often undertaken under the careful supervision of a guru or rabbi or ayatollah and was part of a process which was as important as familiarity with the texts themselves.

Before printing made the exact text of the scriptures available to everyone, and before there was universal literacy, holy writings were regarded as allegorical. The word of God was infinite and open to interpretation. The belief, for instance, that the Bible is true in every detail is a 19th century view. All the verses of the Koran are 'parables' and its images of paradise and hell are also parables, indicating ideas which are beyond our worldly comprehension.

JUSTIFICATION 3: INTELLECTUAL

I. ST. THOMAS AQUINAS: QUINQUE VIAE (THE FIVE WAYS)

THOMAS AQUINAS (1224-1274)

Philosopher and theologian, Aquinas was born in Italy and when still quite young joined the Benedictine order of friars. His writings display enormous intellectual authority and he became a great influence in the Roman Catholic Church. Much of his prolific work attempts to reconcile Aristotle's rationalism with Christian doctrines of faith and revelation. His best known works are the *Summa contra Gentiles* (1259-64) describing the principles of 'natural religion' and *Summa theologiae* (1266-73) which contains his mature thought in systematic form. He was made a saint in 1323. Thomism, the doctrines based on the teachings and thoughts of St Thomas Aquinas, is still a significant part of catholic doctrine.

Aquinas claimed there are two ways-of-knowing, or understanding faith, through reason and, as we have seen already, through revelation.

FAITH THROUGH REASON

The first way-of-knowing was 'an ascent, by the natural light of reason, through created things to the natural light of God'. This way-of-knowing, 'the natural light of reason', produced five proofs, (known as the *Quinque Viae*) for that which we call God.

1. The world has motion, things move in it, so there must be a first mover 'which we call God' which is not moved by anything.

2. We find in the world an order of efficient causes and therefore there must be some efficient cause, which we call God, which is first in the chain of causes.

3. We find things have the possibility of being or not being because there are things that can be created and destroyed. Not everything can be like this so there must be something, which we call God, which does not have a cause of its necessity outside itself.

4. We find gradations in things, some things are more good, some less, and so on. Therefore there must be something, which we call God, which is the cause of being and goodness and every perfection of things.

5. Things in nature act for the sake of an end even though they lack awareness, therefore, there must be an intelligent being, which we call God, by whom all our natural things are directed to an end.

II. NEWMAN & THE DEEPER TRUTH

JOHN HENRY NEWMAN (1801-1890)

John Henry Newman was born into a Calvinist family, studied at Oxford University and was ordained into the Church of England in 1824. In 1845 he became a catholic and was made a cardinal in 1879. His best known works are his spiritual autobiography, *Apologia pro vita sua* (Apology for his life) (1864) which made a profound impression on many who did not share his religious convictions, and *The Idea of a University Defined and Illustrated* (1873). In this latter work he argued, amongst other things, that the duty of a University was to teach rather than research and to train the mind rather than diffuse useful knowledge.

MAKING FAITH CREDIBLE

One of Newman's main concerns, probably his most compelling concern, was to make faith credible, credible to the intellectual community of the church and the university within which he worked. The increasing awareness of Darwin's Theory of Evolution and the advancement of natural science in the nineteenth century made Newman fear the approach of a new age of atheism. To counteract this advancing atheism he wanted to make faith as convincing as natural science.

THE DEEPER TRUTH OF THE WHOLE PERSON

In his first sermon to the University of Oxford, when he was aged 25, he defined the conflict between the dominant rationality of empirical science and the truth of faith, a subject which he returned to often in his many writings. He argued that the search for religious truth cannot be found using empiricism. Empiricism, a 'tragic narrowing of reason' creates a 'closed and proud mentality' that blocks the search. He saw the attempts of theologians like Thomas Aquinas, with their verification of faith through external evidence, as inadequate as a justification of the truth of faith. In his most well known work, *Apologia Pro Vita Sua*, he states that the traditional proofs of God based on the order of the Universe are unconvincing because what he sees around him is tragedy and conflict. Deeper truth is approached with the 'whole person' and in a spirit of reverence. The attitude with which one seeks religious truth is indispensable for finding it; one comes to receive truth, not to analyse it. Rejection of faith, he wrote to his brother, comes from 'a fault of the heart, not the intellect'.

ACCEPTING WHAT CANNOT BE UNDERSTOOD BY REASON

In his Cardinal's acceptance speech (in 1879) Newman claimed he had spent 50 years fighting 'the spirit of liberalism' in religion. This liberalism, with its exaggerated trust in reason, he defined as the doctrine that there is no positive truth in religion, and that 'no one can believe what he does not understand'. Liberalism reduced non-scientific truths to matters of opinion and this led apologists to present faith as intuitive feeling 'that diminishes its uniqueness as grounded in revelation and history.' Faith, he suggests, cannot be understood in the same way that science is understood.

CONSCIENCE, IMAGINATION AND PROBABILITY

Authentic faith, the faith understood by 'the whole person' is created by 'self-experiencing' rather than the 'external verification' of empiricism. This self awareness is created, by conscience and imagination and supported by probability.

CONSCIENCE

The foundation of Newman's approach to faith lies in conscience. His deep respect for conscience is perhaps best seen in a short passage from his novel (he wrote much poetry and two novels) *Callista*, published in 1855. *Callista* describes conversion to Christianity of a North African sculptor and her eventual martyrdom. She describes her burgeoning awareness of conscience in conversation with a non-Christian philosopher:

> *I feel that God within my heart. I feel myself in His presence. He say to me, 'Do this; don't do that'. You may tell me that this dictate is a mere law of my nature, as to joy or to grieve. I cannot understand this. No it is the echo of a person speaking to me. Nothing shall persuade me that it does not ultimately proceed from a person external to me. It carries with it its proof of its divine origin. My nature feels towards it as towards a person …. I believe in what is more than a mere 'something'. I believe in what is more real to me than sun, moon, stars, and the fair earth, and the voice of friends. You will say, Who is He? Has He ever told you anything about Himself? Alas! no! - the more's the pity. But I will not give up what I have, because I have not more. An echo implies a voice; a voice a speaker. That speaker I love and fear.*

IMAGINATION

One of Newman's basic tenets was that faith must be 'discerned, rested in and appropriated as a reality by the religious imagination'. Truth about God 'lives in the imagination' and when the imagination is not kindled, belief remains simply an idea, and is not a reality. Imagination nourishes our emotional and moral nature. Religion addresses people through the intellect and through imagination and arrives at its own special certainty through arguments 'too personal and deep for words.'

PROBABILITY

Newman is quite open in admitting that there is no one completely compelling argument that leads to faith. He argues that non-rational components such as conscience and imagination create a disposition that make faith 'probable'. In one of his sermons he argues that the personal journey of the mind towards faith is like the fact that the strands of a rope, when bound together, are much stronger than one strand taken on its own.

JUSTIFICATION 4: 'JOY'

THE JOY OF C.S. LEWIS

C(LIVE) S(TAPLES) LEWIS (1898-1963)

From 1924 Lewis taught at Oxford and in 1954 became Professor of Medieval and Renaissance English at Cambridge University. His novel, *The Screwtape Letters* (1942), a Christian apologetic is his most popular adult work. His *Chronicles of Narnia* which started with *The Lion, the Witch and the Wardrobe* (1950) have become children's classics. An autobiography, *Surprised by Joy*, describes his conversion to Christianity.

The young Lewis read a lot and walked a lot. He loved landscape and twilight, myth and fairy tales. These things evoked in him an emotion bigger than mere pleasure, a kind of shining sense of goodness and romance and light. Lewis called this emotion, simply, the 'Joy'. With it came the feeling that both the words and the world were trying to tell him something - not just that there is something odd out there but that there is something *big* out there. 'They taught me longing' he said and made him a 'votary of the Blue Flower' after a story by the German poet Novalis in which a youth dreams of a blue flower and spends his life searching for it. The Christianity he knew in childhood, by contrast, seemed the opposite of magic and joy: dull sermons and dry moral questions to be solved.

At Oxford he befriended Tolkien. The liberal humanism in which he had been raised as a thinker did not allow him to understand the 'Joy' that came to him on country walks and in pages of poetry. In company with another friend Tolkien and Lewis took a long and now famous walk arguing from early evening until early morning. Tolkien argued that Lewis's 'Joy' was what underpinned Christian faith. One had to become religious to understand the Joy. All existence, Tolkien argued as they walked that night, was intrinsically mythical. The stars were the fires of gods if you chose to see them that way, just as the world was the stories you made from it. If you were drawn to myth at all, as Lewis was, then you ought to accept the Christian myth just as you accepted the Northern ones. By the end of the walk, Lewis was a convinced Christian.

'The story of Christ is simply a true myth' he writes, 'a myth working upon us in the same way as others, but with this tremendous difference that it *really happened.*'

Converted to faith as the means to Joy, Lewis never stops to ask why this faith and not some other. His favourite argument for the truth of Christianity is that Jesus had to be crazy to say the things he did or what he said must be true, and since he doesn't sound like someone who is crazy, he must be right.

THEORIES OF TRUTH APPLIED TO FAITH

Deeply faithful, religious people, let's call them Believers, say "Of course God exists, there is no doubt about that". A statement which is at the heart of major religions.

What arguments could you get by applying each of our three theories of truth (Chapter 2.2) to this statement?

PRAGMATIC THEORY
Believers accept their belief on a pragmatic basis; that is, their belief in God works for them, gives meaning and purpose to their lives and actions, moral courage, comfort, etc. Therefore, for them, with this theory, the statement is true.

COHERENCE THEORY
They also accept this statement as true using the Coherence Theory. That is, their belief undoubtedly coheres with numerous other accepted statements from the Bible or the Koran or the Torah. Therefore, for them the statement is true.

CORRESPONDENCE THEORY
While it would be extremely difficult or impossible to discover the objective reality referred to as God, you can be certain that Believers are convinced that such objective reality exists, and in fact, they say as much. Therefore, for them, with this theory, the statement is true.

So, is it?

Non believers say, just a strongly as the Believers, "I don't believe your God exists".

Applying the same truth theories to their statements could produce these arguments.

Using the Pragmatic Theory they claim that the concept of God is not meaningful to them, hence not true for them.

Using the Coherence Theory they claim belief in the existence of God does not harmonise with the reality of the world as Believers understand it, i.e. it is incompatible with your Jewish or Islamic or Buddhist faith. It is false, therefore, for them.

Using the more objective Correspondence Theory they state they don't believe that God is real. If believers know that indeed God is real they challenge them with "Prove it", meaning that they want to be shown some evidence that there is an objective reality called God.

THREE POSTSCRIPTS TO THIS CHAPTER

POSTSCRIPT ONE: INTELLIGENT DESIGN OR GOD OF THE GAPS?

Stephen Hawking has famously written that if and when we understand the universe completely we would understand the mind of God. It seems that when they reach a point in their researches that takes then beyond their understanding, scientists, particularly astronomers and physicists, have made connections with their empirical findings and the existence of a supreme 'designer'.

In his greatest work *Principia* (1687) Isaac Newton wrote:

> *The six primary Planets are revolv'd around the Sun, in circles concentric with the Sun, and with motions directed towards the same parts, and almost in the same plane …. But it is not to be conceived that mere mechanical causes could give birth to so many regular motions …. The most beautiful System of the Sun, Planets, and Comets could only proceed from the counsel and domination of an intelligent and powerful Being.*

The 17th century Dutch astronomer Christiaan Huygens, who was confident of his astronomy but not his biology, wrote in *The Celestial Worlds Discover'd*:

> *I suppose no body will deny there's somewhat more of Contrivance, somewhat more of Miracle in the production and growth of Plants and Animals than in the lifeless heap of inanimate Bodies ….. For the finger of God, and the wisdom of Divine Providence, is in them much more clearly manifested than in the other.*

This idea has led to the theory of intelligent design, known by today's secular philosophers as *God of the gaps*. Because of the gaps in their knowledge, scientists have often taken consolation in 'the finger of God', the intelligent design of the universe.

As long ago as the early 17th century Galileo had no time for a God of the gaps. In a famous letter to the Duchess of Tuscany he wrote:

> *In expounding the Bible if one were always to confine oneself to the unadorned grammatical meaning, one might fall into error …..*

> *Nothing physical which demonstrations prove to us ought to be called in question (much*

less condemned) upon the testimony of biblical passages which may have some different meaning beneath their words ...

I do not feel obliged to believe that the same God who has endowed us with senses, reasons and intellect has intended us to forgo their use.

Later he came out with a more cryptic comment: *The Bible,* he said, *tells you how to go to heaven not how the heavens go.*

Contemporary American astrophysicist Neil De Grassse Tyson[4] states his support of Galileo strongly and clearly. There is no place for intelligent design, for the God of gaps, in his thinking.

I don't want the students who could make the next major breakthrough in renewable energy resources or space travel to have been taught that anything they don't understand, and that nobody yet understands, is divinely constructed and therefore beyond their intellectual capacity.

POSTSCRIPT TWO: CAN MUSIC HELP US TO UNDERSTAND FAITH?

That music can be spiritually uplifting seems beyond doubt. National anthems inspire patriotism and great religious truths and mysteries are explored in oratorios and symphonies. Music plays an important part in marriage ceremonies and funerals and in many other religious services. Music touches the spirit; it is capable of giving us a unique and profound experience that we cannot describe in any other way.

Is it in this sense like faith, taking us to new places, challenging our reason and our imagination and giving us a sense of what might be? Does it bridge the space between our sense of the present and the eternal?

Shakespeare thought it did:

Here we will sit, and let the sounds of music

Creep in our ears; soft stillness and the night

Become the touches of such harmony.

Sit, Jessica: look, how the floor of heaven

Is thick inlaid with patines of bright gold:

There's not the smallest orb which thou behold'st

But in this motion like an angel sings

Still quiring to the young eyed cherubins;

Such harmony is in immortal souls;

(from **The Merchant of Venice**)

---

4. In *Natural History* Vol 114 No 9 Nov 2005 Natural History Museum New York.

POSTSCRIPT THREE: FAITH AND LOVE, A PERSONAL STATEMENT

Faith is often an elusive idea for those of us without it. Once, in discussion with a friend and colleague who had been for nine years in training as a Jesuit priest, I expressed my own inability to understand the concept of faith and somewhat aggressively, I suspect, challenged him to explain it to me. The nearest thing, he suggested, was human love, (not passionate sexual love) but the love we feel, not for, but *from*, our parents, our children, those nearest and dearest to us. Faith is a response to a mysterious but real experience of being loved and loved unconditionally: of being loved rather than loving.

I must admit I find his sincere and thoughtful answer helpful. When I start the school year with a new class of students I don't know, I certainly have no love for them, or them for me, but as the year progresses, and I get to know them, despite their weaknesses and foibles, I grow fond of them. Not that they would ever know: they see me as a grumpy old man who can't tolerate classroom chatter, late arrival at class and carelessly worded statements which begin with 'Like ..'. And I sense too that they begin to accept me for what I am. And that experience of being accepted is what I think my ex-Jesuit friend would call faith.

FIVE MAJOR RELIGIONS OF THE WORLD

HINDUISM

Hinduism, the major religion of India, is one of the world's oldest religions, dating back almost 4000 years. It is difficult to define because there is no single founder or text which is acknowledged by Hindus as being the source of their faith. They refer to their belief as Sanatarna Dharma, which translates as 'eternal law'. Sanatarna Dharma suggests a commitment to an ideal way of life which is dependent on knowing the duties of one's class and station.

A major belief of Hinduism is the passage of a person's soul from body to body determined by one's actions or karma. Hindus also believe the universe is populated by many gods, and they may worship several. The image of one of these gods, usually a family god, is often worshipped in a small shrine within the house. Hindu festivals include Dipavali, the Festival of Lights, at which burning lamps welcome Lakshmi, the goddess of prosperity into the house; Holi, a festival of springtime; and a ten-day period in autumn which ends with Dashara, a day of processions and celebrations.

BUDDHISM

Buddhism, started in India in the 6th century BC by Siddharta Gautama, the Buddha, is practised throughout the world, especially in Asia. There are more than 300 million Buddhists worldwide.

The Buddha's teachings are based on what he called the four Noble Truths. The first Noble Truth is duhka, or suffering: human existence is occasionally painful but all living things, humans, animals and the gods are in a cycle of rebirth, in which their karma (actions) keeps them wandering. The second Noble Truth is the understanding that suffering has a cause, and that everything is part of a chain of events, each event creating further events. The third Noble Truth is that this chain can be broken, and the end of suffering can be reached. The fourth Noble Truth is that, through meditation and ethical practices, enlightened wisdom can be achieved.

Buddhist monks and nuns live in celibate communities relying on support from their followers. Through their generous acts the monks, the nuns, and the laity, are reborn into a life which could lead to enlightenment.

ISLAM

Islam was founded, in the 6th century AD, in what is now Saudi Arabia. Islam, which means submission to the will of God, has over 700 million followers, or Muslims, world wide.

Islamic practices and beliefs are based on the text of the Holy Qu'ran which is regarded as containing the infallible message of God as revealed to his prophet, Mohammed. There are five essential practices for every Muslim, known as the Pillars of the Faith. The First Pillar is Shahada, which is reciting the creed which is at the heart of the religion: There is no God but the One God; and Mohammed is the messenger of God. The Second Pillar is Salat, the ritual of prayer. Muslims must pray five times a day facing in the direction of Mecca, the birthplace of Mohammed. The Third Pillar, Zakat, emphasises compassion and mercy and the sharing of wealth. The Fourth Pillar, Sawm, makes it obligatory to fast during daylight in the Holy Month of Ramadhan, at the end of which is the festival of Id-ul-Fitr. The Fifth Pillar, Haj, states that Muslims are expected, once in their lifetime, to undertake a pilgrimage to the sacred city of Mecca.

CHRISTIANITY

The Christian faith was founded by Jesus of Nazareth who lived two thousand yeas ago, in what is now Israel. Christian belief and practice is based on the writings contained in the Holy Bible. Divided into two parts, the Old and New Testaments. The first four books of the New Testament tell the story of Jesus and his teachings as recorded by four of his contemporary followers, or disciples. Christians believe that Jesus was the son of God, sent to save the world from wickedness. They believe that Jesus, who was crucified by the Roman rulers of that time, died and suffered and in so doing atoned for evil in the world. The ethical code of Christians is based on the Ten Commandments of the Jewish Old Testament and the Sermon on the Mount, a speech Jesus made which is reported in the New Testament. In this speech Jesus advocates, amongst other things, humility and neighbourly love and understanding. Equally important is the 'greatest commandment' of Luke 10:25-28 'You must love the lord ... with all your heart ... and your neighbour as yourself'. The two major Christian festivals are Christmas, in which they celebrate the humble birth of Jesus in a stable, and Easter, which commemorates his death and his living on with a new reality.

JUDAISM

Judaism is the religion of the Jews. According to the Bible Judaism is based on the covenant made between God and Abraham. This covenant ordained the Jewish people's special relationship with God. The first five books of the Bible, the Torah, reveal God's laws and the ways in which they should be obeyed. Judaism is a religion strong on ritual centred on the synagogue and the home. The central time for worship is the Sabbath (sunset on Friday until sunset on Saturday). Annual festivals include Yom Kippur, (or Day of Atonement), Rosh Hashanah, (the Jewish new year), Hanukah (commemorating the rededication of the temple in 165 BC after its desecration by the Syrians), and Passover, (celebrating the release of the Jews from Egyptian slavery)

Now *you have read Chapter 4 ...*

consider or undertake the following:

1.

Now this one is a challenge. Meditate in silence for 15 minutes, either alone or preferably with a small group. Spend the 15 minutes thinking seriously of the ways in which, if there is a God, he or she shows him or herself in our everyday lives. After your meditation discuss your experience and your conclusions.

2.

The justification of faith

For many people with a strong faith, Muslims, Christians, Jews, Hindus and others, to attempt to rationalise their faith is to misunderstand the nature of their faith. Muslims believe in Allah, His angels, His books and His apostles. Christians believe in The Lord their God and that Jesus, the son of God, came to earth to save us. Their belief, their faith, is unquestioning and unquestionable. To question it is a denial of the faith itself. For these people they believe, therefore it is.

However there are always people, often committed to a religion or simply to the concept of God, that feel they must justify their faith in an intellectual way.

Is this necessary?

3. Which of the four justifications for faith outlined in this chapter can you most easily relate to?

Is there another justification which you could add to the list?

4. Look again at the application of the three theories of truth and their application to the question 'Does God exist?'. Is the application of the theories too simplistic?

5. What is your response to Postscript One: Intelligent Design or God of the Gaps?

And to Postscript Two: Can music help us to understand faith?

6. Is my personal comment (Postscript Three) out of place in a school text book?

Or is faith so intensely personal that a personal comment like this is the only way to help other people to understand it?

Want to know more?

You may find the following books helpful:

The Bible.

The Koran.

... and other sacred texts.

For the alternative view, *A Devil's Chaplain*, selected essays by by Richard Dawkins (published by Phoenix).

Finally, if you want a rest from study, there is always *Monty Python's Life of Brian* (film). Often described as an attack on Christianity, it is more a satire on the tendency of people to follow prophets without having much of an idea where they are heading. Also suffering significant collateral damage are crowd behaviour, Roman noses, feminism, ingratitude, Latin teachers etc .

SECTION ONE
WAYS-OF-KNOWING

LANGUAGE

5

CHAPTER CONTENTS

- What is Language?
- Language as communication.
- The Bewitchment of Language:

Before

you read Chapter 5 ...

discuss or undertake the following:

1. Try this in groups of three: each one of you writes down an interesting thought you have had today. Give the written thought to a second person who must then tell the third person what you have written, but without using any language. Each of you take turns to send and receive the thoughts. After you have tried this, discuss what was easy to communicate with gestures and what was difficult. Did you use sign language? Did you use symbols? In what ways do you think your non-language communication was in any way similar to the ways animals communicate?

2. Most of us have at some time or other been confused by something we have read. Using the information given below, make a sketch of the animal described. 'Small with a long nose, ears and tail, the latter being naked and prehensile. The opposable first hind toe is clawless and the tip is expanded into a flat pad. The other digits all bear claws. The best known species is about the size of a cat, grey in colour the fur being woolly.'

Compare your interpretation of the words with interpretations of others in your group. What additional information would enable you to draw the animal accurately? What conclusions can you come to about the way language conveys information?

3. Spend a minute or two thinking about the last essay you wrote. When was it written? What was it about? Were you pleased with it? How could you have improved it? Was it well structured? Was the language appropriate to the subject matter?

4. Now try to explain how you thought about your essay. As you thought, did you use words? If so, how? Did you order them as you would in speech or did you use groups of words? Or did you just use mental images? Are you able to think without using words? When you are thinking about math do you use words? Do you use words when you visualise journeys in airplanes or ships? How important is language in your thinking? If you are fluent in more than one language, do you think in both those languages? Is one language easier for thinking certain things?

5. You probably speak your mother tongue fluently and perfectly and yet have had to learn, perhaps with difficulty, the grammar of a language you learned at school. What possible reasons could there be for you to have learned your mother tongue grammar so easily?

6. Find an example (perhaps an advertisement or a cartoon or a sports report, or a political comment) - from a magazine or newspaper - of language used in an interesting or unusual or amusing or misleading way. Explain to your group what you think the writer has attempted to achieve and whether he or she has been successful.

5.0 LANGUAGE

Language is not logic ..... nothing in language "corresponds with the world" or reflects "the grain of reality". Languages can be translated only roughly. None is ideal. There is no clear standard for perfection or adequacy .....

Abel: **Man is the Measure**.

Language is not only not logic, it is seldom even logical. And yet it is through language that knowledge is created and promulgated. Without the description there would be no knowledge-by-description. We come to understand the complex disciplines we study at school and university using a set of chaotic, undisciplined symbols we call 'language'.

5.1 WHAT IS LANGUAGE?

We all know what language is, what the word 'language' means. We use the word everyday in all sorts of contexts, so we can, presumably, offer a definition of it; a definition which covers its meaning as it is used, frequently and normally, everyday, a definition; for example, which is acceptable to everyone who uses this book.

So, what is your definition?

As you pause and sigh before attempting to answer this question, aren't you in a position you know only too well? You use a word frequently, knowing what you mean when you use it, and then hesitate and sigh, when you have to define it.

We all know what 'language' is, and yet we have difficulty in defining the word 'language'. When challenged we probably rush to the dictionary and there we find an approximate definition, using more language, of what it is we already know. *The New Shorter Oxford English Dictionary* (NSOED) has five major definitions of the word 'language', divided into fifteen minor sub-divisions. How do you know which one to select for your definition? You have to select the definition which is most appropriate for the context in which you are being asked to define the word. You are probably familiar with all fifteen usages of the word and, through your knowledge of the usage of the word, you select the appropriate definition from the fifteen on offer. But even then you are probably not quite happy with the definition, it is not exactly what you understand by 'language' in this context, and the definition itself raises other questions of the meaning of other words used in the definition.

Linguists themselves, who surely know what language is, generally agree on a definition. E. Sapir, a pioneer linguist, defined language as 'a purely human and non-instinctive method of communicating ideas, emotions and desires by means of voluntarily produced symbols'. This definition is probably similar to the definition you arrived at before you began to read this chapter. A later linguist, R.A.Hall, defined language as 'the institution whereby humans communicate and interact with each other by means of habitually used oral-auditory arbitrary symbols.[1]

---

1. In contrast, A.N.Chomsky, another linguist, defined language as 'a set of rules and infinite sentences, each finite in length, and constructed out of a finite set of elements.'

LINGUISTICS

Linguists study linguistics, which they describe as a field of scientific research with language analysis as its focus. Universities began teaching linguistics in the 1960s. Studies are divided into three main sections.

- Theoretical linguistics establishes general principles for the study of all languages.
- Descriptive linguistics establishes the facts of a particular language system and
- Comparative linguistics focuses on the similarities and differences between languages.

Be careful to understand the difference between the everyday meaning of the word *linguist* - a person who is fluent in several languages - and the more specific meaning of the word - a person who studies linguistics.

Most linguists agree on the significant features of language.

Language, they say

1. is uniquely human;
2. communicates; and
3. uses symbols.

The NSOED definition which is closest to this consensus definition is 'a system of human communication using words, written and spoken, and particular ways of combining them'.

Let us look at these three features of language and see what implications they have for us as knowers.

5.2 FEATURES OF LANGUAGE

LANGUAGE AS UNIQUELY HUMAN

When linguists and philosophers claim that language is 'uniquely human' they are claiming only humans have, and use, language. Other living things, mammals, birds, insects do not have language. Of course they do not claim these other living things do not communicate; only that they do not communicate with language. Before you read further it is worth asking yourself, at a common sense level, if you agree with these linguists and philosophers. Have you any personal empirical evidence that animals do use language? There is no animal system of communication that even suggests a complicated and sophisticated system of language. There have been attempts to teach chimpanzees and gorillas a limited and very simple sign language but these attempts, despite the teachers' optimistic claims, have failed. Scientists have claimed that dolphins have a language of their own but have completely failed either to learn it or to codify it. Language does seem to be uniquely human and to differ from animal communication in that it is not produced automatically by external stimuli or internal needs.

CHARACTERISTICS OF ANIMAL COMMUNICATION

1. Animals can produce only a fixed number of signals; they do not have the ability to generate new signals. Each of their signals is for a specific purpose. The communication system of bees, for instance, has been thoroughly investigated. Bees dance when they return to their hive, and this dancing communicates information to other bees. But no bee ever generates new information, it simply repeats the dance which is appropriate for the information it is communicating.
2. Animal communication is instinctive. There is no evidence animals think before they communicate. Certain monkeys scream warning signals when an enemy is sighted and the warning signals can vary according to the nature of the enemy. The communication is entirely automatic; it cannot be repressed and it cannot be falsified.
3. When animal communication varies in volume or intensity, when it gets louder or more frantic, or the pitch varies, the strength of the volume or intensity reflects the degree of fear or hunger or sexual determination.

Most human language is not motivated by external stimuli or internal needs, although of course, it can be. It is not instinctive in its patterning and use. It can be repressed and falsified. Neither is it restricted to communicating factual information. It is immensely creative. Humans can generate and understand an infinite number of new sentences. Language variations in volume and intensity can be for a multitude of reasons other than the instinctive. Language, it seems, is as unique a human attribute as having a trunk is a unique attribute of elephants.

The claim that language is uniquely human does not automatically imply that all human communities use language but there is no known human community without it. What no one seems to be able to determine is how language originated. There have been many fanciful and imaginative theories put forward but none of them have been taken seriously by scholars. A typical example is the Tarara-boom-dee-ay Theory. This theory is based on the idea that when a group of early humans wanted to celebrate, say, the killing of a mammoth, one of them would spontaneously burst into chant, which the others would join in, exactly like modern day soccer supporters when their team scores.

Is language really uniquely human? Many linguists and psychologists question the claim that language is unique to humans. Such an idea, they argue, is incompatible with the Darwinian Theory of Evolution. Evolutionary theory states that animal and plant species are created by the gradual development over many thousands of years of genetic patterns that increase their chance of survival. If humans have learned to use language, it is argued, why haven't other animal species? Why should humans have a unique claim to language?

The photograph shows *Tursiops truncatus* (Bottlenose Dolphin), a large brained mammal that some have claimed uses a simple language.

A convincing answer to this question, supporting the uniqueness of human language, is given by Stephen Pinker, a Canadian psychologist and linguist. In addition to casting doubt on the claims of animal psychologists to have taught any animal to use language, he further argues that the evolution of language is not incompatible with evolutionary theory.

LANGUAGE AS COMMUNICATION

The second of the defined features of language was that it 'communicates'. Communication must be between at least two 'things', animals or people, a sender and a receiver, and must involve a message.

Basic communication takes this form:

SENDER ⟶ MESSAGE ⟶ RECEIVER

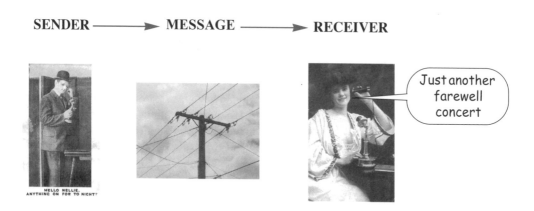

We have already seen that animals communicate. In what sense is human use of language different from animal communication? If the message is in language, it uses words, symbols of reality or ideas, in a way that animal communication does not. Using language, the messages are much more sophisticated, much more complex, than animal communication could possibly be.

LUDWIG WITTGENSTEIN (1889-1961)

Wittgenstein is the most distinguished of 20th century philosophers of language, and, reading around the subject you will soon come across his name. Born in Vienna, he studied engineering at Berlin and Manchester and then studied logic at Cambridge where he later became a professor. His *Tractatus Logico Philosophicus* (1921) argued any sentence is a picture of the fact it represents, and, any thought is a sentence. In *Philosophical Investigations* (1953) he rejected the *Tractatus*, coming to the conclusion that the meaning of language depended on the use to which it was put, and that the 'language game' was a form of life.

An infinite variety of messages can be communicated using language. The way language is used to create and communicate these messages has been the life-time study of many linguists. After analysing the way humans use language, linguists have grouped language use into broad categories which they call language functions. There are almost as many classifications of the function of language as there are books about the subject. These functions range from the 'objective transactional' to the 'emotive poetic'. Each function has rather fuzzy edges and is not necessarily independent. Transactional language, for instance, may have within it social functions, and, expressive communication can have social elements. Here is a selection of these functions.

FUNCTION 1: LANGUAGE AS TRANSACTIONAL COMMUNICATION

The most obvious function of language (i.e. the messages it communicates) is that it is transactional. Transactional here means to get things done. In this category it is used, amongst other things to:

1.   give information (Sun Yat-sen was proclaimed President of the Republic of China in 1912);

2.   give instructions (Stop when the light is red);

3.   set up a hypothesis (If these plants do not receive water they will die);

4.   solve problems (Add the lengths of the sides of the field together and you have calculated the amount of fencing you need).

In these examples of the transactional use of language, the meaning of the language is in the message. If the message is to communicate clearly, it must be unambiguous. The communication will only be clearly understood by the receiver if both the sender and the receiver have exactly the same understanding of the meaning of the words used. The message will then inform the receiver in the exact way that the sender intended. In simple cases, like those given above, there are normally few problems in communication, but as we will see, especially when abstract ideas are part of the message, different understandings of the meaning of words, and the way they are presented, can interfere seriously with the communication.

Lenin tells it his way

FUNCTION 2: LANGUAGE AS EXPRESSIVE COMMUNICATION

Language can also be used to communicate expressively, to express the feelings of the sender and to affect, not just inform, the receiver. In this kind of communication we pay special attention to the words themselves and the feelings and atmosphere they create. We find this kind of language used in poetry.

Consider this poem by Edward Thomas:

> *Adlestrop*
>
> *Yes. I remember Adlestrop -*
> *The name, because one afternoon*
> *Of heat the express-train drew up there*
> *Unwontedly. It was late June.*

The steam hissed. Someone cleared his throat.

No one left and no one came

On the bare platform. What I saw

Was Adlestrop - only the name

And willows, willow-herb, and grass,

And meadowsweet, and haycocks dry,

No whit less still and lonely fair

Than the high cloudlets in the sky.

And for that minute a blackbird sang

Close by, and round him, mistier,

Farther and farther, all the birds

Of Oxfordshire and Gloucestershire.

The poet wants to share that moment with you. He wants you to be emotionally involved; to enjoy the train unexpectedly stopping and giving him an unforgettable chance to see the world about him in a new and wonderful way. Words used in this way, to communicate expressively the feelings of the sender of the message (in this case the sender is a poet) and to affect the listener, are connotative.

Connotative means *imply more meaning to a word than its primary meaning*. Obviously when meaning is implied the message is going to be open to interpretation, each receiver understanding it slightly differently according to his or her own connotation.

FUNCTION 3: LANGUAGE AS SOCIAL COMMUNICATION

Language can be used to communicate socially, both formally and informally. Shortly after moving from London to New York I was asked by an accountant with whom I worked 'How ya doing'?' I was having a bad time with, amongst other things, his accounting and told him so at great length. When I paused for breath he said, quickly, 'In America when somebody asks you 'How ya doin'?' just answer 'Fine'. The communication 'How ya doin'?' was intended as a perfunctory social message. It was not intended to tell me anything other than the fact that he knew I was there in the room with him. The message was purely ceremonial.

Introducing a rhythmical pattern into a message is often an aid to communication. Rhythm arouses attention. Rhyme and alliteration also arouse interest and often reinforce rhythm, establishing patterns of sound that are often difficult for the mind to cast aside. A good example of this is the 1964 presidential campaign slogan of Lyndon B. Johnson. 'All the Way with LBJ' which has rhythm, alliteration and rhyme. The same slogan writers might have created the message which haunted Johnson when he was president and the Vietnam war was raging: 'LBJ, LBJ, how many kids have you killed today?' One of the most comprehensive lists of the functions of language was given by Wittgenstein. Language he writes, can be used to give orders; describe the appearance of an object or give its measurement; report an event; speculate about an event; form and test a hypothesis; present the results of an experiment; make up a story; play act; sing catches; guess riddles; make a joke and tell it; solve a problem in practical arithmetic; translate from one language to another; ask, think, greet, cure and pray.

Roman Jakobson, (1896-1982) a Russian, later American, linguist, developed a classification of the functions of language which is often used. He states that there are six main language functions and dignifies his findings by giving each function an impressive name; referential, emotive, conative, phatic, poetic, metalinguistic.

THE JAKOBSON FUNCTIONS

REFERENTIAL.
When a language is used referentially it is referring to everyday things in a neutral way. 'That is my car'.

EMOTIVE.
This describes those language messages that in themselves express emotion. The communication is the message. 'Oh hell! *@!'

CONATIVE.
Conative expressions are those which attempt to make the receiver do something. 'Come here, my sweetie pie. Now, just relax.'

PHATIC.
These are the communications we make when we give feedback as we listen. 'Yeh!' 'Really!' 'No.' 'Wow.'

POETIC.
When language is poetic, the quality of the sound is more important than the meaning. 'My Love is like a red, red, rose.'

METALINGUISTIC.
When language is used to communicate about language. 'In the nominative case the nouns ...'

Jakobson does not claim each of these functions occurs in isolation. Referential language can be combined with poetic and phatic with emotive and so on.

FUNCTION 4: LANGUAGE AS COMMUNICATION WITH ONESELF

When you sit at home in the evening and settle down to your homework do you organise the thoughts in your head using language? Do you say to yourself, in your mind 'First I'll do the math and then, if I have time I'll do the French, but before I do anything I'll just call Maja and see what she's doing'? Do you ever actually say your thoughts out loud or find yourself moving your lips as if you were speaking but not making the sounds? Do your thoughts, your communication with yourself, need to be put into language?

Some 'thinking' obviously doesn't need to be put into words. Visual artists and composers can 'see' and 'hear' what they eventually produce, without using words, and our response to the smell of freshly baked bread or the sight of a mangled car after a crash is independent of words, although the extent to which these last two examples are 'thinking' in any sense at all is questionable.

Thinking which seems to require language, at least for some of us, is like knowledge-by-description. If we can't put it into words, we can't be sure what it is we are thinking. This idea was summarised by Russian linguist Vigotsky who was quite clear in his opinion:

'Thought is born through words ... a thought unembodied[2] remains a shadow. We seem to need to put our thoughts into some sort of linguistic order and language seems to enable us to do that.'

He used the word 'seem' twice in the last sentence deliberately because the relationship between language and thought is a matter of speculation. There are two conflicting theories about the relationship. The first theory claims that thought and language are entirely separate, but dependent. This can mean that either language is dependent on thought or thought on language. The second theory claims that language and thought are absolutely meshed together, thinking without language is impossible. The most well known discussion of the language - thought relationship is The Sapir-Whorf Hypothesis, which suggests that our thoughts are controlled by our language. It is worth looking at the Sapir Whorf Hypothesis in a little more detail. Here are some comments on it by an Irish linguist, Dr. Tina Hickey:

Does our language affect how we think about the world? Many people assume that thought is primary and language depends on it. According to this view, thought happens separately from language and is only encoded in words later. The pioneer linguist Edward Sapir claimed that Human beings do not live in the objective world alone but are very much at the mercy of the particular language which has become the medium of expression of their society.

Whorf, Sapir's pupil, went on to develop this argument further. Whorf studied a language of the American Indians called Hopi, which is very far removed from English indeed. He came to believe that speakers of Hopi and English could not possibly perceive the world in the same way. Whorf argued that speakers of different languages will have different conceptions of and experiences of the world. So in its strongest form his argument is that we are intellectually imprisoned by the language we speak.

When Whorf looked at Hopi he found that something that had just a brief duration, like lightning or a wave, can only be expressed as a verb, not a noun. In English we treat time as a mass as in 'I have a lot of time' and we carve it up into units we can count. You can't do this in Hopi, as they don't see time as a quantity but as duration. This means they don't have forms like our tenses; instead they talk about duration from the point of view of the speaker.

There are many other examples of differences in the way languages code aspects of the world. In Navaho, for example, if I tell you I am passing you a stone I would have to add the endings to the verb to tell you that the stone I am passing is flat and round, something that is not necessary to the English speaker. But Whorf's claim was most appealing when he looked at word differences rather than grammar differences. The language of Lesu Islanders has more than a dozen words for pig. Speakers of Hananoo, a Philippine language, have a large number of words for rice. The most famous of Whorf's example is the fact that Eskimo has different words to describe snow, like snow that is falling, and snow that has fallen but hasn't become compacted, and snow that is thawing, which Whorf contrasted with our single word snow. But wait a minute. English speakers who are particularly interested in snow - skiers for example - do have more terms to describe it: powder, corn, ice, slush, though the rest of us may normally use just snow. This is where some of the criticisms of the Whorfian hypothesis come in. Specialists in particular areas develop words to describe distinctions that non-specialists might not be aware of.

2. 'Unembodied' here is interestingly metaphorical. Presumably it means 'put into words'.

For the purpose of understanding ourselves as knowers it is not necessary to takes sides although it is certainly worth spending a little time discussing the controversy. What is clear is that language is part of our thinking process. We use language to express our thoughts, to communicate and clarify our thoughts to ourselves and to others.

5.3 THE BEWITCHMENT OF LANGUAGE

That language communicates, and that it communicates in a variety of ways, is clear. What isn't always clear, as I have hinted, is how clearly language communicates.

Wittgenstein wrote:

> *'Philosophy is a battle against the bewitchment of our intelligence by means of language. It is not only philosophy that is a battle against the bewitchment of our intelligences by language; rather all human activity seems bewitched by language. Language casts spells on all our communication, it bewitches with its connotations, flux, grammatical structures, origins, vagueness, contexts, implications, imperfections, irregularities, limited and unlimited vocabulary and because it is an enigmatic, imperfect human enterprise.*

Language bewitches us all and the first bewitchment we should look at is implied in our original definition. Language, as defined by linguists is uniquely human, communicates and uses symbols. We have looked at the significance of the first two features of our definition: its uniqueness to humans and its ability to communicate. The third and final feature, its use of symbols, is certainly bewitching. Let us look at that bewitchment before moving on to others.

BEWITCHMENT 1: LANGUAGE USES SYMBOLS

Humans can make certain things stand for other things. In math you are familiar with this idea. In the statement

Let h stand for the length of the hypotenuse

h is a symbol for a finite number representing the length of all the hypotenuses you can imagine. In English grammar you have probably found the formula for a simple sentence,

$$S>V>O,$$

in which the symbol S stands for the subject, V for the verb and O for the object.

We can, by agreement, make symbols stand for anything we wish.

As part of our evolutionary development we have agreed that when we make certain sounds, when we use language, those sounds, language, are symbols. Those of us who speak English have agreed on one set of sounds as symbols and those of us who speak Chinese have agreed on another set of sounds as symbols. The sounds are agreed symbols within our language communities. A member of the English speaking community might make a sound which we write as 'Look! A small green snake'[3]. Any members of the community who heard the sound could, if they so chose, look

---

3. Writing is of course a set of symbols itself, symbols representing sound. Writing therefore is a symbol of a symbol.

and see an object which they would recognise as a small green snake. The sounds small and green and snake are symbols which would be meaningful to members of that speaking community and they would know what to expect when they looked. But there is not necessarily a connection between the sound symbol and the thing or idea it stands for. The sound symbol for snake is not the reality of the snake.

This may seem a fairly obvious statement to make and with the example of the snake of course it is. But at a more abstract level, the difference between the symbol and idea or thing the symbol represents is not always obviously apparent. The word or sound can become confused with reality and the spell of language can begin to bewitch. The words green and small are beginning this process. What does green symbolise? You describe your new pet snake to me as green and I have an approximate idea of its colour, based on my experience of green snakes I have seen, but your snake might be a bright lime green and the snakes I have seen may be dark bottle green. I might have entirely the wrong idea of the colour of your snake. And what about small? Now the last snake you had, which escaped into the local sewage system last week may have been a six metre long anaconda, and this one, a baby anaconda to replace the monster that escaped may be only one metre long. Sure, your new snake is small compared to the one that got away, but to me a metre long snake is huge. The words, the symbols, we are using to communicate mean different things to different people in different contexts. The sender of the symbol is clear what message he or she is sending. The receiver is clear what message he or she is receiving. But the received signal is fundamentally different from the sent signal. The words have bewitched our intelligences: we have begun to interpret the symbols as representing reality, but there is no reality. What is green? What is small? As our acquaintance with words - symbols of reality but not reality - grows more abstract and those ideas the words symbolise become more abstract, the more we are likely to be bewitched. Because a word exists we expect it to correspond to the reality we know. Scientists have pointed out this danger as they seek to name newly discovered phenomena with old words. Black Holes are neither black nor holes but for most of us these words cast a spell. We apply the everyday meaning of the words and struggle to understand how anything black and shaped like a hole (and what shape is a hole?) can be floating around there in outer space. We are bewitched into conceptualising a reality that doesn't exist.

And it is not the individual words alone that bewitch. The pattern of the language, the way the symbols are joined together, can also cast a spell. 'This path leads to the banana plantation' is a realistic straightforward statement that symbolises reality. 'This path leads to damnation' is a similar structure but the ideas implicit in it are quite different. The path of the second sentence is as different from the path of the first sentence as a banana plantation is different from damnation but the structure of the sentences can bewitch us into thinking they are quite similar: a path is a path is a path and a banana plantation is damnation. Beware the snake wrapped round the banana tree tempting you with the banana of knowledge!

BEWITCHMENT 2: THE MEANING OF WORDS

It is a generally held belief that words have a true meaning and to be able to use a word accurately we must be aware of that true meaning. To appreciate this meaning we are advised to look at words, see how they are used, and then come to an awareness of the true meaning. What often happens is a word can mean so many things in so many situations that we simply can't do this. Many words have no true meaning; rather they have so many different meanings which can only be appreciated in context. The potential power of such words to bewitch is immense: how can your intelligence function clearly if the words you use to think and to express your thoughts can mean many different things?

Dictionary makers know this. They obtain their definitions from the way words are used. The full title of the *Shorter Oxford English Dictionary* is *The New Shorter Oxford Dictionary on Historical Principles*. The historical principles are important. The editors of the dictionary read widely and they note every interesting or unusual word and unfamiliar uses of common words within the context of the sentences they read. When the word is defined for the dictionary the editors look at all the uses of the word they have compiled, and the dates these usages were current, and come to their definition based on the meaning of the words in the context, both now and in the past. The changes in the meaning of a word are traced historically. In time the meanings of words shift and change for many reasons and we can only be sure of the meanings when we know their time contexts as well as their contexts within sentences. Several hundred years ago the word *lust* meant *innocent delight*. The entry for *gay* in the NOED has thirteen definitions, the first dating back to Middle English, (the language spoken in England between 1150 and 1349)[4]. Only the last entry, from the mid-20th century, has anything to do with the meaning homosexual.

THE IMPORTANCE OF THE SOUND OF A WORD

If *cockroaches* were called *cuddlebugs*, would they seem nicer? Would Hitler have done quite so much damage if his name had been *Schicklgruber*? In the sound of a word you can sometimes hear the destiny of a thing.

According to Marshall Blonsky, a Wolfson Fellow in semiotics at the New School, "The sound of a word is of enormous importance. The sound is the lubricant that gets the signifier and its meaning into our consciousness."

"If you've got a lot of names for something," Blonsky says, "none of them euphonious, then it's as if you don't have any name. And if you don't have a name for a thing, then as far as most people are concerned, you don't have the thing at all."

When her teacher says Maja is a 'good' student she means 'diligent' but when the same teacher says Maja gets 'good' grades she means 'high'. When her mother says Maja is a 'good' daughter she might mean 'keeps out of trouble'. When Maja's friend says Maja is a 'good' friend she means 'faithful', when her grandfather says she has a 'good' deal of common sense he uses the word differently from when he says she is a 'good' girl. We must look at the context of each statement to understand the meaning of 'good'. A multitude of words have meaning only in context. When we isolate them to define them they become meaningless. Even in context they still bewitch. What could Maja's mother mean when she says Maja is a 'good' girl? It might just mean she doesn't smoke or that she brings her a cup of coffee every morning or it might mean Maja is a model of conventional morality.

Sometimes the meaning of words is so vague it is difficult to understand their meaning at all. We have already seen small and green. Giving instructions to someone is fraught with difficulties. What does 'Turn right just as you enter the village' mean? Does it mean turn sharply right or fork to the right? And 'just' means what? 'As soon as'? 'Immediately'? And does 'village' mean where the village boundary is signposted or where the houses begin?

---

4. Old English is not the language used by Shakespeare. He used the Elizabethan form of modern English. Old English is the form of English spoken in England up to the middle of the 12th century. *Old* here has a technical meaning within the history of language. Another example of the bewitching meaning of words.

Words that have almost the same meaning can also bewitch. Hint, intimate, insinuate, suggest, imply can be very similar in meaning and we would probably not agree on the subtle differences, if any, in the meaning of each one unless we were aware of the exact context in which it is being used. Poets, of course, delight in the uncertainty of the meaning of words and weave them together in fascinating patterns to further reinforce their ambiguity. Here is the start of a poem by Gerard Manley Hopkins, a poem which bewitches with its choice of words and images.

> *Glory be to God for dappled things -*
>
> > *For skies of couple-colour as a brinded cow;*
> >
> > > *For rose-moles all in stipple upon trout that swim;*
> >
> > *Fresh-firecoal chestnut-falls; finches' wings;*
> >
> > *Landscape plotted and pieced - fold, fallow and plough;*
> >
> > > *And all trades, their gear and tackle and trim.*

You will not find *rose-moles* or *chestnut-falls* in a dictionary. All this bewitchment about the meaning of words doesn't mean dictionaries are of no use and we should throw them away. Dictionaries can indicate the possible meanings of words; meanings the reader has to take and put into contexts. Beware of them, though. Dictionaries cast their own spell: you think you have the meaning, after all it is written there in the dictionary, and what you have is only a possible meaning.

BEWITCHMENT 3: LANGUAGE CREATES REALITY

In the 1990s it became fashionable to mock 'politically correct' (PC) language. The classification 'politically correct' is itself an example of words bewitching. 'Socially correct' might be more appropriate but that could be interpreted as a guide to good manners. In some ways that is what PC language is, an attempt to prune offensive, sexist, prejudiced, racist terms from the language because they create offence. But they also create reality. Recently I re-read Mark Twain's Huckleberry Finn, and as I was finishing it I visited New York and stayed with an old friend who had just retired. His wife still goes off to work everyday and at breakfast on the first day of my visit I asked him, as he sliced the bagels and perked the coffee, what it was like being the house nigger. (Remember I was reading *Huckleberry Finn*). My friend stopped cutting his bagel, paused, and said very seriously to me, 'Don't use that word'. And such was the intensity of his command I have not used it since. The word has gone out of use. And for good reason. It was offensive to the people it described and it reflected a social and economic status that no longer exists. And one of the reasons that status no longer exists is because the word is no longer used. The language that reflected reality also created and maintained it. The feminists are right, if we always read of doctors as 'he' and nurses as 'she', we eventually begin to expect reality to reflect that situation. The words create the reality; our intelligences are bewitched.

If you have any doubt that language creates reality, perhaps George Orwell can persuade you. Here are his famous Principles of Newspeak (selected from the Appendix to *1984* by George Orwell).

The purpose of Newspeak was not only to provide a medium of expression for the world-view and mental habits proper to the devotees of Ingsoc, but to make all other modes of thought impossible. It was intended that when Newspeak had been adopted once and for all and Oldspeak forgotten, a heretical thought - that is a thought diverging from the principles of Ingsoc - should be literally unthinkable, at least so far as thought is dependent on words.

Its vocabulary was so constructed as to give exact and often very subtle expression to every meaning that a Party member could properly wish to express, while excluding all other meanings and also the possibility of arriving at them by indirect methods.

This was done partly by the invention of new words but chiefly by eliminating undesirable words and by stripping such words as remained of unorthodox meanings, and so far as possible of all secondary meanings whatever. To give a single example. The word free still existed in Newspeak but it could only be used in such statements as 'This dog is free from lice' or 'This field is free from weeds'. It could not be used in the old sense of 'politically free' or 'intellectually free' since political and intellectual freedom no longer existed even as concepts, and were of necessity nameless. Quite apart from the suppression of definitely heretical words, reduction of vocabulary was regarded as an end in itself, and no word that could be dispensed with was allowed to survive. Newspeak was designed not to extend but to diminish the range of thought, and this purpose was indirectly assisted by cutting the choice of words down to a minimum.

THE A VOCABULARY

The A Vocabulary consisted of the words needed for everyday life - for such things as eating, drinking, working, putting on one's clothes, going up and down stairs, riding in vehicles, gardening, cooking and the like. It was composed almost entirely of words that we already possess - words like hit, run, dog, tree, sugar, field - but in comparison with the present day English vocabulary their number was extremely small, while their meanings were far more rigidly defined. All ambiguities and shades of meaning had been purged out of them. So far as it could be achieved, a Newspeak word of this class was simply a staccato sound expressing one clearly understood concept. It would have been quite impossible to use A Vocabulary for literary purposes or for political or philosophical discussion. It was intended only to express simple, purposive thoughts, usually involving concrete objects or physical actions.

THE B VOCABULARY

The B vocabulary consisted of words which had been deliberately constructed for political purposes: words, that is to say, which not only had in every case a political implication, but were intended to impose a desirable mental attitude upon the person using them. Without a full understanding of the principles of Ingsoc it was difficult to use these words correctly. In some cases they could be translated into Oldspeak, or even into words taken from the A vocabulary, but this usually demanded a long paraphrase and always involved the loss of certain overtones. The B words were a sort of verbal shorthand, often packing whole ranges of ideas into a few syllables, and at the same time more accurate and forcible than ordinary language.

The B words were in all cases compound words. They consisted of two or more words, or portions of words, welded together in an easily pronounceable form. The resulting amalgam was always a noun-verb, and inflected according to the ordinary rules. To take a single example: the word goodthink, meaning, very roughly, 'orthodoxy', or, if one chose to regard it as a verb, 'to think in an orthodox manner'. This inflected as follows: noun-verb, goodthink; past tense and past participle, goodthinked; present participle, goodthinking; adjective, goodthinkful; adverb, goodthinkwise; verbal noun, goodthinker.

THE C VOCABULARY

The C vocabulary was supplementary to the others and consisted entirely of scientific and technical terms. These resembled the scientific terms in use today, and were constructed from the same roots, but care was taken to define them rigidly and strip them of any undesirable meanings.

From the foregoing account it will be seen that in Newspeak the expression of unorthodox opinions, above a very low level, was well nigh impossible. A person growing up with Newspeak as his sole language would no more know that equal had once had the secondary meaning of 'politically equal', or that free had once meant 'intellectually free', than, for instance, a person who had never heard of chess would be aware of the secondary meanings attaching to queen and rook.

BEWITCHMENT 4. LANGUAGE INFERS AND JUDGES

An inference is a conclusion you come to about the unknown based on something you know. 'Maja is clever', you might infer, from the facts you know. She always gets good grades and hands her work in promptly without any obvious effort. But your statement is not a fact but an inference. Maja may work very hard, she may struggle over every piece of written work she hands in, she may spend hours discussing her work with her parents or her brother. What you are saying when you say she is clever is simply that she gets good grades and hands her work in on time. Your inference that she is clever, because you put it into words, achieves a status it does not deserve. The words have bewitched you into believing something that is open to question is, in fact, a reality.

What you have done is made a judgment and the words of your judgement may imply a disapproval or approval which is not necessarily valid. The bewitchment is that judgements, once they have been put into words, obstruct thought. What does 'Maja is a wonderful human being' actually mean? It probably means that Maja's values, and the way she presents her values, are the same as the values of the person who made the statement.

In extreme cases the judgement is obvious. If someone is called a 'scumbag' or the 'sweetest person on earth' it is clear a judgement is being made. But often phrases and words are used which are just as judgmental but not so obvious. 'He was a typical Wall Street money trader', implies all sorts of judgements and stereotypes. The intelligence is bewitched by the stereotyping, which is simply a generalised judgment.

BEWITCHMENT 5: LANGUAGE CLASSIFIES

'You know the problem with the cafeteria at lunchtime. It's those eighth graders. There are so many of them and they are so noisy and they jump the line. They are awful.'

When you describe the eighth graders in this way you classify them. The individuals belong to no class until we, with our language, put them in it. And in this case our classification will probably lead us to believe the worst of the eighth graders whenever we meet them. If one of them is noisy on the school bus *that's typical*. If one of them doesn't work, *that's typical*. If one of them doesn't turn up for a basketball match, *that's typical*.

Classifying, frequently determines our attitudes and behaviour towards those things which are classified. Eighth graders are no different from ninth, tenth, eleventh and twelfth graders. They have just the same mix of lazy and hardworking, noisy and quiet, extrovert and introvert individuals as any other grade but once they are classified in our minds as a particular set of abstractions the language of the classifications bewitches.

Jews, Arabs, socialists, communists, hippies, drop-outs, saints, valley girls, republicans, these are all generalisations. Do any of these words really mean anything or are they just a set of sounds which trigger in us conventional reactions?

BEWITCHMENT 6: LANGUAGE IS ALWAYS CHANGING

Language is always changing. You know this from your personal experience, as I do. I often sit open mouthed in astonishment and awe at some of the vibrant language I hear used by my Diploma students. I am well impressed.

Changes in usage are often resisted by more conservative (or insecure?) members of a society, but change often brings vibrancy and vigour to a language. Each of the dialects of English - American, Canadian, Irish, Caribbean, Australian, etc. etc., have changed and still change and enrich the language. Slang and unconventional usage also bring dynamism to communication that standard usage doesn't.

To illustrate this point here are some amusing examples from a contemporary dictionary of French slang. The dictionary vividly represents the range of influences on French speech: France's emigrant populations, Anglo-American popular culture, technology, the criminal world and the particular French art of verlan, backslang.

accro,
> hooked on something, dependent. Abbreviation of accroché, a literal translation of the American expression 'hooked'. Origin: drug jargon in the Seventies. You can be accro on zan, zen, zob (liquorice, zen or dick) or anything you want.

avoir l'oreille Van Gogh
> (to have Van Gogh's ear), to have stayed on the phone too long. Astonishing cultural reference, which appeared around the centenary of the master's death in 1990.

barbecue,
> device for 'estimating the speed of a vehicle', as the police say. Good for grilling speedsters.

breaker (pronounced bréquer),
1. Take a break, take a rest.
2. 'Breaker un jeune talent' (showbiz talk) means, as a representative of Sony Music pointed out one day on television, discover a young talent and give him or her a 'break'.

Camembert,
> important figure, big shot. Translation of 'big cheese', the Anglo-American equivalent to the French une grosse légume. Heard at EuroDisney on its opening day, 11 April 1992.

c'est glitter!,
> it's great, superb and above all, showy. "glitter, tes chouzes!" 'Your shoes are really something'. From the English 'to glitter'.

dico,

> intellectual, or, more ironically someone who always knows everything. 'Mais oui, c'est ça, t'es le méga-dico, toi!' "Oh yes, that's right, you're the mega-egghead round here!' From 'dictionary' of course.

faire cheese,

> to smile. First used to make people smile for a photograph. Still very common, especially among young people.

natürlich, Ulrich

> (or natürlich Heinrich), of course! As appropriate, if not yet as common, as 'A l'aise, Blaise!' or 'Tu triques, Patrick'.

pizza!

> warning shouted in the face of imminent danger - going under a bus or out of a window or anything with the potential to leave you flattened. 'Traverser le Sébasto? Houl`a...Pizza!' 'Cross the boulevard de Sébastopo? Whooah ... Pizza!

I have only begun here to explore how language bewitches our intelligences, our ways-of-knowing and the ideas and concepts in those disciplines we study. Language is what the linguists define it as; it is uniquely human. It does communicate and it uses symbols. But it is also a vast unmapped territory fascinating and bewitching your intelligence and casting spells on reason. Use it as a way-of-knowing with great caution.

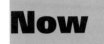 *you have read Chapter 5 ...*

consider or undertake the following:

1. Look at the functions of language defined by Roman Jakobson (page 119). Find examples of each category in the language you have used today. Have you used language in a way that could not be included in one of his categories? Has the classifying of language functions any practical use?

2. All of us have had our intelligences bewitched by language to some extent. Think of examples from your own experience of the ways in which language has confused or misled you. How personally appropriate do you find the argument that language bewitches the intelligence?

3. Read the Sapir-Whorf Hypothesis as presented on page 120. Use examples from your own experience to decide if you agree with the following statements found in the transcript.

i.   Language 'does influence how we perceive the world'.
ii. It is easier to remember things that are encoded in the language we speak.
iii. Using your own experience of learning a foreign language and meeting people who speak languages other than English, would you accept that people who speak different languages live in different worlds?

4. The Principles of Newspeak (page 124) are based on the belief that thought can be controlled by language. Today's tabloid newspapers control the vocabulary of their journalists. Are not tabloid newspapers attempting to do to their readers what George Orwell's Newspeak intended?

5.

This passage suggests the thinking of a language community can be manipulated by language. The authors assume the manipulation they advocate will liberate and expand thought. In your experience is this likely to happen?

By 1975 many major textbook publishers had adopted, or were preparing to adopt, non-sexist guidelines for their authors and editors. The purpose of these guidelines is to give practical examples of how language can be used to liberate and expand thought. Scott, Foresman and Company suggest, for instance, that 'When man invented the wheel...' can become 'When people invented the wheel'; 'congressmen' are more inclusively 'members of Congress'; and 'the typical American......' can be 'typical Americans.....they'. A sentence like "In New England, the typical farm was so small that the owner and his sons could take care of it by themselves" can more accurately be phrased, "In New England, the typical farm was so small that the family members could take care of it by themselves." Amplifying this kind of distinction in more comprehensive guidelines based on an analysis of social studies textbooks, Elizabeth Burr, Susan Dunn, and Norma Farquar wrote, "phrases such as 'the farmer's wife' convey the idea that the female was merely the possession of the farmer and was not herself a farmer, when in fact the wives of most small farmers were themselves farmers in every sense of the word."

6.

Read and enjoy, the examples of contemporary French slang (page 127). Are these the kinds of words you would use or your parents and grandparents would use? Are flexibility and change in the meaning of words desirable? Is there any argument to be made for the meaning of words to be fixed and for people to be discouraged from 'playing' with language.

7.

Does language help or hinder you personally in acquiring knowledge? Are some areas of knowledge easier to understand through language than others?

SECTION ONE
WAYS-OF-KNOWING

CREATIVITY

6

CHAPTER CONTENTS

- Your creativity
- Creativity and natural science
- The Eureka Act
- Creativity in the Arts
- The creative impulse and the artistic impulse

Before *you read Chapter 6 ...*

consider possible responses to these:

1. What are you creating when you take part in so-called 'Creative' writing?

2. What opportunities do you get, in each of the subjects you are studying, to be creative?

3. Do you enjoy being creative or would you rather just be told what to do and get on with it?

4. Do you find you have any opportunities to be creative in the Theory of Knowledge course?

5. Talk to someone you know, who to your certain knowledge, has created something: a painting or sculpture, a poem, an essay on science, a mathematical proof. Try to ascertain the creative process they followed.

6. Think of the most creative thing you have done in your life. Attempt to analyse both the creative process you underwent and the feeling of achievement you had after your creation.

7. Do you ever have creative ideas when you are half asleep or when you are daydreaming?

6.0 CREATIVITY

It is not enough for us to perceive, to reason, to be aware of our emotions and to understand that language is bewitching, we have to bring these ways-of-knowing together in order to create new understanding, for ourselves and for others. When you write a commentary on a poem by Edward Thomas, when you grope your way to understanding the cause of the Second World War, or snappily solve an equation, you are in some little way using your ways-of-knowing to create new knowledge, for yourself if for nobody else.

Here is part of a letter I once received from an ex student. In it you can read how he describes his 'creativity', the application of his ways-of-knowing.

Dear Michael,

I thought you might be interested in reading an essay I wrote for an international essay competition last month. The competition is hosted by the Goethe Institut and something called Lettre International. Submissions were welcomed in Arabic, Chinese, English, French, German, Spanish, and Russian. I thought I would be best off writing in English. The set theme was "Die Zukunft von der Vergangenheit befreien? Die Vergangenheit von der Zukunft befreien?'

I have never written an essay of comparable length. This essay is about six times as long as any piece of work I have ever had to produce for university. I began work in a rather light-hearted manner, not quite realising how much time and thought I would have to invest. As the deadline drew nearer, I found myself completely absorbed in the subject matter. I had no time for any other writing, nor for reading that did not relate to this essay. I took advantage of my seminars and tutorials by turning the discussion towards problems I wished to discuss in my essay, but had failed to think through to a conclusion.

Upon finishing the essay I felt a peculiar combination of emotions. On the one hand I was proud of my work; on the other hand I was convinced it was full of flaws. Because of the time pressure and word limit, I had only been able to outline in very broad terms a solution to the issues I dealt with. I felt I could have continued writing for another couple of weeks. For a few days after the completion of the essay I didn't really know what to do with myself. There had been such a build up in intensity, and then all of a sudden it was over. I found it difficult to return to all the other work I had put aside. Eventually I got back into my normal routine.

In two weeks,,,,,,,,,,,,

Max

Writing the essay was, for Max, hard work. Most creators are likely to agree with the oft misquoted American inventor, Thomas Edison, whose creativity gave us the gramophone player, the electric light bulb and the means to make motion pictures. 'Genius', he wrote, 'is one percent inspiration, ninety-nine percent perspiration'. Max's creativity described above certainly seems to endorse that statement (although let me make it clear that Max has no pretensions to be a genius). But there is plenty of evidence to suggest that creativity is not just brought about by solely 'perspiration'.

CREATIVITY IN NATURAL SCIENCE

The progress of science takes place through a few master architects, or, in any case, through a number of guiding brains which constantly set all the industrious labourers at work for decades.

Friedrich von Schiller (1759-1805) Historian, playwright and poet.

The account of natural science as an area of knowledge outlined in Chapter 7 is an account of 'the industrious labourers at work for decades': diligent, dedicated professional scientists objectively observing, recording and interpreting. But as you have probably already realised, the history of natural science as an Area of Knowledge is not the history of these 'industrious labourers' described by Schiller. It is the history of the 'guiding brains', the stories of the intellectual achievements of such brilliant scientists as Kepler, Newton, Pasteur and Einstein. These geniuses are as rare as they are revolutionary. They are creators, fashioning new and original understandings out of their objective observations of natural phenomena. Other sixteenth century astronomers observed the movement of the planets, Kepler explained them, laying down the principles on which Newton was later to build. Newton defined the laws of gravity which other scientists later refined. Pasteur, as we shall see, through his interpretation of the behaviour of micro-organisms, founded the science of immunology, the development of which has since employed many industrious labourers. The empirical evidence for the Theory of Relativity was available for fifty years before Einstein. Many 'industrious labourers' had all the information to hand before Einstein came along, but it was Einstein's guiding brain that made the necessary connections.

THE EUREKA ACT

The creative process which led to the discoveries of these brilliant scientists has been called the Eureka Act after the victory cry of Archimedes. Archimedes worked under the threatening patronage of Hiero, the so-called Tyrant of Syracuse. Hiero, being the tyrant he was, received an ornate golden crown from some of his subjects, which they claimed was made out of solid gold. Hiero, still the tyrant he was, suspected that the crown was not solid gold but contained some inferior metals. He requested that Archimedes 'check it out', as we now say. Archimedes knew the specific weight of gold, that is, the weight of gold per unit volume (i.e. he knew the weight of the equivalent of a cubic centimetre of gold, although he did not use cubic centimetres). But Archimedes did not know the volume of the ornate crown. He did not know how many cubic centimetres of metal it contained and had no apparent way of finding out. He could, of course, have melted the crown down and then it would have been easy to measure the volume of the solid lump of metal, but that would have destroyed the ornate design and almost certainly have annoyed Hiero, a man not to be annoyed. Luckily for Archimedes he was of clean habits and getting into his bath one day noticed, not for the first time, how the bath water rose as he lowered himself into it. Thinking about this phenomenon he came to the conclusion that the volume of water displaced by his body equalled the volume of the amount of his body below the waterline. If he used the crown instead of his body ...... Eureka! (I have found it!) he yelled and dashed down the street to the palace to get the crown.

Archimedes had created: he had brought together two ideas, the idea of the specific weight of gold and the idea of water displacement, and created a new way of measuring the volume of irregular solids.

ARCHIMEDES 287-212 BC

Archimedes was a greek mathematician and inventor, born in Syracuse, Sicily. He discovered the formulae for the areas and volumes of cylinders, spheres and parabolas and other plane and three dimensional figures (without the use of his bath water?) and founded the science of hydrostatics (with the use of his bath water?). He invented the Archimedes' Screw, a device still used for raising water from one level to another, and designed a siege engine to be used against the Romans. He was killed in the siege of Syracuse when he ignored a challenge from a guard because he was absorbed in a mathematical problem.

The act of creation - creativity - in science, often seems to be the result of chance. If Archimedes had not, by chance, noticed the rise in the water level of his bath, would he have been able to calculate the volume of the crown? But was it chance? Archimedes was highly intelligent, adept at manipulating abstract ideas like 'volume' and 'density'. He was also a careful observer of the physical world around him. He was therefore 'ready' for his discovery: knowledge of the specific weight of gold had been around a long time before Archimedes. Archimedes had known, since he was a child, that his bath water rose when he lowered himself into it. Was it chance that made the connection? Chance may have helped but it was Archimedes' exceptional brain that really connected the two phenomena and enabled him to solve the problem. The history of science seems to be the history of exceptional brains connecting two or more ideas that had not previously been connected.

THE EUREKA ACT FOR IMMUNOLOGY

By the late 1870s Louis Pasteur had shown that rabies, and certain other diseases, were caused by micro-organisms. In 1879 he was studying the effect of bacteria by injecting chickens with a form of bacteria - a bacillus - which caused chicken cholera, a fatal illness in chickens. He accidentally left a collection of chicken cholera bacilli in his laboratory all summer and when he returned to his laboratory in the autumn to continue his research he used these 'old' bacilli to inject a number of chickens. He was surprised that the chickens, although they become ill, did not die. He attributed their survival to the old bacillus which he thought had been 'spoilt' by being

Micrograph of cholera bacilli

in the laboratory all summer. He obtained fresh, virulent supplies of the bacilli and experimented again, using both the old chickens who had survived the 'summer' bacilli and new chickens. The old chickens, the chickens who had been injected with the 'spoilt' bacilli all survived. The new chickens all died. When Pasteur was told about this he is reported to have 'remained silent for a minute, then exclaimed, as if he had seen a vision: "Don't you see, these animals have been vaccinated!" His Eureka Act had occurred.

LOUIS PASTEUR 1822 - 1895

French chemist and microbiologist Pasteur, one of the most distinguished biologists of all time established that putrefaction and fermentation were caused by micro-organisms. In 1881, two years after his Eureka Act, he proved that cows and sheep vaccinated with a weak form of anthrax bacilli gained immunity from the dreaded disease. In 1888 the Institute Pasteur was founded in Paris, specifically to research into the treatment and prevention of rabies. His name has become a laboratory, if not a household, name. *Pasteurisation* is the partial sterilisation of milk which kills most of the micro-organisms in it, making it safe for human consumption and increasing its keeping quality. *Pasteurella* are a group of bacteria which cause plague and other infectious diseases. A *pasteur flask* is a laboratory flask with a long, downward bending neck which reduces the entry of micro-organisms.

Pasteur had known for many years that humans injected with tissue from cows suffering from cowpox were immune from smallpox. (The word vaccination comes from the Latin word *vacca*: cow.) But no one had extended the idea to other tissue or other diseases. Pasteur had done what Archimedes had done: connected two apparently unconnected phenomena. Pasteur's exceptional brain had made the connection between smallpox vaccination and the survival of the chickens. The 'spoilt' weak form of chicken cholera bacillus acted in the same way as the weak form of smallpox found in cowpox and gave immunity to the chickens. Pasteur understood that vaccines, weak forms of micro-organisms, could create immunity from diseases created by virulent forms of the same micro-organisms. The science of immunology had been founded.

THE BASIC SCIENTIFIC METHOD

> He observed
> He gathered information
> He generalised
> He theorised
> He explained

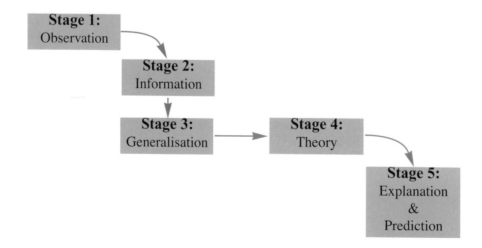

Stage 1:
Observation

Stage 2:
Information

Stage 3:
Generalisation

Stage 4:
Theory

Stage 5:
Explanation
&
Prediction

Pasteur's Eureka Act is compatible with the Basic Scientific Method described in Chapter 7.1.

His great moment of creativity came in his generalisation. He was able, using inductive logic, to go where none had gone before. Later, using deductive logic, he explained and predicted. His creativity was the result of conscious, logical, reasoning.

Not all Eureka Acts, it seems, are so conscious, logical and reasoned. Koestler[1], examining the question of whether the creative problem is solved by the conscious or the unconscious mind, suggests that many scientists and mathematicians are most creative when their rational thought is suspended, for instance, when they are asleep and dreaming or when they are dozing. He describes several Eureka Acts that occurred when the minds of scientists and mathematicians were in this relaxed state. The most convincing is that of Friedrich August von Kekulé, professor of chemistry in Ghent who, one afternoon in 1865 fell asleep and dreamt.

> *I turned my chair to the fire and dozed ...... the atoms were gambolling before my eyes.*
> *This time the smaller groups kept modestly in the background. My mental eye, rendered*
> *more acute by repeated visions of this kind, could now distinguish larger structures, of*
> *manifold conformation; long rows, sometimes more closely fitted together; all twining*
> *and twisting in snake like motion. But look! What was that? One of the snakes had seized*
> *hold of its own tail, and the form whirled mockingly before my eyes. As if by a flash of*
> *lightning I awoke .... let us learn to dream, gentlemen.*

This dream led to the 'revolutionary proposal that the molecules of certain important organic compounds are not open structures but closed chains or 'rings' - like the snake swallowing its tail.'

Is Kekulé's Eureka Act compatible with the Basic Scientific Method?

The difference between Pasteur's generalisation and Kekulé's generalisation is that the former was produced when Pasteur's conscious mind was actively digesting new information and the latter was produced when Kekulé's subconscious mind was apparently relaxed. Neither of these two Eureka Acts, the conscious, logical reasoning or the subconscious dream, is incompatible with the Basic Scientific Method. Both scientists have observed, both have gathered their information systematically and diligently, and both are 'ready' to make their generalisation, to make the creative leap that an exceptional brain can make. Koestler suggests that the more typical creative act is Kekulé's. Most humans are at their creative best, he suggests, when they are free from conscious mental control. Disciplined routines impede creative leaps. Kekulé was able to make his leap, to see his snake biting its tail, because he was relaxed and mentally uninhibited. That being mentally uninhibited can lead to creative connections, to the Eureka act, is corroborated by no less a person then Albert Einstein. In a lecture he gave in Berlin in 1918 he stated:

> *'The supreme task of the physicist is to arrive at universal elementary laws from which*
> *the cosmos can be built up by pure deduction. There is no logical path to these laws; only*
> *intuition, resting on sympathetic understanding of experience, can reach them.'*

Later he is reported as writing that these laws, the universal, elementary laws from which the cosmos can be built, are arrived at by 'free inventions of the mind' rather than by observation, experimentation or logical inference.

---

1. *The Act of Creation* (Arkana 1989)

FREE INVENTIONS OF THE MIND?

Einstein's statement that the laws governing the cosmos are arrived at by 'free inventions of the mind' must be treated with a little caution. The mind must be prepared to freely invent, as were the minds of Archimedes and Pasteur. The 'free inventing' was based on their existing understanding, their awareness of the problems they faced, their 'intuition resting upon sympathetic understanding of experience' to use Einstein's own words. The intuition and experience that Einstein is describing is the educated intuition and experience of natural scientists, keenly aware of the laws governing the external reality of the natural world that exists outside their own minds. All scientific laws must be compatible with that external reality and must be verifiable by experimentation. 'Free inventions of the mind' in natural science must be consistent with existing knowledge, not simply the whimsical daydreams of an imaginative mind. The 'free inventions of the mind' in science must also be impersonal, capable of being replicated by any other natural scientist working under the same conditions as the original 'free inventor'. Einstein's theory of relativity may have been a free invention of his mind but it has to 'correspond to reality' and pass the rigorous tests to which his fellow physicists subject it. His intuition is a very special kind of intuition.

CREATIVITY IN THE ARTS

That creativity in the arts is also dependent on the 'free invention of the mind' is beyond dispute. It is also dependent on 'intuition resting upon sympathetic understanding of experience', but the experience is fundamentally different from the intuition and experience of the natural scientist. Einstein's 'intuition' is not really intuition and his 'experience' is specifically experience of the physical world and its laws. The experience of artists is humanity: humanity in all its emotional richness and diversity, an experience not definable in terms of laws and Platonic knowledge-by-description. This knowledge is also in contrast to the knowledge of the physical sciences because it is personal, rather than impersonal: a work of art evokes and transmits the artist's 'feeling' in a unique way. It depends on the personal intuition and skills of its creator. Great scientists are explorers, mapping territory that exists for them to discover. Artists are explorers too, but they create the territory they explore:

> ... as imagination bodies forth
> The form of things unknown, the poet's pen
> Turns them to shapes, and gives to airy nothing
> A local habitation and a name.

ARTISTIC INSPIRATION: KUBLA KHAN

Koestler, as we have seen, suggests that humans are at their creative best when their minds are free from conscious mental control. This maybe is as true for some artists as it is for some scientists. Samuel Taylor Coleridge, the creator of Kubla Khan wrote a detailed description of how that acclaimed poem came into existence. The creative act Coleridge describes resembles the creative process described so clearly by Kekulé. Here is Coleridge, writing about himself in the third person singular, he is 'the Author' of the passage, describing his creative experience.

> *In the summer of the year 1797, the Author, then in poor health, had retired to a lonely farm-house between Porlock and Linton ...... in consequence of a slight indisposition, an anodyne had been prescribed, from the effects of which he fell asleep in his chair at the moment that he was reading the following sentence .... in Purchas's Pilgrimage: 'Here the Khan Kubla commanded a palace to be built, and a stately garden thereunto. And thus ten miles of fertile ground were enclosed with a wall'.*

The Author continued for about three hours in a profound sleep, at least of the external senses during which time he has the most vivid confidence, that he could not have composed less than from two to three hundred lines; if that indeed can be called composition in which all the images rose up before him as things with a parallel production of the correspondent expressions, without any sensation or consciousness of effort. On awakening he appeared to himself to have a distinct recollection of the whole, and taking his pen, ink, and paper, instantly and eagerly wrote down the lines that are here preserved.

Let us be clear what happened: Coleridge, asleep and under the influence of 'an anodyne' composed, in his mind, 'two to three hundred lines'; the 'images' of his composition he saw as 'things' 'with the parallel production of the correspondent expression'. That is, he saw the objects, visually, in his mind at the same time as he saw the words, the language symbols, that described these things. He could not, of course, write them down, because he was asleep.

Shortly after he 'instantly and eagerly' began to write he was disturbed by a man calling on him 'on business'. When he returned to his writing he was unable to recall the whole vision so Kubla Khan is 'a fragment' of just 54 lines, 54 of the most celebrated lines of English poetry. Inspiration or Perspiration?

And here it is:

Kubla Khan

In Xanadu did Kubla Khan
A stately pleasure dome decree:
Where Alph, the sacred river, ran
Through caverns measureless to man
Down to a sunless sea.
So twice five miles of fertile ground
With walls and towers were girdled round:
And there were gardens bright with sinuous rills,
Where blossomed many an incense-bearing tree:
And here were forests ancient as the hills,
Enfolding sunny spots of greenery.

But oh! that deep romantic chasm which slanted
Down the green hill athwart a cedarn cover!
A savage place! as holy and enchanted
As e'er beneath a waning moon was haunted
By woman wailing for her demon-lover!
And from this chasm, with ceaseless turmoil seething,
As if this earth in fast thick pants were breathing,
A mighty fountain momently was forced:
Amid whose swift half intermittent burst
Huge fragments vaulted like rebounding hail,
Or chaffy grain beneath the thresher's flail:
And 'mid these dancing rocks at once and ever
It flung up momently the sacred river.
Five miles meandering with a mazy motion
Through wood and dale the sacred river ran,

Then reached the caverns measureless to man,
And sank in tumult to a lifeless ocean:
And 'mid this tumult Kubla heard from far
Ancestral voices prophesying war!
The shadow of the dome of pleasure
Floated midway on the waves;
Where was heard the mingled measure
From the mountain and the caves.
It was a miracle of rare device,
A sunny pleasure dome with caves of ice!

A damsel with a dulcimer
In a vision once I saw:
It was an Abbysinian maid,
And on her dulcimer she played,
Singing of Mount Abora.
Could I revive within me

Her symphony and song
To such deep delight 'twould bring me,
That with music loud and long
I would build that dome in air,
That sunny dome! those caves of ice!
And all who heard should see them there,
And all should cry, 'Beware! Beware!
His flashing eyes, his floating hair!
Weave a circle round him thrice,
And close your eyes with holy dread,
For he on honey-dew hath fed,
And drunk the milk of Paradise.

It is hard to imagine that Coleridge's brilliant poem was dependent on his being free from conscious mental control. His 'intuition and experience' were 'ready' for the creative acts he undertook, in the same way Pasteur's mind was 'ready' to understand vaccination. The intuition and experience of artists is the inspiration and experience of creators consciously aware of what it is to be human and consciously able to transmit that awareness through their work.

Clive Bell describes the creation of a work of art as having three stages. These are, to use his words:

1:   a state of peculiar and intense sensibility
2:   the creative impulse and
3:   the artistic problem.

Let's look briefly at each of these.

'PECULIAR AND INTENSE SENSIBILITY'

'A state of peculiar and intense sensibility' he describes as that moment when the artist becomes intensely aware of his emotions. We are all, he argues, intensely aware at some times in our lives, when we fall in love, for example, or when we suffer great loss or when we suddenly become aware of the beauty of the countryside or are overwhelmed by the brightness and clarity of the marine life on a coral reef. Artists, he suggests, are different from the rest of us in that they are constantly intensely aware of their feelings about the world they inhabit. They are intensely 'sensible' to the world about them, not just to the natural world but also the world of human emotions and understanding. Most of us experience the intensity of life rarely. Artists experience it constantly. They respond intensely to the fall of snow outside a window or to the piping of a snake charmer, experiences the rest of us would enjoy, perhaps, but do not respond to intensely.

'THE CREATIVE IMPULSE'

Once the intense feelings have been perceived, Bell claims, artists have a longing to express them. That is the creative impulse. The special perception of artists and their desire to communicate this special perception, he sees as almost a single event.

'THE ARTISTIC PROBLEM'

The artistic problem which is at the heart of the creative act of artists, is matching the emotional experience with the form in which that emotion is expressed. Artists need a specific form, a method or a system, which is exactly right for their emotions. Finding that form is the artistic problem. Having the creative impulse is relatively easy; expressing it in the 'exactly right' way is the problem that demands the Eureka act. Artists must 'sit down to write a play or a poem, to paint a portrait or a still life'.

Bell claims that solving this problem, 'driving emotion through narrow tubes', is at the heart of art. The solution of the problem is the creative act of that artist.

Bell does not concern himself with the question that drives Koestler: the question of whether the creative problem is solved by the conscious or the unconscious mind, and for the purposes of Theory of Knowledge the problem is interesting but not important. Creativity in the arts and sciences seems to have much in common, but is also quite different. Friedrich Nietzsche, a nineteenth century philosopher and critic can have the last word:

> *The activity of genius does not seem in any fundamental way different from the activity of the inventive engineer, the astronomer, the historian or the master of tactics. All these activities can be described as those of people whose mental activity is concentrated in a single direction, who draw their data from all sources, who pay constant and careful attention to their own inner life and to that of others and who are untiring in their efforts to make use of all their resources. Genius is no more than learning first to set one stone on another and then to build; than seeking out first one's materials and then working unceasingly to impose form upon them. All human activity, not merely genius, is miraculously complex; but none of it is a miracle. Whence comes the idea that genius exists only in artists? That they alone have something called 'intuition': a sort of pair of magic spectacles through which they see directly into reality.*

> *The finished work of artistic expression hides from us any idea of the process and its creation; it imposes itself tyrannically on perfection existing here and now. That is why it is creative artists above all rather than scientists who are called geniuses. In reality this over-valuation and under-valuation are no more than childishness.*

Now *you have read Chapter 6 ...*

consider or undertake the following:

1. Based on what you have read in Chapter 6 and your own ideas and experience do you think the process of creativity is the same in the sciences as it is in the arts?

2. 'All artists are creative but only a very few scientists are.'

Is this a statement you could agree with?

3. How convincing do you find the idea that creativity is more likely to occur in the subconscious than in the conscious mind?

4. To be successfully creative do you have to be talented in a special way?

Want to know more?

You may find the following book helpful.

Koestler Arthur: *The Act of Creation* Arkana 1989.

SECTION TWO
AREAS OF KNOWLEDGE

CLASSIFICATIONS OF KNOWLEDGE

7.0

CHAPTER CONTENTS

7.0 AREAS OF KNOWLEDGE

*Histories make men wise; poets, witty; the mathematics, subtle; natural philosophy,
deep; moral [philosophy], grave; logic and rhetoric, able to contend.*

Francis Bacon (Of Studies)

As you can see from the diagram on page 16 the designers of the IB Theory of Knowledge have
divided knowledge into six 'Areas'. Natural Science, Mathematics, Human Science, History, the
Arts and Ethics. Philosophers of education (and others) have been classifying knowledge for many
centuries. Before you look in detail at the six Areas of Knowledge defined by the ToK programme,
you should be aware that there are other ways of classifying knowledge.

As you can see from the quotation above, Francis Bacon (1561-1626) divided knowledge into seven
broad categories shown in the box.

> **Bacon's classification of knowledge**
>
> History
> Poetry
> Mathematics
> Natural Philosophy
> Moral Philosophy
> Logic
> Rhetoric

You are familiar with history, poetry, mathematics and logic. 'Natural philosophy' is what we call
natural science and moral philosophy is ethics. Rhetoric is the art of persuasive speaking or writing
which is probably part of your English program.

Over a hundred and fifty years after Bacon's death his classification of knowledge was still in use.
Thomas Jefferson (1743–1826) when faced with the problem of cataloguing his vast personal
library used Bacon's classification. Jefferson's world was a world in which knowledge was
expanding rapidly but he seems not to have been too frustrated by his task.

THE DEWEY DECIMAL SYSTEM

The first 'modern' attempt at a grand systematic classification of knowledge was made by Melville
Dewey (1851-1931). Dewey, the librarian at Amherst College, was, in 1876, faced with the practical
problem of organising the collection in such a way that students and faculties could have quick and
easy access to it. He developed a method by which books are catalogued systematically according
to their subject matter. So successful was his system that he became chief librarian and professor of
library economy at Columbia University and then director of the New York State Library.

Dewey's ten main 'Classes' encompass knowledge in its entirety. His system is simple and logical
and because of this it is the most widely used library classification in the world. It is used in
135 countries, translated into over 30 languages and is now maintained by the Library of Congress
of the United States of America.

000	Generalities
100	Philosophy & psychology
200	Religion
300	Social sciences
400	Language
500	Natural sciences & mathematics
600	Technology (Applied sciences)
700	The arts
800	Literature & rhetoric
900	Geography & history

FORMS OF KNOWLEDGE

Dewey's classification of knowledge was practical. He wanted to know where to shelve the books in his library. Other attempts at classifying knowledge have been made by philosophers, both for theoretical and practical reasons. Some, like the educators who designed the IB diploma program, have attempted to list knowledge in order to define what is appropriate for schools and universities to teach. One such classification is made by the English philosophers *Hirst & Peters* in their book *The Logic of Education*. They suggest there are seven main areas of knowledge, *forms of knowledge* they call them, and each form has unique ideas (or concepts) and unique ways of testing the validity of the knowledge within its form.

HIRST & PETERS FORMS OF KNOWLEDGE

Formal logic & mathematics
The physical sciences
Understanding of our own and other
people's minds
Morals
Aesthetics
Religion
Philosophy

REALMS OF MEANING

Another 20th Century philosopher, Philip Phenix, again for practical educational reasons, divides knowledge up into what he calls six 'realms of meaning', which, he claims, are the 'foundation for all the meanings that enter human experience'. His realms of meaning have rather grand names (Phenix is, after all, a philosopher) but they correspond to school and university subjects with which we are familiar.

PHENIX: REALMS OF MEANING

Symbolics:	Language, mathematics.
Empirics:	Physical science, life science, psychology, social science.
Esthetics:	Music, visual arts, movement arts, literature.
Synnoetics:	Religion.
Ethics:	Morals, ethics, history.
Synoptics:	Philosophy.

HOW UNIVERSITIES CLASSIFY KNOWLEDGE

One of the main responsibilities of universities is to create knowledge. Universities are first and foremost research establishments where the boundaries of knowledge are extended. Extending knowledge in this way is specialised and universities are usually divided into faculties, each faculty concentrating on a specific area of knowledge. Faculties are often further divided into departments or 'schools' and the names of these faculties and schools indicate how the university classifies knowledge. Universities also teach of course, and the courses they teach reflect, to some extent, the classification of knowledge implicit in that university. Some universities offer courses which combine studies in more than one faculty or school. In 2006 Oxford University, for instance, offers these undergraduate admission courses:

- Archaeology and Anthropology
- Biochemistry, Molecular and Cellular
- Biological Sciences
- Chemistry
- Classical Archaeology and Ancient History
- Classics
- Classics and English
- Classics and Modern Languages
- Classics and Oriental Studies
- Computer Science
- Earth Sciences
- Economics and Management
- Engineering Science
- Engineering and Computing Science
- Engineering, Economics and Management
- English Language and Literature
- English and Modern Languages
- European and Middle Eastern Languages
- Experimental Psychology
- Fine Art
- Geography
- History (Modern)
- History (Ancient and Modern)
- History (Modern) and Economics

- History (Modern) and English
- History (Modern) and Modern Languages
- History (Modern) and Politics
- History of Art
- Human Sciences
- Law (Jurisprudence)
- Materials Science
- Materials, Economics and Management
- Mathematics
- Mathematics and Computer Science
- Mathematics and Philosophy
- Mathematics and Statistics
- Medicine
- Modern Languages
- Modern Languages and Linguistics
- Music
- Oriental Studies
- Philosophy
- Philosophy and Modern Languages
- Philosophy, Politics and Economics (PPE)
- Philosophy and Theology
- Physics
- Physics and Philosophy
- Physiological Sciences
- Theology

Many universities and colleges now offer multidisciplinary first degrees. Subjects such as *American Studies* and *Environmental Studies* involve a variety of 'areas of knowledge'. Princeton, for instance, in 2006, includes (amongst others) the following Programs offering first (bachelor) degrees. Note that it lists its engineering programs separately.

> African Studies, Program in
> African-American Studies, Program in
> American Studies, Program in
> Applications of Computing, Program in
> Applied and Computational Mathematics, Program in
> Biophysics, Program in
> Creative Writing, Program in
> East Asian Studies, Program in
> Environmental Studies, Program in
> European Cultural Studies, Program in
> European Politics and Society, Program in Contemporary
> Finance, Program in

Hellenic Studies, Program in
Humanistic Studies, Program in
Judaic Studies, Program in
Language and Culture, Program in
Latin American Studies, Program in
Linguistics, Program in
Materials Science and Engineering, Program in
Medieval Studies, Program in
Musical Performance, Program in
Near Eastern Studies, Program in
Neuroscience, Program in
Russian and Eurasian Studies, Program in
Teacher Preparation, Program in
Theater and Dance, Program in
Visual Arts, Program in
Women and Gender, Program in the Study of
Writing Program

Program of Study for the Degree of Bachelor of Science in Engineering (B.S.E. Degree)
Engineering and Applied Science, School of

Architecture and Engineering, Program in
Engineering and Management Systems, Program in
Engineering Physics, Program in
Geological Engineering, Program in
Robotics and Intelligent Systems, Program in

Philosophers like Hirst and Peters, and Phenix, argue there are only a restricted numbers of 'areas of knowledge', each with its own tests for validity and truth. This does not mean that interdisciplinary studies in themselves have no value, rather students should be aware of the status of knowledge in each of the components of their course and treat that knowledge with the caution that is, or is not, appropriate. The classification of knowledge is more than a simple practical device for organising libraries and universities and schools. It is an indication of the nature of the knowledge itself.

Examining the nature of the Areas of Knowledge defined in the following pages will help you look more critically at the nature of the programmes you select to study in your college courses.

SECTION TWO
AREAS OF KNOWLEDGE

NATURAL SCIENCE

7.1

CHAPTER CONTENTS

Before

you read Chapter 7.1 ...

consider some possible responses to these questions:

1. Physics is regarded as a challenging school subject, as 'hard', by many students. Why? What is there about physics that has earned it this reputation?

2. What is an 'experiment' in science? Think back to a time when you conducted an 'experiment' in physics, chemistry or biology. What did you do and why did you do it? What did you learn? Was it possible for you to claim, as students often do, that the experiment 'worked' or 'did not work'? What does it mean to say an experiment 'worked'?

3. Who should decide the areas of scientific research which scientists undertake? And on what principles should they make this decision?

4. The word 'mass' has a specific scientific meaning: the quantity of matter a body contains measured in terms of resistance to acceleration by a force. What do *body, resistance, acceleration* and *force* mean in this definition? Is it possible for you to simplify the definition so that an average ten year old could understand it? Can you recall any instances of language bewitching your intelligence as you study science?

5. What image of scientists do you, and others in your group, have?

6. Play the game described on page 153. Are there any ways in which playing the game is 'scientific'?

7.1   NATURAL SCIENCE

Natural Science as an area of knowledge became an obsession in the 20th century. If we want to know something about the natural world we live in, we consult science. Science provides facts. Science is reliable, precise, objective, testable, self-correcting. Science has at its core the unremitting vigilance of scientists examining evidence they collect about the nature of the natural world and ruthlessly applying logic to any analysis of that evidence. We assume the facts science gives us are true and justified. Science is the ultimate justified true belief; the certain way-of-knowing. Science uses 'the scientific method'. Other disciplines model their claims to know on 'the scientific method', seeking to achieve the status and certainty of natural science.

What is Natural Science?

Ernest Nagel (1901-1985) a professor of the philosophy of science at Columbia University, New York, emphasised the potentially wide range of scientific enquiry when he described *science* (without the 'natural' before it) as seeking to 'discover and formulate in general terms the conditions under which events occur'. 'Events' here presumably covers all happenings, all those things which we can observe in the world around us, whether they be the rise and fall of air temperature, the rise and fall of stock market prices or the rise and fall of empires.

Natural Science has a rather more restricted meaning, the study of the 'phenomena of the physical universe', that is the natural world about us, that world which is independent of human behaviour. The natural world is such a vast entity that no one scientist is capable of understanding it all, so scientists have specialised. At school you are probably familiar with four broad scientific categories: physics, chemistry, biology and earth science. Within each of these categories there are numerous further specialisations.

biology,
> the study of living organisms, includes the following:

aerobiology,
> the study of the nature and distribution of the living organisms, spores, pollen and seeds carried by the air;

agrobiology,
> the study of soil and plant nutrition;

astrobiology,
> the search for, and study of, extraterrestrial life;

bacteriology,
> the study of bacteria;

biochemistry,
> the study of the chemical processes which occur in plants;

biometry,
> the application of statistical methods to biological investigations;

biophysics,
> the application of the laws of physics to organisms;

cybernetics,
> the study of control and communication systems within organisms;

cryobiology,
> the study of organisms at temperatures below which they normally function;

cytology,
> the study of the structures and functions of the cells of organisms;

electrobiology,
> the study of the electrical phenomena of organisms;

embryology,
> the study of the development of organisms up to the time of birth or hatching;

enzymology,
> the study of the proteins (enzymes) produced by living cells;

gnotobiology,
> the study of organisms free from bacteria normally present in their environment;

microbiology,
> the study of micro-organisms;

molecular biology,
> the study of the function of macromolecules essential to life;

palaeontology,
> the study of extinct animals and plants;

pharmacology,
> the study of the effects of drugs and medicines on organisms;

physiology,
> the study of the normal functioning of organisms;

radiobiology,
> the study of the effect of radiation on organisms;

taxonomy,
> the systematic classification of living organisms;

virology,
> the study of viruses.

What is it about the scientists' way of acquiring and establishing scientific knowledge that makes it the ideal model, the model other disciplines seek to imitate? Much has been written by scientists, historians of science and philosophers about the nature of scientific knowledge. The 'scientific method', the process by which scientific knowledge is acquired, has been scrutinised so intensively that every attempt to define it has led to counter-definitions and redefinitions and reservations.

THE SCIENTIFIC METHOD 1

THE BASIC SCIENTIFIC METHOD

There is, however, a generally accepted popular understanding of the scientific method. For convenience let us call this the Basic Scientific Method, although its more formal name is *naive inductivism*. This is the most generally held view of the scientific method, the view most non-scientists hold and the view shared by many scientists too.

Scientists observe the world through their senses and record the information their senses provide. They collect as much of this sensory information as they can, from as many observations as possible. Using this information they make generalisations about the things they have observed. These generalisations form the basis of a theory which explains why the information they have collected is as it is. The theory will also predict what is likely to happen in similar circumstances in the future.

AN EXAMPLE

Scientists make observations about the rise and fall of marine tides at various places throughout the world. Using the information they collect, they make generalisations about the rise and fall of tides and use the generalisations to create a theory describing why seas behave in the way they do. They then use this theory to explain the rise and fall of the tides and to predict their rise and fall in the future.

BECOME A SCIENTIST: COLLECT DATA AND CREATE A THEORY

PETALS AROUND A ROSE

You will need four dice and this initial information.

If you rolled a set of four dice and scored 1, 5, 4 and 6 your number of petals around a rose would be 14.

If you rolled a second time 3, 3, 6, and 5 your petals would also be 14.

2, 2, 1 and 6 would give you 10 petals.

Here are some more scores with the four dice in this game.

```
3 4 1 2 score 8
1 6 4 3 score 12
2 3 4 2 score 10
6 5 4 4 score 18
5 3 5 3 score 12
2 1 5 3 score 8
6 6 6 6 score 24
```

To play the game you have to discover the rule which determines the number of petals. Each player uses the scores above to develop a theory that explains the scores. Don't tell any one else your theory. Write it down. Place the dice in any position you wish and then tell the rest of the group the score according to your theory, but don't tell them the theory. If your are satisfied you have a theory that explains all the scores, show new combinations on the dice to help the other players and then retire from the game to allow the other players to demonstrate their theories.

When all the players have discovered a theory that works, share your theories, as you have written them, so that they can be publicly tested.

After the game, discuss your processes and difficulties. How did you go about working out your first and subsequent theories?

Here then is the Basic Scientific Method:

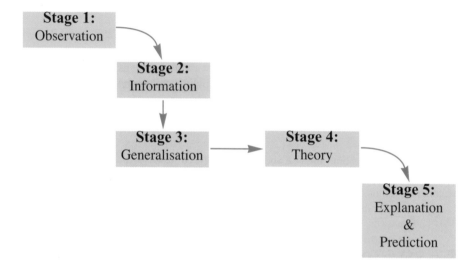

It is not difficult to understand why this view is popularly held. The natural world is in many ways predictable. There is a regularity in nature. Predictions made using this Basic Method can be accurate and in practice the Method works. Mostly.

PROBLEMS WITH THE BASIC METHOD

But you already know a little about the problems of sensory observation; the unreliability of empirical information. You already know too the problem with inductive logic; the unreliability of generalisations. Based as it is, firstly on empirical knowledge and secondly on inductive reasoning, couldn't our trust in the reliability and precision of science be a little misplaced?

Let's examine briefly these two problems, sensory observation and inductive logic, with reference to the Basic Scientific Method.

THE OBSERVATION PROBLEM

The Basic Scientific Method begins with observation. At least three factors influence the reliability, or otherwise of the information we obtain through observation.

1. PERCEPTUAL PROBLEMS

To be valid, scientific observations must be accurate and unbiased. We know already how easy it is for our senses to be deceived, making our observations inaccurate and misleading. (See Perception; Some Complications, page 21).

Our visual, auditory, olfactory, taste and tactile experiences are frequently inseparable from what we believe we are seeing, hearing, smelling, tasting and touching. Our senses cannot be trusted.

2. THE OBSERVATION STATEMENT

Observations have to be described in language. There has to be what is called an observation statement. This statement will be scrutinised and used by other scientists. But even the simplest observation statement, because it uses language, assumes theories embedded in the language. For instance, here is an observational statement about tides, in simple everyday language: *The highest tide was recorded at 14.42*. Much is assumed in this statement. It is assumed there is such a thing as a tide, an immense concept in itself. It is also assumed that it is possible to have a highest tide, which implies a lowest and a mean and the concept of height. Is the concept of height really appropriate in describing the movement of water? Isn't there an implication that the sea level is constantly changing? The precision of the observational statement is as accurate as the language used and the ideas that are embedded in that language. However neutral the initial observation is, the language of the observation statement inevitably influences that neutrality.

3. THE CHOICE OF WHAT IS OBSERVED

Scientists are human. They don't just observe whatever is there to be observed, they choose what they observe. They 'choose' for as many reasons as there are scientists. They choose for financial reasons (what industry will pay for); for social reasons, (what societies see as important); for political reasons, (what governments want) for practical reasons (what equipment is available); for personal reasons (to advance their career) and so on. Sometimes the observations scientists make are by chance. Fleming discovered penicillin almost by accident. Science is also influenced by trends: at the moment it is fashionable to concern oneself with the problems of global warning. The observations scientists make are inevitably influenced by the reason they are observing.

THE LOGIC PROBLEM

The significant differences between deductive and inductive logic are explained in Chapter Two. The 'Basic Scientific Method' requires both kinds of logic. After scientists have observed and collected information they make generalisations. In doing this they use inductive logic to create scientific laws and theories. They then apply deductive logic to these laws and theories to make explanations and predictions.

The use of deductive logic between Stage 4 and Stage 5 presents no problems. Deductive logic, you will recall, guarantees that if the premises of an argument are sound, then the argument must be valid. The logical problem of course is that the premises are based on the theory generated at Stage 4. That theory is based on inductive logic. Inductive logic, as we have seen, is not reliable. This creates what is known, rather grandly, as the Problem of Induction.

THE PROBLEM OF INDUCTION

We earlier attempted to use inductive logic to test the generalisation that in every country's capital city there is an international school. Using three tests, the Sufficient Number Test, the Varying Circumstances Test and the Exceptions Test, (see page 65) we decided not to accept the generalisation but to modify it. Our new statement suggested a probability rather than a certainty.

Science is looking for certainty. Inductive logic does not give certainty. It can give good reasons for supporting a conclusion but it can never guarantee it.

Deductively one might argue:

- The scientific method demands certainty
- Inductive logic can never be certain.
- Therefore the scientific method cannot use inductive logic.

All of us, of course, use inductive logic in our everyday lives. Just as you are about to go shopping you look out the window and see heavy, grey clouds. In your experience heavy, grey clouds mean it is going to rain. You decide not to go shopping because you know, through your experience, that if you go out in the rain you get wet. You know, again through your experience, that shopping when you are wet is unpleasant. Lots of inductive reasoning there. But, of course, the heavy, grey clouds are not a guarantee it is going to rain. Even if they always, in your experience, signify it is going to rain, it is possible on this occasion they will not. The clouds might be blown rapidly away. The best one can claim is that it will probably rain. And the Problem of Induction is that 'probable' is not good enough. Science wants to be certain.

SOME SUGGESTED SOLUTIONS TO THE PROBLEM

SOLUTION ONE: IT WORKS
Science works. It delivers. The Internet is alive and well. Our standard of living is improving almost daily. Prozac is there for the asking. Our predictions about the tides have always been proved to be right so far. It may not be perfect but it's pretty good and it's the best we have. We don't have a better way than induction so let's go with it.

An interesting objection to this argument is its own internal inductive argument. This justification is based on a generalisation about the inductive workability of science. An inductive argument cannot provide an argument for induction.

SOLUTION TWO: PROBABILISM
Laws of nature may not be certain but they probably are. The more observations we make, the more information we have confirming what we know, the more likely it is to be true. So, the tide may not rise and fall tomorrow but it probably, very probably, will.

SOLUTION THREE: DENIAL
The Basic Scientific Method is not really the basis of scientific knowledge. The real model is different. If the real model, Falsification, doesn't use induction then the Problem of Induction doesn't exist.

THE SCIENTIFIC METHOD 2

FALSIFICATIONISM
The scientific method associated with the name Karl Popper side steps the Problem of Induction. Popper and his colleagues argued that the Basic Scientific Method does not describe the way scientists work. Popper argues that scientists do not begin by making basic scientific observations, rather they begin with an idea, an informed theory based on previous theories about the natural world and the events that naturally occur in it. Using this idea or theory they create a hypothesis, a proposition made as a basis for reasoning, about the natural world, without assuming the proposition to be true.

This hypothesis is then tested with the sole aim of proving it to be false, (hence the name of this method, Falsificationism). Popper argued that science is effective because it attempts to show that hypotheses are false rather than that they are true.

KARL POPPER'S PRINCIPLE OF FALSIFICATION

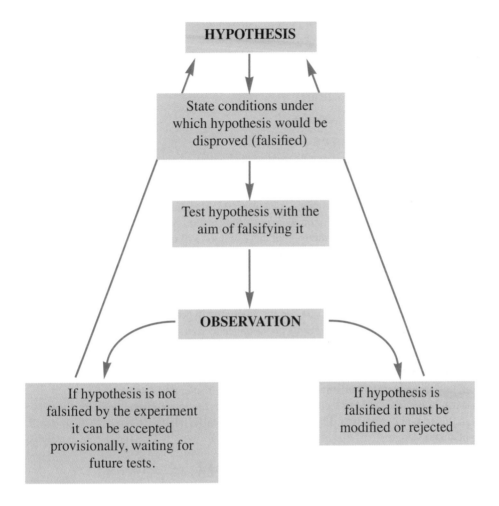

From the diagram you can see that Falsification depends as much on observation as the Basic Scientific Method. The difference, amongst other things, is that this method does not begin with observation. The observation, the empirical experiment, is undertaken after the theory has been stated and with the sole view of falsifying. Popper's method is just as dependent on observation, and therefore, just as subject to the problems of sense perception, as the Basic Scientific Method. What it is not subject to is the Problem of Induction. No generalisations, and therefore no inductive logic, are used.

ADVANTAGES OF FALSIFICATIONISM

1. CERTAINTY

Falsification has one clear advantage over the Basic Scientific Method. If one single false example shows the hypothesis to be unacceptable, it is unsatisfactory, it cannot be 'scientific', therefore a certainty is achieved. The certainty there is no certainty. With the Basic Scientific Method no matter how many observations are made which support a hypothesis, there can never be certainty. The next, as yet unmade observation, may disprove the theory.

The empirical basis of objective science has thus nothing 'absolute' about it. Science does not rest upon rock bottom. The bold structure of its theories rises, as it were, above a swamp. It is like a building erected on piles ...... driven down from far above into the swamp, but not to any natural or given base; and when we cease our attempt to drive our piles into a deeper layer, it is not because we have reached firm ground. We simply stop when we are satisfied that they are firm enough to carry the structure, or at least for the time being.

Karl Popper

2.   SCIENTIFIC RELEVANCE

Falsification has another advantage. It can be used to distinguish scientific valid hypotheses from non-scientific hypotheses. A hypothesis that cannot be falsified cannot be scientific. *Earthquakes under the Pacific Ocean always occur in June* is an easy hypothesis to test by empirical experimentation, by observation, and to falsify or not, so it has scientific potential. *That there will, or will not, be earthquakes under the Pacific Ocean in June* is not a scientific hypothesis because it cannot be falsified. You cannot test the theory that there will, or will not be, an earthquake under the Pacific in June. The statement is true by definition.

More controversial hypotheses come from disciplines which claim to be scientific in their methods. It is not possible to test many of the conclusions that psychiatrists arrive at in diagnosing the cause of their patients' illnesses. For instance, one cannot falsify the hypothesis *People became mass murderers because of certain traumatic events they experienced in their childhood.* What possible experiment or observation could be used to prove, or disprove, this hypothesis?

3.   SCIENTIFIC GROWTH

Falsification, it is argued by Popper, encourages the growth of scientific knowledge. Science progresses when hypotheses are falsified and new, and better, theories replace them. Science progresses in this trial and error way. If you cannot, theoretically, falsify a hypothesis then it will not lead to new knowledge.

FALSIFICATION: HISTORICALLY ACCEPTABLE?

Does Popper's Principle of Falsification reflect accurately how science has progressed in the last two thousand years? Two major developments in the history of science would suggest the answer to this question might be 'No'.

For about 1500 years the Ptolemaic view of the universe put the earth at its centre. In the late 15th century Copernicus after observing the sun and the planets, conceived the idea that the earth and the other planets in our solar system, moved round the sun. Despite the considerable evidence he presented to his fellow scientists falsifying the Ptolemaic view, it was several centuries before his ideas were accepted.

Sir Isaac Newton's laws of gravity and motion were accepted and applied for over two centuries. They had, in part, been falsified soon after they were published, by observations of the moon's orbit. Only in the 20th century did Albert Einstein, through falsification of parts of them, show they had to be revised or modified.

FOUR OUTSTANDING SCIENTISTS

'PTOLEMY' CLAUDIUS PTOLEMÆUS (FIRST HALF OF THE 2ND CENTURY AD)

A Greek who lived and studied in Alexandria, Egypt, was the greatest astronomer of ancient times. In his treatise, *Almagest*, (The Greatest), he describes an elaborate system of circles and ellipses that explain how the motions of the Sun, the Moon and the five known planets Mercury, Venus, Mars, Jupiter and Saturn revolve around the Earth, the centre of the universe.

NICOLAS COPERNICUS (1473-1543) – THE FOUNDER OF MODERN ASTRONOMY

Born in Poland, Copernicus studied mathematics in Krakow before moving to Bologna where he studied church law. In 1530 he completed his vast treatise *On the Revolutions of the Celestial Spheres*. In this book he presents the idea of the earth rotating daily on its own axis and annually orbiting the sun. When it was published in 1540 it received a very hostile reception, both from his fellow scientists and from the church, because it challenged the Ptolemaic theory of the Earth being the centre of the universe.

ISAAC NEWTON (1642-1727)

Born in England, Newton studied at Cambridge and became the Lucasian Professor of Mathematics there when he was 23. Tradition has it that an apple falling to the earth from a tree inspired him with the idea that the same force that made the apple fall made the moon 'fall' towards the earth in its elliptical orbit. The theoretical proof of this he wrote in *The Mathematical Principles of Natural Philosophy* (published 1687). The impact of this book was immense. The 'three laws of motion' described in it formed the basis of all subsequent scientific exploration of moving bodies.

ALBERT EINSTEIN (1879-1955)

Born in Germany, Einstein studied at Munich and Zurich. He published papers on theoretical physics while working at the Patent Office in Zurich. One of these papers included a description of his Theory of Relativity which he had drafted when he was sixteen. In 1916 he published *The Foundation of the General Theory of Relativity*. This paper included an explanation of the slow rotation of the elliptical path of Mercury, which Newton's theories failed to do. In 1921 he was awarded the Nobel Prize for Physics, although the citation did not mention his still controversial Theory of Relativity. In the early 1930s he left

Germany and became a US citizen, working at Princeton University, New Jersey. Einstein is one of the greatest scientists of all time. He devised new ways of understanding space and time and gravitation. He was undoubtedly a falsificationist for he wrote: No amount of experimentation can ever prove me right, a single experiment can prove me wrong.

THE SCIENTIFIC METHOD 3

SCIENTIFIC REVOLUTIONS

A physicist turned scientific historian, Thomas Kuhn, argues that neither the Basic Scientific Method nor Falsification reflect what happens in reality. Kuhn argues that science progresses through 'revolutions'. A scientific revolution, like any other revolution, is a movement in which one system is replaced, dramatically, by another system. Reduced to its simplest level Kuhn's argument is this:

> *Within a restricted scientific community, say taxonomy within biology, the acceptance of what Kuhn calls a* paradigm *emerges. All the scientists working within this taxonomic community work within a collection of assumptions; laws and theories which they accept as rigorous and normal. Taxonomists agree on certain principles for the classification of, say, insects. As they go about their scientific work of classifying insects they relate their observations of insects to their paradigm. This paradigm is the normal science of that particular scientific community. They adjust and modify their paradigm if falsifications become apparent but consistently stay within it. But eventually there comes a point when new observations are no longer compatible with the existing paradigm. It may be that progress in another branch of biology, say knowledge of the DNA of genes, gives them information about insects which is incompatible with the existing paradigm. Revolution! The old paradigm goes and a new one takes its place. This new paradigm, which is based on the new assumptions, laws and theories arising from knowledge of DNA, attracts more and more taxonomists and becomes the paradigm, the new normal science. This paradigm becomes the accepted one until it too is overthrown. And so it goes on ...*

Umbrellaology: A genuine science?

> *Dear Sir,*
>
> *I am taking the liberty of calling upon you to be the judge in a dispute between me and an acquaintance who is no longer a friend. The question at issue is this: Is my creation, Umbrellaology, a science? Allow me to explain .... For the past eighteen years assisted by a few faithful disciples, I have been collecting materials on a subject hitherto almost wholly neglected by scientists, the umbrella. The results of my investigations to date are embodied in the nine volumes which I am sending to you under a separate cover. Pending the receipt, let me describe to you briefly the nature of their contents and the method I pursued in compiling them. I began on the island of Manhattan. Proceeding block by block, house by house, family by family and individual by individual, I ascertained (1) the number of umbrellas possessed, (2) their size, (3) their weight, (4) their colour. Having covered Manhattan after many years, I eventually extended the survey to cover the other Boroughs of New York, and at length completed the entire city. Thus I was ready to carry forward the work to the rest of the state and indeed the rest of the United States and the whole known world.*
>
> *It was at this point I approached my erstwhile friend. I am a modest man, but I felt I had the right to be recognised as the creator of a new science. He, on the other hand, claimed that Umbrellaology was not a science at all. First, he said, it was silly to investigate umbrellas. Now this argument is false, because science scorns not to deal with any object, however humble and lowly, even to the 'hind leg of a flea'. Then why not umbrellas?*
>
> *Next, he said that Umbrellaology could not be recognised as a science because it was of no use or benefit to mankind. But is not the truth the most precious thing in life? Are not my nine volumes filled with the truth about my subject? Every word in them is true. Every*

sentence contains a hard, cold fact. When he asked me what was the object of Umbrellaology I was proud to say, 'To seek and discover the truth is object enough for me'. I am a pure scientist; I have no ulterior motives. Hence it follows that I am satisfied with the truth alone.

Next, he said, my truths were dated and that any one of my findings may cease to be true tomorrow. But this, I pointed out, is not an argument against Umbrellaology, but rather an argument for keeping it up to date, which exactly is what I propose. Let us have surveys monthly, weekly, or even daily, to keep our knowledge abreast of the changing facts.

His next contention was that Umbrellaology had entertained no hypotheses and had developed no theories or laws. This is a great error. In the course of my investigations I employed innumerable hypotheses. Before entering each new block and each new section of the city, I entertained an hypothesis as regards the number and characteristics of the umbrellas that would be found there, which hypotheses were either verified or nullified by my subsequent observations, in accordance with proper scientific procedure, as explained in authoritative texts. (In fact, it is of interest to note that I can substantiate and document every one of my replies to these objections by numerous quotations from standard works, leading journals, public speeches of eminent scientists and the like.)

As for theories and laws, my work represents an abundance of them. I will here mention only a few, by way of illustration. There is the law of Colour Variation Relative to Ownership by Sex. (Umbrellas owned by women tend to great variety of colour, whereas those owned by men are almost all black.) To his law I have given exact statistical formulation (See vol.6 Appendix 1, table 3, page 582.) There are the curiously interrelated Laws of Individual Ownership of Plurality of Individual Umbrellas. The interrelationship assumes the form, in the first law, of almost direct ratio to annual income, and in the second, in almost inverse ratio to annual income. (For an exact statement of the modifying circumstances, see vol.8, p.350.) There is also the Law of Tendency Towards Acquisition of Umbrellas in Rainy Weather. To this law I have given experimental verification in chapter 3 of volume 3. In the same way I have performed numerous other experiments in connection with my generalisations.

Thus I feel that my creation is in all respects a genuine science, and I appeal to you for substantiation of my opinion ....

From J. Sommerville 'Umbrellaology' in Philosophy of Science

A HUMAN NOTE......

It would seem that philosophers, scientists and science historians find it difficult to agree on 'the scientific method'.

Whatever inadequacies as a way-of-knowing science may have are inadequacies caused by the fact that it is a human construct. Scientific observations are made using our human senses and these observations are processed through our human intelligences. Scientists create paradigms both from, and for, human thinking, human rationality. No way-of-knowing created by humans will ever be entirely reliable, entirely precise, entirely objective.

The scientific method, the way we develop our scientific knowledge, science as a way-of-knowing is pragmatic. It is reliable, precise, objective, testable and self correcting. Other disciplines model their claims on science for good reason. But is it the most reliable way-of-knowing? Is it the best justified true belief? The answer to that question is an unqualified 'yes' if we are limiting our ways-of-knowing to the physical, natural world around us. But ways-of-knowing are not limited to the physical, natural world around us. There is an absolute way-of-knowing in which justification is absolutely independent of observation. For good reasons this way-of-knowing has long held a privileged place in universities and schools. In the next chapter we examine it: mathematics.

IS SCHOOL SCIENCE REAL SCIENCE?

A talk given by David Pritchard, Head of Science, Munich International School, to 11th and 12th grade ToK students.

My aim in this talk is to identify some of the key features of scientific knowledge and to pose some discussion questions about that knowledge using school science as a starting point. I am doing this for three reasons.

1. For many, if not most of you, the science you study at school will be your only direct experience of science.

2. A number of recent studies in the UK have shown that children's and young people's view of science and scientists is strongly affected by their own experience of science.

3. In the ToK course you are challenged to be critical and reflective. If you are going to do this successfully when discussing the nature of science, you need to be aware of the limitations of your own experiences of science, so that you don't make invalid generalizations about them.

I intend first to look at the kind of science we teach in school, to compare this with real science and finally to see the relationship, if any, between the two.

THE CHARACTERISTICS OF SCHOOL SCIENCE

How would you describe the experience of science you have had or are having at school? In outlining a number of features of school science, I am not intending to make any value judgements but only to indicate the extent to which those features are likely to help or hinder your understanding of science as a way of knowing the world. After all, science education has a fundamentally different purpose from the activities of professional scientists.

- The most obvious feature of school science is that every student is, for the most part, engaged on similar, if not identical, activities. This is less likely in the 11th and 12th grades but almost invariably true up to 10th grade.

- Those identical activities are directed by one individual, the teacher. The purpose of and motivation for the activity are often determined by the teacher - if indeed, they are not created by the teacher.

- The activities undertaken by students, whether experimental or theoretical, have an outcome which is either completely predictable (at least by the teacher) or are bounded in some way. This is, of course, because they have nearly all been done before.

- The need to examine and assess your understanding of science imposes a further constraint on science in the school laboratory. Every question has a 'right' answer. Science in schools can very easily become a game which involves you, the students, finding and learning the correct answer and in which I, the teacher, try to find ways of conveying that answer as efficiently as possible. So if you were to use your experience of science in the school class room as the basis for describing science as a way-of-knowing, you might come up with something like the following: Scientific ideas and theories are true statements about the world which can be justified on the basis of observation and experiment.

In this view of science, theory is seen as providing the correct interpretation of empirical data. According to two recent studies in the UK, which involved interviewing 9-16 year olds about their view of science, this is a view held by nearly all students. Furthermore, it is probably a view of science which only a minority pass beyond. It is easy to see how this view of science develops from school science.

School science deals almost exclusively with the core scientific theories about which there is no serious dispute, or there is no longer any serious dispute, e.g. conservation of energy, the atomic theory of matter, the role of DNA in cell replication.

Experiments in the school laboratory are conducted which conform to these theories and, where experimentation is not possible (e.g. evolution, nuclear fission) evidence is presented which, again, conforms to the accepted theory.

You may, therefore, be forgiven for expecting certainty from science because certainty is what you are often presented with. However, even a cursory look into the past will reveal how uncertain an activity science is.

Inspired by the falling apple, Newton developed his Law of Gravitation which, as simple and far reaching as it was, could not explain all the evidence which astronomers gathered.

The Atomic Theory of Matter is a fairly recent creation that we all accept today, but, at one time, it was a matter of dispute, even to the extent that Ludwig Bolzmann (after whom the Bolzmann Constant is named) apparently committed suicide because he could not persuade his colleagues of the reality of atoms.

The Theory of Evolution, whether biological or cosmological, is not a monolithic theory which answers all questions. In both cases there are unresolved questions and many interpretations. So, if science isn't a collection of facts, incontrovertible statements and 'right' answers, then what is?

THE CHARACTERISTICS OF REAL SCIENCE
One of the best statements I have ever read is as follows:

Science is an enterprise in which explanations are sought for why phenomena happen in the way they do. In seeking explanations, scientists use previous knowledge, new observations, imaginative analogies, and carefully designed experiments.

Einstein once said:

Scientists are people with a passion to explain.

This suggests to me that uncertainty is the driving force which creates and sustains interest in science. An unresolved question or a contradictory piece of evidence invites investigation. Real science differs from school science in several ways.

- You will probably not find in any science laboratory anywhere 23 people carrying out identical procedures and undertaking identical activities. What you are more likely to find are groups of people working co-operatively on different aspects of the same problem (e.g. AIDS research, protecting buildings against earthquakes, green house-effect, etc.)

- The purpose and motivation for an activity are different, arising from the individual's 'passion to explain' rather than being imposed by someone else (e.g. research into the age of the universe and how we got from the Big Bang to here).

- Experiments are not 'standard', simply repeated activities that hundreds have already done (as experiments done in school usually are). However their results may be predictable, to the extent to which they are hinges on the explanatory power of the theory being tested.

- When seeking to explain the unexplained there is no teacher or examination board that knows the right answer. A scientist, or team of scientists, has to convince equally knowledgeable people of the validity of their explanations. (Remember Cold Fusion!).

THE LINK BETWEEN SCHOOL SCIENCE AND REAL SCIENCE

So where does that leave school science? Is school science real science? It may seem that I have come down on the side of NO! However, before I conclude I feel I should redress the balance a little and justify my existence as a science teacher.

I said earlier that science education has a different purpose from the activities of professional scientists but let us review again the statements I showed you earlier:

Science is an enterprise in which explanations are sought for why phenomena happen in the way they do. In seeking explanations, scientists use previous knowledge, new observations, imaginative analogies, and carefully designed experiments.

There are two points about it I wish to make.

Firstly, there is a sense in which each of us is, or at least has a potential to be, a scientist. We are faced from birth with a myriad of unfamiliar and initially inexplicable happenings. Evidence from studies on how babies and young children learn, indicates that we have an innate predisposition which enables us to make sense of the world around us. We identify links between events. We perceive causes and effects. We construct an internal representation of the world which is consistent with our experience. This internal representation of the world enables us to relate to other people and to the world around us with a certain amount of coherence and predictability. However, the view of the world we construct for ourselves tends to act at what we might call the level of common sense. For example, we very quickly learned that when we stopped pushing our building blocks across the floor they stopped moving. We might have formulated this relationship to ourselves as:

> pushing = moving;
> not pushing = not moving.

This was quickly confirmed by other everyday experiences - to the extent that, when we see an object moving, we are very likely to ask 'What is pushing it?'. The question led the Ancient Greeks to put the sun in a chariot drawn by horses. Now if we look at theories in science we will see that the theories do not always support common sense. If I were to say to you now (as I would say to you in a physics class):

"Once a body is moving it will continue moving the same way until stopped", you will probably respond "that does not make sense"; your experience tells you the opposite. However, for lots of reasons I haven't got time to go into now, this rather counter intuitive statement is part of the accepted scientific explanation for why and how things move.

Take another example, the Atomic Theory of Matter which is the basis for understanding chemistry and most of biology. That theory too is not readily obvious. Our common sense experience is of matter as continuous and infinitely divisible. It took a considerable amount of careful experimentation before evidence became sufficiently convincing to persuade poor Bolzmann's intransigent colleagues.

I'm afraid that common sense, (i.e. our everyday intuitive approach to generating working hypotheses and assumptions that work in everyday life) cannot stand up to careful and critical inspection.

- The school science laboratory is the place where you are challenged to think carefully and systematically about natural phenomena. It is probably the first, and for many of you unfortunately the last, place where your intuitive and common sense explanations about the natural world are put to the test.

The second point I wish to make about the value of school science is this. Scientists build upon existing knowledge. Isaac Newton, Alexander Fleming, Watson and Crick, did not produce their theories in vacuo. They used the knowledge acquired by others. Newton spoke of standing on the shoulders of giants. If you read the background to any scientific discovery, and you should, you will find out how much had to be discovered first. Our emphasis, in school science, on the tried and tested core theories is designed to give you access to existing knowledge and to broaden your own knowledge and understanding in a systematic way.

I hope you can see now that maybe the answer to my question Is School Science Real Science? is both YES and NO.

I want to finish by posing two questions because, I believe, your exploration of them will take you to the heart of the scientific endeavour.

1. What part do theory and experiment play in the acquisition of scientific knowledge? What is the interplay between the two? What is the connection between them?

2. To what extent is the acquisition of new scientific knowledge a social as distinct from an individual activity? Is the expression 'scientific community' of very recent origin?

THE LANGUAGE OF SCIENCE AND THE SCIENCE OF LANGUAGE

And to complete this chapter, three cautionary notes about natural science and the bewitchment of language.

The first from T H Savory in *The Language of Science*

THE MATHEMATICAL PHYSICIST

The mathematical physicist is guilty of linguistic rape of a family of related words - force, work, power and weight. In mechanics, force does not mean strength, as it does when the ordinary man says that he is perhaps impressed by the force of an argument. It is given a rather precise and intricate definition .... quite different from anything that the word force implies in everyday life .... A weight, one is surprised to learn, is not ... the familiar block of metal with a ring on the top ... the weight of a thing has to be the force with which the earth attracts it. Work gives even more trouble, because a physicist has decided that a force works, or does not work, only when it moves something. I may push and pull in vain at an immovable object, make myself hot and tired by my efforts, and find that mathematically I have done no work. But if I seize the dangling reins of a runaway horse and pull them, and find that nevertheless the animal continues on its course, I have had work done on me, and I, panting and dishevelled, have done less than no work. After this it is quite easy to accept the idea that power has come to mean the rate at which work can be done.

And these two from *The Cambridge Encyclopaedia of Language*

INTELLIGIBILITY GAP

The gap between scientific language and everyday language is a large one, which is difficult to bridge. Scientists are often unable to express themselves in terms the lay person can understand, or take the time to bother. Not surprisingly, therefore, there is a widespread mistrust of scientific language, which is only partly alleviated through popular science publications and radio or television programmes. It is still the exception to find popularizations of science that maintain intelligibility while avoiding oversimplification, and that come to be acclaimed by specialist and lay person alike.

LINGUISTICS

Linguistics shares with other sciences a concern to be objective, systematic, consistent and explicit in its account of language. Like other sciences, it aims to collect data, test hypotheses, devise models and construct theories. Its subject matter, however, is unique: at one extreme, it overlaps with such 'hard' sciences as physics and anatomy; at the other, it involves such traditional 'arts' subjects as philosophy and literary criticism. The field of linguistics includes both the sciences and the humanities, and offers a breadth of coverage that, for many aspiring students of the subject, is the primary source of appeal.

Now *you have read Chapter 7.1 ...*

consider or undertake the following:

1. Which of the three models of 'the scientific method' described in this chapter do you find most convincing?

2. Now you have read a little about 'the scientific method' can you draw any parallels with *your* hypothesising when you played Petals Round a Rose and *scientific* hypothesising?

(Just in case you are still frustrated one 'law' you might have deduced which would explain the scores was that the central mark on the dice were never counted. The central mark was the 'rose' and all other marks were 'petals'. Thus 1 scored 0, 2 scored 2, 3 scored 2, 4 scored 4, 5 scored 4 and 6 scored 6. You may of course, have come up with a more imaginative 'law'). Did you find any relationship between your scientific method and those described in this chapter?

3. Scientists, of course, use instruments to enhance their observational abilities. Are these instruments themselves capable of being deceived in the same way as human senses are?

4. The claim for Umbrellaology to be a science seems to be reasonable. The research method described seems to fit the Basic Scientific Method. Are problems with observation and inductive logic the only reservations you would have about supporting this as a science? Consider your answer to the request in the letter.

5. Do you agree that science 'linguistically rapes' words we use everyday? Does science need its own language? To what extent is the specialised use of words by scientists a reason why physics, for instance, is 'hard'? Is linguistics really a science at all or is it one of those disciplines that would like the status of being a science?

6. Read the talk given by David Pritchard to the ToK students at Munich International School and discuss possible answers to the questions he poses at the end of his talk (page 162 on). How convincing is David Pritchard's argument that science is counter intuitive? Isn't he really just sitting on the fence trying to justify school science as real science?

Want to know more?

You may find the following books helpful.

Kuhn Thomas S: The *Structure of Scientific Revolutions* University of Chicago Press 1962

Popper K R: *The Logic of Scientific Discovery* Hutchinson 1968

SECTION TWO
AREAS OF KNOWLEDGE

MATHEMATICS

7.2

CHAPTER CONTENTS

Before

you read Chapter 7.2 ...

consider possible responses to these:

1. What have been the advantages, for you, of learning mathematics?

2. In what ways is mathematics helpful to you?

3. Why is so much time in schools allocated to mathematics?

4. What does it mean to get the 'wrong' answer in mathematics? Can you get 'wrong' answers in other subjects?

5. Why is mathematics so difficult for many students?

6. What would you consider to be the characteristics of those people you know who are good at mathematics?

7. Mathematics has been described as both the 'queen' and the 'servant' of science. What could 'queen' and 'servant' mean in this context?

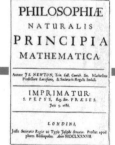

PHILOSOPHIÆ
NATURALIS
PRINCIPIA
MATHEMATICA

Autore JS. NEWTON, Trin. Coll. Cantab. Soc. Mathefeos Professore Lucasiano, & Societatis Regalis Sodali.

IMPRIMATUR
S. PEPYS, Reg. Soc. PRÆSES.
Julii 5. 1686.

LONDINI,
Jussu Societatis Regiæ ac Typis Josephi Streater. Prostat apud plures Bibliopolas. Anno MDCLXXXVII.

7.2 MATHEMATICS

Pilate's question 'What is truth?' has become a rhetorical cliché. When we hear it we wash our minds of it and move on, knowing we are not going to get a straight answer or even any answer at all. If there had been a mathematician around when Pilate was drying his hands he would have had an immediate answer. American mathematician Jerry King[1] has no doubt of that. Mathematicians know what truth is. Truth, Mr. Roman Governor, is what you find at the end of mathematical arguments.

Natural science, to many mathematicians, is a vast compost heap of uncontrolled induction and observation. The worms of prejudices and false ideas thrive there until they are gobbled up by younger and fitter worms with different prejudices and false ideas and these in turn are eaten by younger and fitter worms. Mathematics is not like that, they claim. Mathematics does not depend on precarious observation for its justification as an area of knowledge. Nor is it dependent on inductive logic, which isn't logic at all. Mathematicians do not set up a theory and then sit around until a better theory replaces it. Mathematics as an area of knowledge is not subject to trendy paradigm changes. Mathematics is not about the natural world. If the natural world was quite different from the way it is now, mathematics would not in any way be changed. Mathematical theories are for all time. Pythagoras defined his famous theorem 2600 years ago and it is as valid today as it was then. New mathematical ideas may develop but they do not do so at the expense of earlier mathematical ideas. Mathematics is an exquisitely cultivated, worm-free *Jardin des Plants*. Mathematics, Mr. Roman Governor, is Truth. (And most mathematicians would add that it is also Beauty.)

This claim, that mathematics is 'ultimate truth' is based on the nature of mathematical knowledge. Logic and mathematics are what philosophers call a formal system of knowledge. The foundations of both logic and mathematics are axioms[2]. If you apply rules of inference to these axioms you create mathematical knowledge, called theorems:

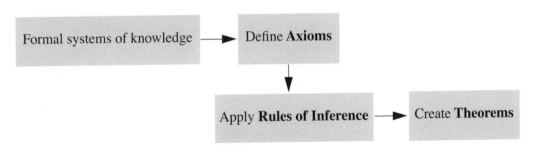

This is the mathematical method. There are no alternative 'mathematical methods' awaiting the wary reader on the next few pages. That's it. But the bewitchment of language is ever with us: we can be bewitched into believing we understand by using words. *Axioms*, *rules of inference* and *theorems*, are special ideas in a specific area of knowledge. Ideas that need to be considered with caution.

---

1. *The Art of Mathematics* 1992.
2. The difference between logic and math is the nature of the axioms.

AXIOMS

All mathematics is based on a small collection of fundamental laws. These fundamental laws are called *axioms*. If mathematical knowledge has ultimate truth then clearly the axioms on which it is built must be ultimately truthful. So where do these axioms come from?

Axioms are obtained by reflecting rationally on what we know. They are examples of *a priori* knowledge, accepted by all mathematicians. Some mathematicians claim they are self evident and their truth can be recognised by anyone who understands and reflects on them. Because mathematical knowledge is based on axioms the 'truth' of mathematics is determined by the fundamental truth of these axioms.

Most mathematicians are not directly concerned with axioms. They know they are the rock bottom foundations of mathematics but would find it difficult to define them. They assume them as 'given' and work only with theorems developed from them. Most mathematicians would probably claim that, if necessary or desirable, they could define the particular axioms on which their work is based, but they seldom have reason to do this.

There are, of course, different axioms for different parts of mathematics. One set of axioms is set down in Euclid's '*Elements*' along with the theorems that are inferred from them. Much publicity has been given in recent years into what is known as non-Euclidean geometry, the geometry of space and time. A casual reader may be tempted to assume that a mathematical version of the Scientific Revolution has taken place. But non-Euclidean geometry is not a new paradigm which has replaced an old one. Non-Euclidean geometry is not in conflict with, nor has it replaced, Euclid's Elements. It is based on a different set of axioms.

Another more recent set of axioms are the Seven Axioms of Set Theory defined by mathematicians Ernst Zermelo and Abraham Franker in 1908. The truth of these Zermelo-Fraenkel axioms, it has been argued, 'is established by intuitions which lie too deep for proof since all proof depends on them'.

Probably the most well publicised set of axioms is known as the Peano Postulates, named after the 19th century Italian Giuseppe Peano (1858-1932). These axioms define the 'fundamental laws' from which the number system is developed. Peano postulates[3] that there are such things as 'numbers' and then assumes they can be defined by five axioms.

PEANO'S POSTULATES

1. 0 is a number.
2. Every number has at least one and at most one successor which is a number.
3. 0 is not the successor of any number.
4. No two numbers have the same successor.
5. Whatever is true of 0, and is also true of the successor of any number when it is true of that number, is true of all numbers.

---

3. *Postulates* means *assumed as a basis for reasoning*. I use the word here carefully because the words *axioms* and *postulates* (used as nouns) are interchangeable. The phrase *Peano's Postulates* is pleasantly alliterative and flows more smoothly off the tongue than *Peano's Axioms*. Bewitchment.

Peano's Postulates were not, originally, presented in words but rather in symbols. The concepts 0, number and successor were not defined. Using these five axioms Peano was able to infer an infinite series of whole numbers and to further infer all the theorems of arithmetic based on numbers. These are the fundamental rules, the axioms of arithmetic. It is not necessary (or simple) to go into the details of the meaning of each of these postulates. They are presented so you can see that a set of axioms really does exist.

BEWITCHED BY WORDS AND AXIOMS

The discovery that all mathematics follows inevitably from a small collection of fundamental laws is one which immeasurably enhanced the intellectual beauty of the whole; to those who have been oppressed by the fragmentary and incomplete nature of most chains of deduction, this discovery comes with all the overwhelming force of revelation; like a palace emerging from the autumn mist as the traveller ascends an Italian hillside, the stately storeys of the mathematical edifice appear in due order and proportion, with a new perfection in every part.

Bertrand Russell (1872-1970), philosopher and mathematician

RULES OF INFERENCE

Inference is the forming of conclusions from the information available. Rules of inference, therefore, are those rules which mathematicians apply deductively to the mathematical information available to them: axioms. Mathematical knowledge is created by deductively applying rules of inference to axioms. The rules of inference themselves, like the axioms, are *a priori*. The 'mathematical information available', of course, is not limited to axioms. Rules of inference generate theorems from axioms, and to these new theorems the rules of inference can also be applied.

if .... then

A well known rule of inference, one we are all familiar with in some form or other, is the if ... then rule. Here is a simple example of the if .... then rule in action.

Arithmetically, *if* $1 + 6 = 7$ and $5 + 4 = 9$

         then $(1 + 6) + (5 + 4) = 7 + 9$

         or

Algebraically, (algebra is simply arithmetic with variables instead of numbers)

         if $x = y$ and $p = q$

         then $x + p = y + q$

In bewitching language: equals added to equals are equals. To continue in language rather than numbers or variables, what rules of inference do, is imply.

That $x = y$ and $p = q$ implies that $x + p = y + q$.

Applying rules of inference deductively to axioms creates new mathematical statements. Each new statement must be consistent with the original axioms and must use only the original axioms and the new statements generated by the application of the rules of inference. The rules of inference control the process of creating mathematical knowledge.

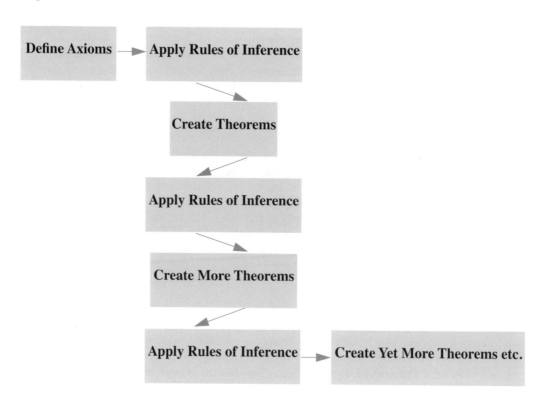

Mathematical operations deductively change one set of marks on a piece of paper to another set of marks. These sets of marks trace the deductive process of the application of the rules of inference. Because mathematicians restrict their reasoning to deductively applying the rules of inference to axioms and then theorems, mathematics can extend its subject for ever. New theorems are generated and these theorems provide new opportunities for further theorems, without any reference to the natural world.

A (VERY) BRIEF HISTORY OF MATHEMATICS

Beginning with a few ways in which various civilisations have written 'FOUR'.
The dates are very approximate. Some notations are still in use. Can you say which?

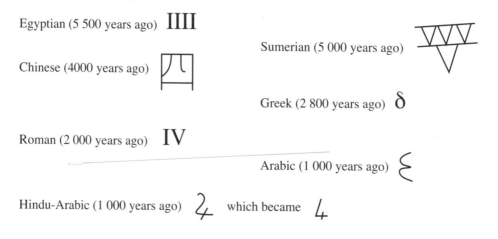

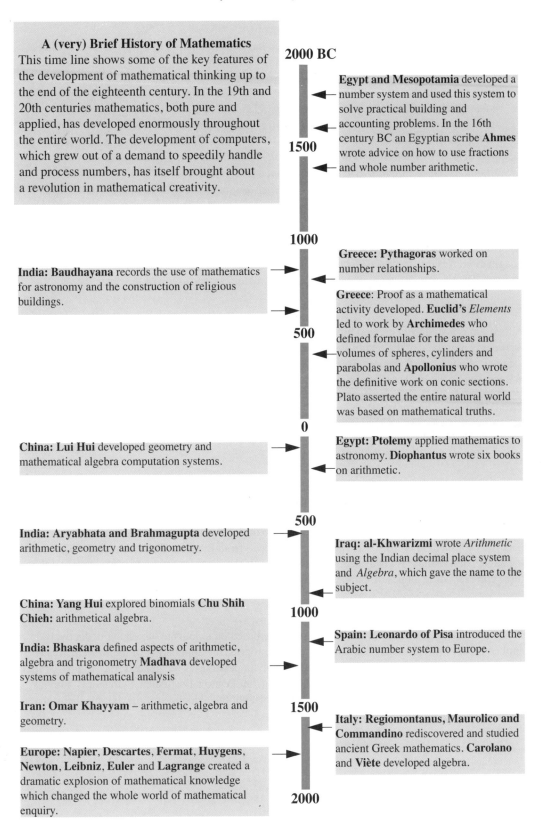

A (very) Brief History of Mathematics
This time line shows some of the key features of the development of mathematical thinking up to the end of the eighteenth century. In the 19th and 20th centuries mathematics, both pure and applied, has developed enormously throughout the entire world. The development of computers, which grew out of a demand to speedily handle and process numbers, has itself brought about a revolution in mathematical creativity.

2000 BC

1500

Egypt and Mesopotamia developed a number system and used this system to solve practical building and accounting problems. In the 16th century BC an Egyptian scribe **Ahmes** wrote advice on how to use fractions and whole number arithmetic.

1000

India: Baudhayana records the use of mathematics for astronomy and the construction of religious buildings.

Greece: Pythagoras worked on number relationships.

Greece: Proof as a mathematical activity developed. **Euclid's** *Elements* led to work by **Archimedes** who defined formulae for the areas and volumes of spheres, cylinders and parabolas and **Apollonius** who wrote the definitive work on conic sections. Plato asserted the entire natural world was based on mathematical truths.

500

0

China: Lui Hui developed geometry and mathematical algebra computation systems.

Egypt: Ptolemy applied mathematics to astronomy. **Diophantus** wrote six books on arithmetic.

500

India: Aryabhata and Brahmagupta developed arithmetic, geometry and trigonometry.

Iraq: al-Khwarizmi wrote *Arithmetic* using the Indian decimal place system and *Algebra*, which gave the name to the subject.

China: Yang Hui explored binomials **Chu Shih Chieh:** arithmetical algebra.

1000

India: Bhaskara defined aspects of arithmetic, algebra and trigonometry **Madhava** developed systems of mathematical analysis

Spain: Leonardo of Pisa introduced the Arabic number system to Europe.

Iran: Omar Khayyam – arithmetic, algebra and geometry.

1500

Europe: Napier, Descartes, Fermat, Huygens, Newton, Leibniz, Euler and **Lagrange** created a dramatic explosion of mathematical knowledge which changed the whole world of mathematical enquiry.

Italy: Regiomontanus, Maurolico and Commandino rediscovered and studied ancient Greek mathematics. **Carolano** and **Viète** developed algebra.

2000

JUST LIKE WRITING A NOVEL?

This process of creating mathematical knowledge has been compared to the process of writing a novel[4]. The process is

> .... *not quite that of inventing a game, but rather that of the continued invention of a game in the very course of playing the game. This kind of game-inventing is akin to writing a novel, and the parallel is quite close up to a point. There never was a person called Sherlock Holmes, not even a person like Sherlock Holmes. Yet this character was well defined by the description of his consistent behaviour in a series of fictitious situations. Once Conan Doyle had composed a few good stories with Sherlock Holmes as their hero, the image of the detective - however absurd in itself - was clearly fixed for the purposes of any further such stories.*

The main difference between a fictitious mathematical entity, like a complex number, and a fantastic character like Sherlock Holmes, lies in the greater hold which the latter has on our imagination. It is due to the far richer sensuous elements entering into our conception of Sherlock Holmes. That is why we acquire an image and not merely a conception of the detective.

THEOREMS

A theorem is a statement created by deductively applying the rules of inference to axioms. The theorem is presented at the end of the deduction, following the representation of the application of the laws of inference. A theorem is a statement of mathematical knowledge. The process of arriving at a theorem is the mathematical way-of-knowing.

We all know the Theorem of Pythagoras:

> *The sum of the squares on the arms of a right triangle equals the square on the hypotenuse.*

This theorem is derived from the 10 Axioms defined in Euclid's *Elements*. But mathematicians, and budding mathematicians in schools, do not think of Euclid's axioms every time, or even anytime they use it. They take the deductive logic, the application of the rules of inference that arrived at the theorem, as a given. They know, if pressed, they could justify their use of the theorem, but it is not necessary for them to do so. Other theorems developed from Euclid's *Elements* include 'The sum of the angles of a triangle is always equal to 180°' and 'If three angles of one triangle are equal to the three corresponding angles of another triangle then the two triangles are similar'.

A priori knowledge: the source of axioms?

Mathematics then is a formal system of knowledge based on axioms to which are deductively applied rules of inference to create theorems. The process, the application of the rules to create theorems, is easily understood. What is not so easily understood is the genesis, the origins, of the axioms. Arithmetical theorems follow deductively from Peano's Postulates. Pythagoras' famous theorem follows deductively from Euclid's Elements, but the evidence for the axioms themselves seems to be rather vague.

---

4. Michael Polanyi in *Personal Knowledge*.

A MAGNIFICENT SEVEN

Seven modern mathematicians who have influenced the progress of mathematical thinking in the last two hundred years are described below. In common with all successful mathematicians, their best work was done when they were young. It is safe to say that if you haven't distinguished yourself as a mathematician by the time you are thirty, you probably never will.

Bernhard Riemann (1777-1885). Born in Breselenz, Germany, he became professor of mathematics at Göttingen in 1859. As a young man, Riemann worked with the theory of functions but he is famous for his later development of non-Euclidean geometry. His theories in non-Euclidean geometry were significant for the subsequent development of the Theory of Relativity. The Riemann Hypothesis (1857) concerning the distribution of prime numbers is still awaiting proof.

Nikolay Lobachevsky (1792-1856). Born in Nizhny Novgorod, Russia, he became professor at Kazan in 1816. He too developed a theory of non-Euclidian geometry in which Euclid's parallel Postulates did not hold.

Henri Poincaré (1854-1912). Born in Nancy, France, he became professor of mathematics in Paris in 1881. He was the first mathematician to predict Chaos Theory and he also defined the foundations of topology and triangulation. Some of his late work, like Riemann's, anticipated Einstein's Theory of Relativity.

David Hilbert (1862-1943). Born in Königsberg, Germany, he became a professor there in 1893. His early work included a critical examination of the foundations of geometry as well as important contributions to number and invariant theories and algebraic geometry. At the International Congress of Mathematicians in 1900 he listed 23 problems which he regarded as important for contemporary mathematicians, some of which are still unsolved.

John von Neumann (1903-1957). Born in Budapest, Hungary, he emigrated to America in 1933 and joined the Institute for Advanced Study at Princeton. He wrote a major work in quantum mechanics and defined a new set of axioms for set theory. During the Second World War he provided a mathematical description of shock waves caused by bombing. His work on high speed calculations contributed to the development of the computer. He defined Game Theory, a mathematical concept much used by economists.

Bertrand Russell (1872-1970). Born in Trelleck, Wales, he studied at Cambridge and became a fellow of Trinity College there in 1895. Convinced of the objectivity of mathematics Russell published *Principles of Mathematics* (1903) and, with A. N. Whitehead, *Principia Mathematica* (1910-1913). Russell's claim to the complete objectivity of mathematics was based on two principles: 1. Mathematical truth is pure logic and 2. because of this Mathematics has no subject matter.

Kurt Gödel (1906-78). Born in Brno in the Czech Republic, he emigrated to America in 1940 and joined von Neumann at the Institute for Advanced Study in Princeton. He is famous above all for his proof, known as Gödel's Proof, that any formal logical system adequate for number theory must contain propositions not provable in that system, a problem at the very heart of mathematics. Gödel's proof persuaded Russell that his conviction of the logical truth of mathematics was questionable.

Roger Scruton, a professor of philosophy at Oxford, describes the Zermelo-Fraenkel axioms as 'established by intuition which is too deep for proof since all proof depends on them.' Is this not similar to some arguments you have heard for the existence of God?

Axiomatic knowledge is *a priori* knowledge, knowledge created by reasons other than observation. Most mathematicians claim their axioms are 'self evident', but this seems simply to be their way of claiming them to be *a priori*. If they are self evident the very evidence for this must be *a priori* rationalism. Plato was one of the first philosophers to suggest that mathematical axioms, and the numbers they use, were *a priori*, although he did not use that term. He saw numbers as belonging to a 'separate and eternal realm' to which humans had a privileged access because of their ability to rationalise.

Immanuel Kant (1724-1804) is the philosopher whose name is most often associated with *a priori* knowledge. He accepted the then currently held view that there were two ways of knowing, *matters of fact* (empirical knowledge) and a kind of *a priori* knowledge which he called *knowledge by definition*. Knowledge by definition is found in statements like 'All cats are animals'. If cats are not animals then clearly there is a misunderstanding about the meaning of the words. He called this *a priori analytic* knowledge, because by analysing the meaning of the words within the statement you could arrive at its truth.

To these two ways of knowing Kant added a third way which he called *synthetic a priori* knowledge to differentiate it from *analytical a priori* knowledge. This *synthetic a priori* knowledge is necessarily true, true in its own right, and not dependent on other knowledge. It is also known independently of experience and yet is knowledge which we could not get through either empirical knowledge or *analytic a prior* knowledge. Mathematics, Kant argued, is an example of *synthetic a priori* knowledge. It is necessarily true, it is not *analytic a priori* and it is not empirical. 7 + 5 =12 is a *synthetic a priori* statement.

His rationale for *synthetic a priori* knowledge is explained in *Critique of Pure Reason* (1781)[5]. It is impossible for us to know what the world is really like, Kant claimed. We base all our knowledge on what he calls the *phenomenal world*. This phenomenal world is both spatial - it has space,

---

5. This is, of course, a very simple account of Kant's arguments. *Critique of Pure Reason* is a very challenging book.

distance, size - and temporal - events occur in it in a time sequence. Both of these features, space and time, are only how our intuition constructs what we perceive. We are incapable of conceptualising anything that doesn't conform to our intuition. Our perceived space has only length, breadth and height because that is all our intuitive mind can cope with. We perceive time as the same everywhere because that is the way our intuition perceives it. Another category of this perceived world is number. Numbers, and mathematical axioms, are created by our intuition. Whether they really exist or not is unimportant. Our intuition creates them because we need to use them to make sense of our phenomenological world. *A priori* knowledge is a series of structures in our mind and mathematics axioms are created by one of those structures.

This explanation of Kant's *synthetic a priori* knowledge leaves much out. But isn't Kant simply arguing that numbers are concepts that humans create? There isn't such a thing as a number as a physical object. When we need numbers we create them. And any 'truth' about numbers we also create when we use them in theorems. This is what *a priori* really means. Numbers are like school grades: they don't exist until someone, in this case a teacher, creates them. Did Peano's Postulates exist before he created them? Clearly not. But the conditions under which anyone could have created those Postulates did exist.

Don't we hear an echo of the Scruton claim 'intuition too deep for proof'? Perhaps it would be easier to accept that axioms are 'self evident'. Certainly there is cause here to question the ultimate truth of mathematics. The genesis of the axioms needs to be thought about very carefully.

CONTRADICTORY LOGIC

Even the rigorous deductive logic of the process of mathematics is not entirely certain. Set Theory is a branch of mathematics with which many of you are probably familiar. A set is any defined group of objects. You can have a set of all the people who live in Japan or a set of the three highest mountains in Peru or a set of all the people in Senegal who eat fried bananas for breakfast everyday. Until Bertrand Russell described his paradox it was assumed that you define a set by naming its characteristic, e.g. all the people who live in Japan. But Russell showed that set theory was flawed: it isn't always possible to define a set in this way, thus questioning the deductive logic of the application of the rules of inference.

RUSSELL'S PARADOX

There is a regimental barber, himself a member of the regiment, who shaves all and only those members of the regiment who do not shave themselves. Does the barber shave himself?

That is, we are looking at ...

Set of
all and only those members of the
regiment who the barber shaves and who
do
not shave themselves.

Think for moment before you read on. Does he shave himself?

If you answered 'Yes, he does shave himself,' that means he doesn't shave himself because he only shaves those people who don't shave themselves. If you answered 'No, he doesn't shave himself,' that means he does because he shaves all members of the regiment who don't shave themselves.

So, if he shaves himself, he doesn't shave himself. If he doesn't shave himself he does shave himself. There cannot be a set of members of the regiment that the barber shaves. If the set includes the barber it doesn't include him because he shaves himself. If the set doesn't include him he doesn't shave himself.

The example may seem trivial but it should make us wary of the application of the rules of inference. If they lead to contradictions, as they do in Russell's Paradox, should we be a little cautious too in accepting the claim that they lead to ultimate truth? Perhaps Pilate was right not to wait for an answer, even a confident answer, from a mathematician.

The claim of mathematicians to find truth at the end of mathematical arguments is perhaps something of an overstatement. A more modest claim, that mathematics is a conceptual technique for making explicit what is implicitly contained in a set of premises, seems much more acceptable. This definition concentrates on the process of mathematics, the application of the rules of inference and implies no absolute truth for the axioms or 'set of premises'.

THE OBJECTIVITY OF MATHEMATICS

One of the reasons why mathematics is so highly esteemed as an area of knowledge is because it is objective. Science, we have seen, is a human construct which strives to be objective, but scientists are aware of the problems of objectivity created by observation and experience-based induction. Mathematics, as an area of knowledge, is free from both observation and induction. The only subjective influence in mathematics would seem to be the mathematician's personal choice of the process of applying the rules of inference: which rules are to be applied and in what order and for what end. Perhaps it is for its objectivity that mathematics is so highly esteemed. And it is possibly also for this reason that it is a compulsory school subject. As an area of knowledge it demands precise and rigorous objective intellectual understanding. Despite the fact that most adults do not need more than elementary arithmetical skills in their daily lives, a considerable part of our education is devoted to mathematical knowledge. Its objectivity and the intellectual rigour required for its understanding seem to be the reasons why this is so.

APPLIED MATHEMATICS

The mathematical way of knowing explored in this chapter is the way-of-knowing of pure mathematics. No reference has been made to the natural world and it might seem that mathematics has no connection whatsoever with anything other than itself. Applied mathematics, as distinct from pure mathematics, is the use of mathematics in the natural world. Applied mathematics enables humans to construct models of the universe or the trajectory of satellites or the nature of radio waves. This is not mathematics as an area of knowledge as it has been described in this book, rather the use of an area of knowledge to further knowledge in other areas, whether it be physics, economics or even stage design. Perhaps the value of mathematics lies in its ability to be the handmaiden of other ways-of-knowing.

THE LANGUAGE OF MATHEMATICS

Philosophy is written in this grand book, the universe, which stands continually open to our gaze. But the book cannot be understood unless one first learns to comprehend the language and read the letters in which it is composed. It is written in the language of mathematics, and its characters are triangles, circles and other geometrical figures without which it is humanly impossible to understand a single word of it; without these, one wanders about in a dark labyrinth.

Galileo Galilei *(1564-1642) Astronomer and mathematician*

180

By 'Philosophy' Galileo means natural science. Whether or not natural science is written in the language of mathematics or whether the human construct of mathematics is used to describe what exists in the natural world is problematic[6]. To call mathematics *a language* is less problematic. Many people, mathematicians included, talk about the language of mathematics. What do they mean?

We have already defined language as being uniquely human; as communicating and using symbols. Within that definition mathematics is certainly a language. As far as we know, no animals use mathematics. Your dog might go for the bigger of two bones but that means merely that she recognises one has more pleasure in it than the other, no precise measurement is attempted. What mathematics communicates in the form of axioms, rules of inference and theorems is restricted, but communicate it certainly does, clearly and precisely, and the more clearly and precisely the better.

The symbols of the language of mathematics are as precise as the concepts embedded in them.

$$= \text{equals} = (\text{or more mathematically} = = =).$$

$$\sqrt{} = \sqrt{}.$$

$$\neq \; = \; \neq \; .$$

$$3 = 3.$$

$$3 = 2 + 1.$$

There is no bewitchment here. Mathematical symbols communicate specific statements that have precise meanings.

A language like this, with carefully defined symbols and rules for using those symbols, is called a *formal language*. Mathematics is a formal language. There is no danger of bewitchment in a formal language. What it communicates, it communicates precisely and completely and unambiguously. A neat example of the advantage of a formal language over natural language is given in *The Cambridge Encyclopaedia of Language*.

Take the mathematical expression $\sqrt{\dfrac{250}{3}} + 7$

In this form, in the language of mathematics, this expression is clear, precise and unambiguous. When we attempt to read it aloud, in a natural, as distinct from a formal language the precision of the mathematical language is appreciated. We would read it as the square root of two hundred and fifty divided by three plus seven. In the imprecise natural language into which we have translated it this could mean one of four things.

1. $\dfrac{\sqrt{250}}{3} + 7$

2. $\dfrac{\sqrt{250}}{3 + 7}$

---

6. *Problematic* is a bewitching word. Here it is used to mean *supporting what is possible but not necessarily true.*

3. $\sqrt{200} + \dfrac{50}{3} + 7$

4. $\sqrt{200} + \dfrac{50}{3 + 7}$

In the speech of natural language, careful use of emphasis and pausing could possibly get rid of some of the bewitchment but the precision of mathematical language would never be possible.

But most of us are not mathematicians and we do not use precise mathematical language even when we attempt to communicate mathematical ideas. Describing mathematical processes in the words of a natural language is one of the main reasons why mathematics is something of a mystery to many people. Without looking back to page 176 attempt to describe this theorem in your natural language.

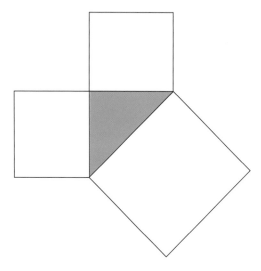

Mathematicians use language precisely and frugally. How near are you to *the sum of the squares on the arms of the right triangle equals the square of the hypotenuse?*

Precision and meaning can cause problems. What is a right triangle? Of course we know a right triangle is a triangle with a 90° angle in it. But why should 90° be right? And the sum of the squares, what does that mean? We do sums in elementary school, but here the word does not mean sum in that sense but total. And squares? What squares? A triangle doesn't have squares. (The triangle drawn above has squares but they have been added for the sake of the theorem. Right triangles do not normally have squares sticking to their sides.) And arms? A triangle has arms? The only words in the stated theorem that have not been bewitched are *the* (used five times) *of* (used three times) *on, a, equals, triangle* and *hypotenuse*, and the last one is a technical term from the vocabulary of mathematics. Even *triangle* is a little bewitched. It could mean a musical instrument.

The language of mathematics is itself a bewitching phrase. It could mean the formal language of symbols used by mathematicians to communicate precisely with each other. It could be a metaphor for that precision. It could even be a metaphor for the relationships within mathematics. It could mean the specialised use of everyday words within a mathematical context. The formal language of mathematics is a tool perfected by mathematicians to communicate exactly and precisely what they want to communicate. When natural language is used to communicate mathematical ideas, the precision of mathematics begins to fade.

THE BEAUTY OF MATHEMATICS

Beauty is the first test. There is no place in the world for ugly mathematics.

Godfrey Harold Hardy 1940.

Mathematicians frequently talk of the beauty of mathematics. Russell described mathematics as 'supreme beauty, like that of a sculpture'. Mathematicians seem united in their awareness of the beauty of mathematics. They have an instinct for it which is part of their mathematical awareness. Like all definitions of beauty, in art or music or the human body, the definition of mathematical beauty presents difficulties. Mathematicians do seem to agree though that beauty in mathematics is in the elegance of the presentation of a theorem.

A good proof, of course, must be deductively valid but it should also be elegant, to be beautiful. Elegance here seems to mean:

1. It must be as brief and concise as possible. It should not contain any material which is not absolutely essential.

2. It should contain mathematical ideas that can be applied to mathematics outside the theorem. The theorem should, in essence, have implications for mathematics outside itself. These implications are not for the natural world but for the mathematical world.

3. It must be powerful or complex but underpinning this power and complexity it should be direct and plain.

4. It should contain some idea or approach or device which is surprising and gratifying and there should be a twist in it that is intellectually satisfying.

John von Neumann describes elegance in mathematics in *The World of Mathematics:*

One expects a mathematical theorem or a mathematical theory .... to describe and to classify in a simple and elegant way numerous a priori disparate cases. One also expects 'elegance' in its 'architectural', structural makeup. Ease in stating a problem, great difficulty in getting hold of it and in all attempts at approaching it, then again some very surprising twist by which the approach or some part of the approach, becomes easy, etc. Also if the deductions are lengthy or complicated, there should be some general principle involved, which 'explains' the complications and detours, reduces the apparent arbitrariness to a few simple guiding motivations, etc. These criteria are clearly those of any creative art.

HOW MATHEMATICAL ARE YOU?

According to Kerry King three characteristics separate those people who understand mathematics from those who do not.

1. 'Mathematical' people understand mathematics consists of assertions and they also understand some propositions imply some other proposition. That is they understand the meaning of p implies q.

2. 'Mathematical' people understand the word 'only' is essential in the sentence. 'Each new assertion must use only the axioms and assertions which have already been proved'.

3. 'Mathematical' people understand the need for complete precision in the statement of the axioms, the definitions and the proofs and assertions of mathematics.

Test your mathematical aptitude by solving these three problems in the simplest way possible.

THREE MATHEMATICAL PROBLEMS

1. The Inspired Pure Thought Tennis Club has 1025 members. Every member has to take part in the Club's Annual Championship Tournament. They draw lots for the first matches and because there is an odd number of members the odd[7] player, the one whose name is not picked in the first round, sits out. The winners from the first round, plus the 'odd' member proceed to the second round and so on .... until the Championship is decided. How many matches were played altogether in all the rounds of the tournament?

2. What is the total of all the numbers between, and including, 1 and 100?

3. Express the perimeter of the figure below in terms of the radius of the largest semicircle, r.

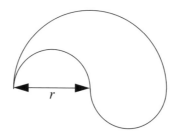

MATHEMATICIANS ON MATHEMATICS

TEN DEFINITIONS AND A QUESTION

Mathematics ....

> ... is the study of quantity.
>
> Aristotle

> ... is the science of order and measure.
>
> René Descartes

> ... is the science of self-evident things.
>
> Felix Klein

> ... is the most exact science and its calculations are capable of absolute proof.
>
> Charles P Steinmetz

---

7. Beware bewitchment: many of the members of the Inspired Pure Thought Tennis Club are odd, why else would they join a tennis club with that name and that exact number of players, but here the word means *odd* as in *odd* and *even*.

... is the Queen of Sciences

Carl F. Gauss

... is relations between objects; it does not matter if we replace one object by another provided that the relationship between them does not change.

Henri Poincaré

... is a game played according to simple rules with meaningless marks on paper.

David Hilbert

... is the subject in which we never know what we are talking about, nor whether what we are saying is true.

Bertrand Russell

... is the gate and key of the sciences...he who is ignorant of it cannot know the other sciences or the things of this world.

Roger Bacon

rightly viewed, possesses not only truth, but supreme beauty - a beauty cold and austere, like that of sculpture.

Bertrand Russell

and a question:

How can it be that mathematics, a product of human thought independent of experience, is so admirably adapted to the objects of reality?

Albert Einstein

 you have read Chapter 7.2 ...

consider or undertake the following:

1. Consider each of the statements by mathematicians on page 184 on. Which of them reflect your awareness of mathematics as an area of knowledge?

2. Is mathematics the perfect example of Justified True Belief?

3. How convincing do you find the explanation of Kant's synthetic *a priori* knowledge on page 178? Have you any alternative suggestions about the genesis of axioms?

4. Read again Russell's description of mathematics (*Bewitched by Words and Axioms*) on page 173. When you became aware of the nature of mathematics was it for you 'like a palace emerging from autumn mists'?

5. How appropriate, in your experience, is Professor King's description of the three characteristics of people who understand mathematics? Has he really got to the core of mathematics in these three characteristics?

6. Read *The Beauty of Mathematics* on page 183. Could the four points of elegance be used to describe elegance in other subjects? Can natural science be elegant? Can poetry? Can the answers to a comprehension exercise?

7. Solve the three problems on page 184 and compare the different ways members of your group arrive at the answer. Are some solutions more elegant than others?

8. Has learning mathematics trained your mind?

9. Is mathematics really a language?

Want to know more?

You may find the following book helpful:

King Jerry *The Art of Mathematics* Fawcett Columbine 1992

and this one a little more challenging:

Polanyi Michael *Personal Knowledge* University of Chicago Press 1958

SECTION TWO
AREAS OF KNOWLEDGE

THE HUMAN SCIENCES

7.3

CHAPTER CONTENTS

- What are the human sciences?
- Verstehen
- The Cassandra Paradox
- Free will and determinism
- Experimentation
- The Hawthorne Effect
- An alternative to experimenting
- The origins of human science
- Statistical analysis
- Is economics a science?
- The human sciences in action

Before

you read Chapter 7.3 ...

consider some possible responses to these:

1.
a. List five examples of human behaviour that you are convinced would hold true for all people in all circumstances.

b. List five examples of human behaviour that you believe would hold true for 80% of all people, 80% of the time.

2. What problems do you think might arise if you use the Basic Scientific Method described in Chapter 7.1 for studying human behaviour?

3. How would you go about finding out, as accurately as possible, the attitude of people between 70 and 80 years old to the Internet?

4. How would you attempt to measure the success of your school?

7.3 THE HUMAN SCIENCES

Natural science, we know, is the study of the natural world or the 'phenomena of the physical universe' as philosophers call it. Human beings are certainly 'phenomena of the physical universe' and social scientists, those scholars who work within the academic disciplines that study the behaviour of human beings, appear to use the same basic method of enquiry as the natural scientists. They observe a selection of 'the phenomena of the natural world', they use inductive logic to generalise and they create theories which explain and predict. But, despite these apparent similarities of subject matter and method, the knowledge generated by social scientists does not have quite the same status as knowledge generated by natural scientists. It is not that knowledge generated by social scientists is not valued, rather that it is valued in a different way. It is regarded rather more as a guideline to what is 'probably' the truth rather than the 'firm' truth of natural science.

WHAT ARE THE SOCIAL SCIENCES?

The social sciences are the academic disciplines that study human behaviour, human society and social relationships. The best known of these disciplines are:

anthropology
the study of human societies and customs,

economics
the study of the production and distribution of wealth,

political science
the study of the state and systems of government,

sociology
the study of the structure and functioning of human society and

psychology
the study of the human mind and its behaviour in specific contexts.

In recent years many colleges and universities have developed degree courses which use knowledge from the social sciences for specific purposes. Business studies borrow from economics and psychology, for instance, and education courses are composed of material from psychology and sociology. Geography, an interestingly hybrid discipline, borrows from economics and politics, as well as from the natural sciences.

The social sciences are sometimes called the 'human sciences'. The reasons for this are a little obscure. The use of the name 'human sciences' is relatively new and seems to be in reaction to the word 'social'. The IBO ToK curriculum planners obviously prefer the word 'human' to 'social'.

Some social scientists resent this. The social sciences they claim are sciences. They apply the same standards of objectivity, of precision and testability, and reliability as natural scientists and the knowledge they create deserves the same status as knowledge created in the natural sciences. They further argue that life would be impossible if people didn't behave in a more or less predictable way.

There are, for example, rules we all follow for self preservation and advancement. Studying human behaviour can help us understand these rules and enables us to generalise about human behaviour in the same way as natural scientists generalise from their observations about other features of the natural world. Of course, they agree, there are exceptions, but in general we have enough consistent knowledge of human behaviour to justify it as being as objective, precise and testable as any other scientific knowledge. Basically, their view is that human behaviour can be described by a set of rules or laws in much the same way as other aspects of the physical world are described by, for instance, the laws of physics. Human actions, they argue, are simply a division of the phenomena of the natural universe and the action of humans must be governed in the same way as other phenomena. Human behaviour can be studied by a psychological science which is just a part of natural science.

But despite these claims social science is not quite as reliable, as precise, as objective, and as testable as natural science. Nor is it able to explain and predict with the same accuracy as natural science. Why? Are there some 'phenomena of the physical universe' that are different from others? Some phenomena that cannot be accurately observed? Some phenomena whose behaviour is not entirely predictable? Some phenomena that are different in a fundamental way from the phenomena studied by physicists, chemists and biologists?

The answer to these questions is a clear 'Yes'. Human beings are unique 'phenomena of the physical universe'. Social scientists studying those areas of knowledge concerned with understanding human behaviour should use the scientific method with caution. The raw material they are studying is different from all other phenomena. Human behaviour, for a whole variety of reasons, is inconsistent and immeasurable; it is imprecise and subjective. The precise, objective methods of natural science are not entirely suitable for its study. To further complicate matters social scientists are themselves humans; they are part of what they are observing. It is extremely difficult, almost impossible for them to separate their own understanding and awareness of themselves as human beings from the subjects they study. Therefore the methods used to create knowledge in the social sciences differ from the methods used by natural scientists. These methods, objectively attempting to study human behaviour but understanding the challenges created both by its diversity and by the observer being part of what is observed, are called by philosophers, *Verstehen*. Verstehen in German means simply 'to understand'. Used as a philosophical term it means the method social scientists use to create knowledge within the social sciences. Verstehen has its roots within the scientific method but differs from it in several ways. To understand the social sciences as a way-of-knowing we should look at those differences.

VERSTEHEN

OBSERVATION

The Basic Scientific Method begins with observation. Using either their own senses or instruments which measure beyond their sensory range, natural scientists 'see' the natural world from which they create knowledge. Can social scientists observe in the same way?

Observing 1. Seeing what can't be seen

Much of what social scientists concern themselves with cannot be 'seen', in the sense of being observable through the senses, with or without instruments to aid the seeing. You cannot 'see' 'motivation' or 'leadership' or 'concentration'.

To understand these, and the many similar characteristics of human behaviour, social scientists have to rely on their own 'empathy and introspection', rather like the proverbial 'sixth sense'. Why didn't you attend class yesterday? Were you lazy? Ill? Bored? Otherwise engaged? Rebellious? Doing your own thing? Social scientists cannot be sure of your reason for being absent. They can ask you of course, (but what would the answer be worth?). Instead, they must consult their own repertoire of motives to understand your behaviour. But their 'repertoire of motives' may be misleading. They may pick the wrong one or not even have the correct one in their repertoire. Or the behaviour may be a blend of motives which are impossible to separate from each other. Social scientists can make some well informed attempts to define the reason you were not in class yesterday and their empathetic analysis will probably give them some accurate insights into your behaviour. But *probably* is not *definitely*. You can't see what can't be seen.

Observing 2. Being seen by the seen.

If you knew your behaviour was being watched by social scientists researching into the effectiveness of homework, would you act entirely normally? You might sense what it is they hoped to know (even if you were wrong) and give them that information. Or, depending on a variety of factors, including possibly your character or mood, or how sympathetic you find the researchers, you might deliberately ensure they don't get the information you sense they are looking for. You might also deliberately deceive the researchers to protect a secret or two you have. Or you might distort information to present yourself in a more flattering way. Or again, you may believe, rightly or wrongly, the researchers are going to provide the school administration with information which will lead to your homework load being increased, so you make sure your behaviour indicates that you already work six hours every evening and couldn't possible manage any more.

THE CASSANDRA PARADOX

Social scientists are all familiar with the The Cassandra Paradox. Cassandra was a Trojan princess. The god Apollo fell in love with her and was so pleased she returned his love that he gave her the gift of accurately predicting the future. However, she cheated on him so he turned his gift into a curse. She could still accurately predict the future but no one would believe her. (There's an interesting knowledge problem there: if she knew what was going to happen in the future did she know, when she cheated on Apollo, that the gift would become a curse? And if she did ...?). The Cassandra Paradox works like this: social scientists predict, based on the knowledge of your behaviour, that you will be absent from school next week. You hear of this prediction and it so annoys you that you make sure it doesn't come true. An astronomer's prediction of the appearance of Halley's Comet doesn't influence the Comet. A social scientist's prediction of human behaviour might influence human behaviour. Being seen by the seen distorts what is seen.

Observing 3. Seeing what you want to see.

Both the natural sciences and the social sciences are human constructs: methods of creating knowledge and the knowledge itself, created by humans. These humans have values, values which classify actions and achievements, goals and aspirations, as good or bad, just or unjust, worthy or worthless. Any personal values or biases based on these values that scientists, natural or social, bring to their research should be made explicit and compensated for. Physicists looking for an all-embracing Theory of Everything must be extremely careful that their desire to find such a theory doesn't interfere with their observations and deductions. Social scientists face the same kind of problems as physicists. But their researches are even more vulnerable to personal values because they, the social scientists are themselves human and part of their own subject matter. Social scientists researching the effectiveness of homework have themselves experienced homework. Their own experience may lead them to believe that homework is fundamental to success later in life or that it is simply a device used to keep young people busy and to control them or train them to work hard or one of a thousand other things. They may make their values explicit and compensate for them, may overcompensate perhaps, but it is impossible for them to ignore them completely. Total, value-free objectivity is not possible in either natural or social science. But in social science it is more difficult to achieve than in natural science. Seeing what you want to see, distorts.

CONCLUSION:
Observing in the social sciences is not the same as observing in the natural sciences.

1. Social science is concerned with concepts that may not be observed through the physical senses.
2. What is observed can be distorted, either deliberately or otherwise, by what or who is being observed.
3. Objective value free observation is even more difficult than it is in the natural sciences.

WHAT ARE YOU GOING TO DO THIS EVENING?

WHO, OR WHAT, DECIDES YOUR BEHAVIOUR
The central problem of the social sciences is the unpredictable behaviour of human beings. What determines our behaviour? Do we determine ourselves the way we behave or are we in some way programmed to behave the way we do? Is this unpredictability, predictable? Philosophers and others, including theologians, have argued long and hard in an attempt to answer these questions. Their debate centres round the ideas of Free Will and Determinism.

FREE WILL AND DETERMINISM
Some philosophers, Determinists, claim that natural laws determine what will happen, including how humans will behave. All events, they claim, are caused by previous events and nothing happens by chance. Once we have discovered the natural laws that determine events, and are aware of the conditions before an event, we can, theoretically know about an event before it happens. Magical as this may seem it is the way natural science works: if x under y conditions then z. Determinism is accepted widely in the natural sciences. The same predictability, Determinists argued, should apply to human behaviour. Everything we do has a cause. We just do not know enough about these causes. We do not know what events lead to our making the decisions we make and the actions we do based upon those decisions. Other philosophers claim that human behaviour is not always caused by previous events. We are free to behave in the way we choose. We have free will.

DETERMINISM
Determinism is based firmly on the belief that every event must have a cause. The cause or causes determine what is going to happen. These causes in turn have causes and these causes have causes and so on. There are two main Determinist arguments, physical Determinism and psychological Determinism.

PHYSICAL DETERMINISM
Physical Determinism implies that behaviour is determined by something physical, in this case physical activity in the brain. Brain processes, physical Determinists claim, are physical events caused by previous physical events. These brain processes direct our behaviour. They determine what we do. Brain processes are governed by natural laws, in the same way as physics is governed by natural laws, so it must follow that human behaviour is governed by natural laws. Decision making, by this argument is physical, based on the predetermined processes of the brain, which themselves have a cause. This means that there cannot possibly be any choice in the way we behave. There can be no free will.

An obvious objection to this claim is that there is no evidence that brain processes are physical. We do not know what causes brain 'events' or even what brain events are. Until such time as we know more about the way the brain works, physical Determinism must be a theory in search of evidence.

PSYCHOLOGICAL DETERMINISM

To overcome the objection that there is no physical evidence, psychological Determinists claim that the psychological state of the brain, rather than the physical state, determines the decisions we make. The psychological state of the brain, it seems, is an inert state rather than an event. An inert state which has been determined by the sum of its experiences to make each of us the thinking, learning, emotional individuals that we are. Psychologists investigate, amongst other things, our emotions, moods and abilities and the causes that determine the way we think and act. They argue that our human psychological makeup is a result of heredity and environment: we behave the way we do because of the genes we have inherited from our ancestors and because of the place, manner and time of our upbringing. Psychological Determinists argue that if they could compile a complete set of causes explaining the way we behave the unpredictable would become predictable and psychological Determinism could confidently justify and predict human behaviour.

The main objection to psychological Determinism is that it simply doesn't fit with reality. When you decide what you are going to do tonight you choose from several alternatives. You may choose to study, or go to the movies or a disco, or go swimming or simply stay at home and persuade your parents that all your actions are predetermined so you can't be responsible for anything you do. Is your choice determined by the way your brain has been programmed? Do you decide to study because you have been brought up to want good grades? Or because you feel guilty if you don't get them? Do you go swimming because your genes are screaming at you to exercise your body? Are good grades, guilt, exercise important to you and what makes you decide between them? Do you sense any predetermined decision? Is your behaviour predictable? We do not know what we people will do in any particular case and to claim behaviour is controlled by previous events, even if those events are psychological states of mind, seems not to match experience. And, of course, your debate with your parents about your behaviour being determined by causes beyond your control means you are not responsible for your actions. Can you accept that you are not responsible for the choices you make?

FREE WILL

Free will is based on the belief that humans are free to decide some, not necessarily all, of the ways they behave and that these decisions are not determined by previous events.

A DELIBERATE CHOICE

Philosophers and theologians who claim that human behaviour in not predetermined, that we do have free will, are called Libertarians. Libertarians claim that you decide for yourself, regardless of any internal forces driving you, what you are going to do. You exercise your free will when you make a conscious and deliberate decision to do one thing rather than another, having thought out the consequences and alternatives. Free will makes you responsible for your actions. Having weighed up all the options for tonight, having considered all your desires and values and emotions, you decide to go swimming. You exercise your free will and thus bring uncertainty into human behaviour.

PARALLELS IN NATURAL SCIENCES:

THE HEISENBERG UNCERTAINTY PRINCIPLE

Libertarians claim that free will has a parallel in modern science. The Heisenberg Uncertainty Principle in physics states that you can either know with certainty the position of a particle of matter or you can know with precision its velocity. If you are sure of its position you are uncertain of its velocity and if you are sure of its velocity you are uncertain of its position. Libertarians argue that if there is uncertainty in the natural non-human world there can be uncertainty in the natural human world. And free will is part of that uncertainty.

AN END TO THE DEBATE?

Determinists must believe that Libertarians have no choice in believing in free will. They are, after all, predetermined to believe in it. So why do they bother to debate it?

The consequences of human behaviour being either determined or a matter of free will affect our attitudes to morality. We look at the moral consequences of free will and determinism when we examine Ethics.

EXPERIMENTATION

EXPERIMENTATION 'IN THE LABORATORY'

Observation in the natural sciences often means experimenting. The chemists, physicists and biologists set up experiments and observe. The replication of the experiments, confirming the knowledge generated by earlier experiments is the test that natural scientific knowledge has to pass. If the findings of other natural scientists are the same as the original experimenter then the knowledge has validity. In the ideal experiment in natural science all variables except one are controlled. In a biochemical experiment testing the effect of fertiliser on tomato growth all the variables except the fertiliser would be constant. It is true that one cubic meter of soil is never exactly like another but for the purpose of the experiment it can be made so. Its texture, water and chemical composition and so on can be kept constant as must the quality and type of tomato plant, heat, light and water. If the biologists tried to conduct the experiment in any other way they could not be sure which features of the plant or its environment affected the growth, or non-growth, of the tomato plants. If the biologists' observations of the experiment indicated that a certain composition and amount of fertiliser produced maximum growth and other experimenters found the same thing in identical circumstances then they have generated scientific knowledge.

In the social sciences this kind of experiment is impossible. Controlled experiments with very small groups of people, experiments which concentrate on all possible variables, are extremely difficult to run. Could research into attitudes to homework in any one class in your school or college be replicated? It might indicate attitudes for that particular group at that particular time, and these attitudes might reflect more general attitudes throughout the school or college or even schools and colleges generally. But replication in the rigorous sense of the biology experiment is not possible. The external variables of such things as time and place and mood and levels of cooperation will never be exactly the same.

THE HAWTHORNE EFFECT

Aware as they are of the possible problems, social scientists do attempt laboratory type tests. A well known example of such a test took place at the Western Electrical Company's factory in Hawthorne in California. The management was concerned about efficiency, so they hired a team of social scientists to investigate the effects of changing working conditions on productivity and morale. A group of workers was installed in an assembly line in a room separated from the main assembly line. In this separate room variations in working conditions could be altered and carefully monitored. The researchers changed certain working conditions, for instance the level of lighting and the frequency of breaks, but changed only one variable at a time, in the best experimental tradition. The results at first seem self evident: the better the lighting or the more breaks, the 'better' the working environment, the higher the morale and productivity. But then the researchers 'disimproved' the environment: lowered levels of lighting and allowed fewer breaks, and still the productivity went up. Morale and productivity, it was concluded, increased because the workers were singled out for attention: a consequence now known generally as the Hawthorne Effect. The Hawthorne Experiment indicates a major difficulty with 'laboratory' experimenting in the social sciences: the problem of the see-ers being seen by the seen.

'Laboratory experiments' in the social sciences are faced with too many uncontrollable variables. People change from day to day. They worry. Their cars break down. Their crops don't grow. They get excited. They get bored. People change over time. They get older. They get backaches. Their children don't do their homework. And groups of people change and therefore cultures change. Compare your parents' and your grandparents' attitudes to sex, drugs and rock 'n' roll and footwear. Human behaviour is too inconsistent to be part of controlled experiments.

AN ALTERNATIVE TO EXPERIMENTING

PREDICTING

In some of the natural sciences, astronomy for instance, it is not possible to experiment. You observe, you theorise, you deduce, you predict. Further observation of the natural world 'in the wild' either confirms your prediction or it doesn't. Every 76 years Halley's Comet returns, exactly as predicted and those astronomers lucky enough to be alive at that time pat themselves on the back and return to monitoring the radio waves of dying stars in deep space. This kind of 'repeat' prediction, a check on the validity of the knowledge, resembles more closely the way social scientists work, than does the controlled laboratory experiment. Economists observe (the patterns of the rise and fall of prices on the stock exchange); they theorise (when certain conditions are fulfilled prices will drop dramatically); they deduce (these certain conditions are likely to be fulfilled next May); they predict (next May there will be a stock exchange crash). The verification of their prediction (their repeat experiment) takes place in May, when the stock exchange crashes or doesn't crash. But unlike Halley's Comet the timing of the crash, and even the actual crash itself, cannot be accurately determined. Human behaviour is not governed by the wholly predictable forces that control the orbit of Halley's Comet.

THE ORIGINS OF SOCIAL SCIENCE

The Social Sciences were conceived in the Age of Enlightenment. The Enlightenment was an intellectual movement in western Europe in the late 17th and 18th centuries. Influenced by great thinkers like Descartes and Newton, it had at its core the belief that reason was the key to all human understanding and to all knowledge and progress. It encouraged religious tolerance and regarded superstition as a barrier to understanding.

In Germany the leading figures of the Age of Enlightenment included:

*   Gottfried Leibniz (1646-1716), mathematician and philosopher,
*   Immanuel Kant (1724-1824), philosopher,
*   Wolfgang von Göethe (1749-1832), writer and natural scientist,
*   Friedrich von Schiller (1759-1805), historian, playwright and poet.

In France the leading figures were:

- Voltaire (1694-1778) writer and natural scientist,
- Jean Jacques Rousseau (1712-1778), philosopher and essayist,
- the editors of *Encyclopaedia*, a major work of the Age of the Enlightenment,
- Denis Diderot (1713-1784),
- Jean d'Alembert, (1717-1783).

In Britain the leading figures were:

- the Scotsmen Adam Smith (1723-1790), economist and philosopher, and
- David Hume (1711-1776) philosopher and historian,
- the editor of the original *Encyclopedia Britannica*,
- William Smellie (1740-1795) editor, printer and antiquary.

The ideas of the Age of Enlightenment led to the political revolutions in America (1776) and France (1789).

Although Adam Smith is the only social scientist listed above, the Age of Enlightenment produced the first economists and sociologists who strongly believed they were scientists in the same way as natural scientists were scientists. Both economics and sociology developed slowly until the 19th century. Two of the most celebrated social scientists of all time are Emile Durkheim (1858-1917) regarded as the founder of modern sociology because of his book *The Rules of Sociological Method* (1894) and Max Weber (1864-1920) whose treatise *The Protestant Ethic and the Spirit of Capitalism* had a major influence on the development of sociology.

ANOTHER ALTERNATIVE TO EXPERIMENTING

STATISTICAL ANALYSIS OF DATA

A second alternative to experimenting is what Jerry R. Rose in his book *Introduction to Sociology* calls *Statistical Analysis of Data*. He gives an interesting hypothetical example of this which highlights the problems of research in the social sciences and indirectly emphasises the claims of Verstehen.

On large university campuses there appears to be a higher level of student discontent than on small campuses. The obvious explanation for this would seem to be the impersonal treatment of students by college officials working in a large bureaucratic system. An alternative explanation might be large, public universities, cheaper than small private universities recruit lower class students and lower class students are more discontented than middle class students in which case, the size of the campus would have nothing to do with their discontent.

To check the 'truth' of the alternative explanation social scientists could use 'statistical analysis of data'. Researchers would have to examine lower class students in small universities and see if they are discontented in those also, or compare large private universities with large public universities. The problems here are clear: how do you measure 'discontent'? How do you measure class? What is a 'large' university? In addition to these measurement problems, researchers, to be sure of the validity of their findings, must consider all the possible other alternative reasons why student discontent is higher on larger campuses. This is where Verstehen becomes significant. The researchers must, through their own awareness as humans, seek out alternative explanations and attempt to isolate them from their analysis. This is impossible. The social sciences as an area of knowledge offer fascinating and important insights into human behaviour but they do not give definitive information. As Rose says 'Perfect confidence in explanations arrived at in this manner cannot be expected but ..... perfection, if it is to be found elsewhere in life, is not to be anticipated in sociological researches.'

THE SEARCH FOR PERFECTION

Social scientists are aware of the imperfections of social science as an area of knowledge. For this reason they constantly appraise the methods they use. Rose's statement above is an example of this. Social scientists are particularly interested in distinguishing the social sciences from what is known as 'social lore', the kind of traditional common sense beliefs about a society and how it works which members of a particular society hold. Social science, they claim, is different from social lore for three main reasons.

1. Social science is an 'explanatory enterprise of culturally universal validity'. The important word here is 'universal'. If the social sciences do give 'universal' explanations of human behaviour then they would be significantly different from social lore.

2. Social science is an 'explanatory enterprise that is interpretively neutral'. Social science is not subjective and social scientists are neutral when they report and interpret human behaviour.

3. Social science is an 'explanatory enterprise which is evaluatively independent'. Social science looks at human behaviour and explains it without judging it.

IS ECONOMICS A SCIENCE?

Printed below are two short articles originally published in *Chem NZ* (Number 46, February 1992), a journal of the New Zealand Institute of Chemistry. I have included them here because they give interesting, expert insights into the nature of knowing in the human sciences.

An unbiased account from a physical-chemist's point of view Arthur Williamson, First Vice President New Zealand Institute of Chemistry.

Recently I have noticed that economists have begun to draw on some of the jargon and concepts of physical chemistry and are using the ideas of thermodynamics to support their assertions about the possibility of continued economic growth. I guess this gives thermodynamics some reciprocal right to expound on the methods of economics. An aspect of economics which interests me is the relationship between theory and real behaviour. In both fields it appears that one can devise theories about the behaviour of a system and then use them to make predictions about the future behaviour of the system, which can then be compared with the actual behaviour. At this point physical science and economics seem to diverge. When actual and predicted behaviour differ, the physical scientist generally concludes that either the observations or the theory are in error. If the observations are trustworthy, then the theory has to be wrong. In economics there seems to be a third possibility which is illustrated by the current 'free-market' approach. In this case disagreement between prediction and actuality is often ascribed as 'market failure'. I imagine that the equivalent in physical science would be to say that a disagreement between theory and experiment is due to 'reality failure'. Perhaps even more mystifying to the physical scientist is the fact that the economist will then go one step further and propose a measure to 'correct' this 'failure'.

This is the equivalent to the physical scientist attempting to do something to bring reality more into line with the existing theory.

One must conclude that the relationship between theory and reality is indeed different in these two fields. Physical science aims at elucidating characteristics assumed to be inherent in the system and expressed in its behaviour, while economics seems to impose these models on the system. To my mind the ability that the economist has to 'interfere' with the object of his theory adds a dimension of subjectivity that is not present in physical science and suggests that there can be no inherent rightness in any particular economic theory.

Is Economics a Science? A Reply, Seamus Hogan Department of Economics, McGill University, Montreal.

There are a number of similarities in the methodologies of physical science and economics. Unfortunately, the similarities in substance are not as great as the similarities in the language used to express the substance. A lot of our technical language is borrowed from the physical sciences (principally physics, since many of the economists who first brought mathematical rigour to the subject earlier this century had received their original training in physics). Naturally, the borrowed language has taken on its own meaning in economics, adapting to the differences in disciplines. This can lead to misunderstanding if professionals from one area try to read the material from the other. One similarity between the physical sciences and economics is that both involve the systematic investigation of complex phenomena. The human brain has only a limited capacity to comprehend complex systems of interacting forces without an organising framework. One way of providing such a framework is to invent ideal worlds that contain many of the interactions that we wish to comprehend but are still relatively simple and can be used as benchmarks against which the real world is analysed.

For instance, a physicist might consider the dynamics of a body on a frictionless surface attached to an ideal spring (i.e. a spring that has no mass and gives rise to a restoring force that is proportional to the distance the body is displaced from rest). Obviously, ideal springs or frictionless surfaces do not exist, but it is easier to comprehend the observed behaviour of a spring by considering how the presences of friction or spring mass distort the dynamics that it is trying to model. Similarly, modern economic theory is built on a mathematical structure that can analyse the simultaneous interaction of all decision-making agents in an economy (consumers, firms, governments, etc.). This structure makes a number of simplifying assumptions that are palpably false, but, as with the ideal spring, it provides a benchmark, exceptions from which generate our comprehension of the real economic world.

One reason for calling the simplified worlds 'ideal' is that they often contain a number of desirable properties that one would like to approximate in practice (e.g. minimising friction can reduce the amount of energy that one needs to supply in order to achieve a particular amount of work). Since the economic benchmark also has some desirable properties, one set of real-world deviations from this benchmark are termed 'market failures'. To continue with the analogy, an economist's recommendation that economic policy be used to remove a market failure would be equivalent to a physicist's recommendation that a lubricant be used to reduce friction. Professor Williamson's final point is that "the ability that an economist has to 'interfere' with the object of his theory adds a dimension of subjectivity which is not present in physical science."

There are important differences between physical sciences and economics in the methodology of connecting theory (in the physical science sense of the term) and reality. The most important of these is that economists can almost never use controlled experiments. One can think of controlled experiments as being an attempt to create the conditions of an imagined 'ideal' world in order to isolate a small number of phenomena from the distractions of real-world interactions. Economics certainly does have 'a dimension of subjectivity which is not present in physical science', but this is precisely because the economist cannot 'interfere' with the object of his theory in the way that a physical scientist can through the use of controlled experiments.

THE HUMAN SCIENCES IN ACTION

Here is a example of how knowledge is created by social scientists.

ACADEMIC RANKING OF WORLD UNIVERSITIES

Each year The Institute of Higher Education of the Shanghai Jiao Tong University ranks universities by several indicators of academic and/or research performance. Here are the criteria as listed by the Institute:

Criteria	Indicator	Code	Weight
Quality of Education	Alumni of an institution winning Nobel Prizes and Fields Medals	Alumni	10%
Quality of Faculty	Staff of an institution winning Nobel Prizes and Fields Medals	Award	20%
	Highly cited researchers in 21 broad subject categories	HiCi	20%
Research Output	Articles published in Nature and Science	N&S	20%
	Articles in Science Citation Index-expanded, Social Science Citation Index, and Arts & Humanities Citation Index	SCI	20%
Size of Institution	Academic performance with respect to the size of an institution	Size	10%
Total			100%

AND JUST TO BE SURE YOU UNDERSTAND THEY FURTHER DEFINE THE CRITERIA

Alumni. The total number of the alumni of an institution winning Nobel Prizes and Fields Medals. Alumni are defined as those who obtain bachelor, master or doctoral degrees from the institution. Different weights are set according to the periods of obtaining degrees. The weight is 100% for alumni obtaining degrees in 1991-2000, 90% for alumni obtaining degrees in 1981-1990, 80% for alumni obtaining degrees in 1971-1980, and so on, and finally 10% for alumni obtaining degrees in 1901-1910. If a person obtains more than one degree from an institution, the institution is considered once only.

Award. The total number of the staff of an institution winning Nobel prizes in physics, chemistry, medicine and economics and Fields Medal in mathematics. Staff is defined as those who work at an institution at the time of winning the prize. Different weights are set according to the periods of winning the prizes. The weight is 100% for winners in 2001-2004, 90% for winners in 1991-2000, 80% for winners in 1981-1990, 70% for winners in 1971-1980, and so on, and finally 10% for winners in 1911-1920. If a winner is affiliated with more than one institution, each institution is assigned the reciprocal of the number of institutions. For Nobel prizes, if a prize is shared by more than one person, weights are set for winners according to their proportion of the prize.

HiCi. The number of highly cited researchers in broad subject categories in life sciences, medicine, physical sciences, engineering and social sciences. These individuals are the most highly cited within each category. The definition of categories and detailed procedures can be found at the website of Institute of Scientific Information.

N&S. The number of articles published in Nature and Science between 2000 and 2004. To distinguish the order of author affiliation, a weight of 100% is assigned for corresponding author affiliation, 50% for first author affiliation (second author affiliation if the first author affiliation is the same as corresponding author affiliation), 25% for the next author affiliation, and 10% for other author affiliations. Only publications of article type are considered.

SCI. Total number of articles indexed in Science Citation Index-expanded, Social Science Citation Index, and Arts & Humanities Citation Index in 2004. Only publications of article type are considered. When calculating the total number of articles of an institution, a special weight of two was introduced for articles indexed in Social Science Citation Index and Arts & Humanities Citation Index.

Size. The weighted scores of the above five indicators divided by the number of full-time equivalent academic staff. If the number of academic staff for institutions of a country cannot be obtained, the weighted scores of the above five indicators is used. For ranking 2005, the numbers of full-time equivalent academic staff are obtained for institutions in USA, Japan, China, Italy, Australia, Netherlands, Sweden, Switzerland, Belgium, Slovenia, etc.

Using these criteria they create the following knowledge: The world's top ten universities in 2005 were:

1.	Harvard	100
2.	Stanford	77.2
3.	Cambridge	76.2
4.	Berkeley	74.2
5.	M. I .T.	72.4
6.	California I. T.	69.0
7.	Princeton	67.3
8.	Oxford	61.4
9.	Columbia	61.2
10.	Chicago	60.5

They also worked out the top universities in each of the continents. You can find out more by visitng their website: http:/ed.sjtu.ed.cn

Now *you have read Chapter 7.3 ...*

consider or undertake the following:

1. How much respect would Plato have had for the human sciences?

2. Read the articles reprinted on page 197 on. Do you find Dr Hogan's reply convincing? Do his comments on the problem of language reflect a wider problem in the social sciences?

3. Read again the information concerning the ranking of universities. What do you consider the strengths and the problems of the knowledge created? Could you make a similar league table for schools offering the IB Diploma?

4. A Social Science Project. Create your own knowledge in the human sciences.

The aim of this project is to get you to investigate the attitudes, or behaviour, of a group of people towards a given situation, to enable you to understand how knowledge is created in the social sciences. You are welcome to devise your own project or to choose one from the list below. You may work alone or in groups of two or three. The end point of the investigation is a presentation to the rest of the group about your work and findings.

Your project should have:
1. a clearly stated title and purpose;
2. an organised method of approach to the problem; this may include the format of the questionnaire, number of subjects taken as a sample, recognition and control of variables, etc.
3. a clear analysis of the results;
4. an appreciation of the limitations of your investigation;
5. a clear exposition of your findings.

Some suggested areas of investigation. (You can probably think of a project that interests you personally).

Does listening to music while studying help or hinder learning?

Is it easier to remember a combination of numbers or a combination of letters?

How easy is it to persuade somebody they are wrong when they are right?

Design and conduct a survey into the attitude of your colleagues to geography.

How does the perception of age change with age?

Is there a difference between the ability of left handed and right handed people to perform simple tasks?

Is there a maximum number of units (of letters or numbers) beyond which a sequence becomes difficult to remember?

5.

Social scientists use a variety of methods of collecting data. Four of these methods are indicated on the grid below

Method	Possible advantages	Possible disadvantages
Survey/Questionaire		
Observation of unaware subjects 'in the wild'		
Observation of subjects in controlled experiments		
In–depth interviewing of 'experts'.		

Complete the grid specifically for the testing of the hypothesis named. Which areas of research in the social sciences are appropriate for each of the four methods listed?

6.

What are you going to do tonight and how will you decide?

Want to know more?

You may find the following books helpful.

Ryan Alan *The Philosophy of the Social Sciences* Macmillan 1970

Smith Roger *The Fontana History of the Human Sciences* Fontana 1997

SECTION TWO
AREAS OF KNOWLEDGE

HISTORY

7.4

CHAPTER CONTENTS

Before *you read Chapter 7.4 ...*

discuss or undertake the following:

1. Write down what history you have studied in the last two years: the period studied, the geographical area covered, the subject matter (was it political, social economic, military?) and how you studied it. Were you taught directly by the teacher? Did you learn through assignments or projects? Did you look at historical documents? After compiling your list, compare it with the lists others in your group have made and attempt to come to some mutual understanding of what history has been, so far, for you.

2. Why do you think you have studied this particular history?

3. What effect has studying history had on you? Has it made you wiser? Has it given you a guide for any future decisions you might make? Were you fascinated/bored by it? Do you want to study more history? Has your perspective on life been enlarged by studying history?

4. Go to the history section of your school library and select from it what you consider to be a typical history book. Bring your chosen book back to your group and be prepared to explain why you think it is a 'typical' history book.

7.4   HISTORY

WHAT IS HISTORY?

A nineteenth century German historian, Ranke, used the phrase 'wie es eigentlich gewesen ist' to describe how he believed historians should present their records of the past. 'wie es eigentlich gewesen ist' is simple to translate, it means 'how it really was'. Ranke and his fellow nineteenth century historians believed that not only was it possible to present the past 'how it really was' but they also believed they were doing exactly that when they wrote their history books. They regarded history as they regarded the natural sciences, as we have seen certain social scientists regard the social sciences. There were 'historical facts' just as there were 'scientific facts'. In the same way that scientific facts were independent of the scientists, so historical facts were regarded as independent of the historians. The historian's job was to collect together a proven body of facts and present them to the readers.

Modern historians regard this approach not only as impossibly idealistic but also as simply impossible. Why? For most of us isn't that what history is about? What, after all, is history, if it is not about the facts of the past? If it isn't the past 'wie es eigentlich gewesen ist'?

THE DIFFERENCE BETWEEN THE FACTS OF THE PAST AND HISTORICAL FACTS

We all know, or think we know, what a 'fact' is: a reliable piece of information, something we know to be, in the common sense meaning of the word, 'true'. That you are reading this book, at this moment, is a fact. We also know, or think we know, what a historical fact is. We can produce, without too much trouble, at least half a dozen historical facts from the top of our heads: the date of the first arrival of Columbus in America, the year the French Revolution began, the name of the German Chancellor in World War Two, the exact site of the city of Carthage, the name of the Chinese Communist ruler responsible for the purges in the 1960s, and so on. These are facts, definite pieces of historical knowledge, close perhaps to the natural scientific knowledge the nineteenth century historians wanted to use as their model of knowledge.

But these facts are only the start of history; only the foundation on which history is built. History is not the facts of the past alone but the processing of these facts into a coherent, meaningful interpretation of the past with which these facts are concerned.

History is the interpretation of these facts, the processing of them into a narrative with causes and effects.

These 'facts', these pieces of information about the past are important to historians. Historians must be certain of their accuracy, must have confidence in their integrity before they can confidently interpret them for their contemporaries. One could reasonably expect historians to have vigorously applied Plato's tests for justified true belief to these core facts.

Historians collect their facts from wherever they can. Certain historical facts, often obtained from archives[1], may be collected directly by historians themselves. Historians can visit public record offices or churches and examine historical documents directly. Historians sometimes interview people who were directly connected with the historical events the historian is researching, and obtain 'oral' history. Many other historical facts are obtained from the academic disciplines which underpin history, subjects like archaeology, palaeontology, numismatology, and so on.

---

1. *Archives* are collections of documents, private or public, connected with events of the past. The places where the documents are stored are also called *archives*.

Epigraphy is an interesting example of such a discipline. Epigraphy is the study of ancient inscriptions: letters and words and symbols, chiselled, moulded or embossed on stones, metal, clay, even wood. These inscriptions and their interpretation by epigraphists provide some of the basic material from which historians select their 'facts'.

THE ROSETTA STONE

The Rosetta Stone is an inscribed stone found near Rosetta in northern Egypt in 1799. The inscription on the stone, commemorating the accession to the throne of the Pharaoh Ptolemy V, is in Egyptian hieroglyphics and in a simplified form of Egyptian writing called *demotics*. It is also in Greek. In 1822 a French epigraphist, Jean-François Champollion, deciphered the hieroglyphics. This led to the deciphering of many other records from the ancient Egyptian civilisations.

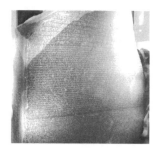

HISTORY IS A SELECTION

And that is the important thing about historical facts: they are selected. It is selection that makes it impossible for history to be 'wie es eigentlich gewesen ist'. If you watched television today your watching television is a fact, just a matter-of-fact fact. It has not yet been selected by a historian to be part of history. It probably never will be. It is not a historical fact. Historians make history by selecting facts and processing them and it is the processing that creates history. History has been described as an enormous jigsaw with lots of bits missing. Historians try to create the missing pieces. But they can only create these missing pieces by selecting from all the information available to them.

PROBLEMS WITH SELECTING

Historians select, but what they select inevitably reflects both the perspective of the original creator of the fact as well as the perspective of the historian who is selecting.

THE PERSPECTIVE OF THE CREATOR OF THE HISTORICAL 'FACT'

A well known example of this is the 'fact' that common people, the 'peasants' in Mediaeval Europe were devout Christians. What evidence we have for this comes, of course, from the people in the Middle Ages who wrote about their own lives and times. And the people who wrote about their own lives and times in the Middle Ages in Europe were monks and priests. Were these people capable of being objective about something so important to them as their religion?

THE PERSPECTIVE OF THE HISTORIAN INTERPRETING THIS 'FACT'

Historians approach Mediaeval documents created by the monks and priests attempting to imaginatively understand - not necessarily to sympathise with - the minds of the creators of the documents. Imaginative understanding is an important part of a historian's skill, but imaginative understanding varies from historian to historian. Can modern historians, coming with their own prejudices and biases, reliably process this piece of information from the past, process it not only aware of the intentions of the creators of the document but also fully aware of the biases and prejudices of the generation to which they themselves belong? Is there any way in which modern historians can guarantee their freedom from bias or prejudice or expectation? Would Japanese historians be able to interpret European feudalism without being influenced by their understanding of the similar social systems in Japan?

Imagine a situation in 50 years time when the history of your school is being written for, say, a centennial celebration. The historian finds in the archives a record of a discussion of mathematics teachers from the year 2000 in which it is clearly agreed among these now long dead math teachers that math is the most appreciated and enjoyed subject in the 12th grade. So the historian includes that 'fact' in the history. A selection has been made, by a historian. But that selected fact might tell us many things, depending on our interpretation, our processing, of it.

- It might tell us what the writer(s) genuinely thought had happened or was happening. The math teachers thought that math was the most appreciated and enjoyed subject. And maybe it was. Perhaps at the time the document was written, a group of students who really enjoyed math were having a good time in the math classes.

- It might tell us what the writer(s) thought ought to have happened. The math teachers thought math ought to be the most appreciated and enjoyed subject. The teachers saw the importance of math in leading students to an awareness of the intellectual beauty of the logical rigour of math and wanted math to be appreciated and enjoyed.

- It might tell us what the writer(s) wanted others to think they thought. The math teachers wanted the students/other teachers/administrators/ parents/ visitors to think the students believed math was the most appreciated and enjoyed subject. Maybe because math was under threat. Perhaps too many students were dropping it and the teachers saw their livelihood threatened.

What those researchers in the year 2050 have to do is critically examine the 'facts' they have before them. They have to imaginatively understand the minds of the math teachers, now alas, long dead. The only way they can do this is by using their own thought processes. Historians recognise that to portray history 'wie es eigentlich gewesen ist' is impossible. They cannot really be sure of the motives of the writers of the archive document. The past can only be seen through the eyes of the present.

EACH GENERATION'S RECONSTRUCTION

History is not a portrait of the past, nor historians' thoughts about the past, but the bringing together of these two things. Reconstructing the past is dependent on selection and interpretation of factual evidence. History is each generation's reconstruction of the past. If history is a jigsaw puzzle, then not only the missing pieces have to be created, the existing pieces need to be continually reshaped to fit together with the newly created pieces. Then both these new and old pieces have to be reinterpreted in the light of new knowledge and changing values.

IS HISTORY A UNIQUE AREA OF KNOWLEDGE ?

We have seen that the natural sciences, mathematics and logic, and the social sciences have distinctive areas of knowledge. Can a similar claim be made for history? Can it claim to be a distinct area of knowledge?

One way of answering that question is to look at the work of historians. As we do this we should ask ourselves the question 'What do historians do that scientists, mathematicians and social scientists do not do?'

Let us simulate the work of a historian and see what historians actually do.

Imagine there lived in the year 1900 a 17 year old by called Holden. Holden was the only child of wealthy parents, who adored him. They lived in a large house in Boston, Massachusetts, in the centre of the city. Holden had his own self-contained section of the house, with his own bedroom, bathroom and study. He was a good student and an avid reader and he was also good at sports and he played the clarinet in his school orchestra. He was indulged by his parents and his clothes and other possessions were numerous. A month after his 17th birthday he was sailing off-shore with his father and some friends when he was washed overboard and presumed drowned. His body was never found. His distraught parents were emotionally unable to handle his death. Without even entering it, they sealed up Holden's section of the house. When they died in the 1940s they willed their house to relatives on the condition that Holden's rooms be left unentered until the year 2000, at which date the entire and complete contents of the room were to be offered to a prominent Boston museum as a memorial to their son. In the year 2000 the relieved descendants approached the museum and the delighted 'historians' moved in.

The making of history from Holden's rooms and belongings can be divided into four stages.

STAGE ONE: RECORDING

Some scholars collect, record and preserve evidence from the past. If we stick to our definition of historians as interpreters of facts these scholars are not historians in our sense of the word. They are archivists and curators, collectors and preservers. Many of these use carbon dating or DNA testing. They scrupulously determine the origin of documents or objects, and when, and in what circumstances, they were written. This empirical accuracy is important for historians, indeed they must be able to depend on it absolutely, but it is not unique to history. The knowledge of archaeologists and curators is 'scientific' knowledge put to use by historians.

These curators are the first historians to visit Holden's room. Their task is relatively easy. Painstaking, but easy. The rooms are exhaustingly and precisely catalogued. Nothing is moved until photographs are taken, measurements made and meticulous records compiled of everything that is there and exactly where it is. That is the work of the historical researchers who record and preserve evidence from the past. Every object is recorded and, as far as possible, identified. The historical knowledge these 'historians' have is no different from the knowledge of natural science: it is empirical and objective.

STAGE TWO: ASSESSMENT

An assessment of the significance of the rooms and their contents has now to be made by historians. Holden's rooms and their contents, the Boston historians have agreed, are important historical events because they are unique. They have no other comparable evidence which supplies them with the detailed information about the life of a wealthy young Bostonian at the very beginning of the twentieth century. These historians assess the evidence they have, compare it to other similar evidence that might be available and come to the conclusion that Holden's rooms are indeed a unique historical event. Only historians can do this. This assessment is a unique way of knowing in history.

STAGE THREE: RECONSTRUCTING THE PAST

Having assessed the evidence and accepted its importance, historians now have to use it, to infer from it and to reconstruct the past. They use the evidence, for instance, to reconstruct Holden's daily life. How did he clean his teeth? How did he keep warm? What time did he get up each day? How did he relax?

Historians also are interested in reconstructing beyond the obvious. They attempt to reconstruct the values of a wealthy youth 100 years ago ..... they attempt to assess the attitude society had to wealthy young men .... they want to know in what ways Holden was still regarded as a child and in what ways he was not.

To do these things the historian must imaginatively understand Holden and his parents and the other people who were part of Holden's life. This imaginative understanding, this reconstruction, is another unique way of knowing in history.

STAGE FOUR: INTERPRETING

Historians, after they have reconstructed Holden's life, want to put him and his artefacts into some wider context. They ask themselves questions like what can these rooms and their contents tell us about the wider community 100 years ago? What, if anything, can these rooms tell us about human communities in general? They might compare the artefacts in Holden's room with the artefacts found in the pyramid tomb of Tut-an-khamoun, who was only a little older than Holden when he died and attempt to make a comparison of the societies from which both young men came. This is a wider interpretation or evaluation of the significance of Holden's rooms and, again, this interpretation is unique to history.

Historians' ways-of-knowing are distinct. They record, assess, reconstruct and interpret in a way that other scholars do not. Historians continually reinterpret the events of the past and reappraise them for each new generation.

HISTORICAL SOURCES

PRIMARY AND SECONDARY SOURCES

The problem with the past is that it has passed. It has gone. Time machines are a wonderfully fanciful idea but as yet we haven't managed to produce one. The idea of all time past, and present, running parallel is intriguing but until we have the technology to explore other times in reality, we have to explore the past through what the past has left us, through the multitude of artefacts surviving from times past. Historians use what they term primary sources as their main access to the past. Secondary sources are also available: these are sources of information provided by other historians.

Gibbon's *Decline and Fall of the Roman Empire* written in the eighteenth century is a secondary source. It is Gibbon's account of the end of the Roman Empire, written more than a thousand years after the event(s) it describes and analyses. Julius Caesar's *The Gallic Wars* is a primary source: Caesar actually was there, fighting those wars.

Primary sources are the bedrock of history. They include every conceivable type of document: maps, treaties, church and temple records, imperial archive documents, letters, legal records, diaries, newspapers, catalogues and even bus tickets. They can be formal or informal, private or public, serious or frivolous. Primary sources also include artefacts. The underground bunkers in Whitehall, London from which Churchill ran his wartime government are a wonderful primary source, as are the pyramids in Egypt and South America and the many cave paintings in central France.

Information from primary sources themselves needs to be treated with great caution.

Can historians be sure they understand the meaning of any document as it was intended by the original compilers? Do the actual words mean what they seem to mean? If the language used has to be translated, has the bias of the translator, however subconscious, affected the interpretation? Historians attempt to overcome these problems by using as many varied primary sources as possible.

Historians are wary of all sources and here are some of the questions they ask when using primary (and secondary!) sources:

> Who produced this source?
> When was it produced?
> Was the creator of the source an eyewitness?
> Why was the source produced?
> Where was the source produced?
> Is there consistency within the source?
> Is there consistency with other sources?

All these questions are aspects of one main question: How reliable is this source?

THE USES OF HISTORY

Many reasons have been suggested for the study of history. Here, selected from the comments of historians, are some of them.

HISTORY MAKES PEOPLE PATRIOTIC

One Frenchman suggested that the study of history was important because it makes people patriotic. This idea might seem strange to you as patriotism is now a little out of fashion, but you can identify from his suggestion the history he had in mind: the glorious military and cultural history of France in the last two centuries. History has always had a prominent place in the curriculum of schools in all parts of the world. Often the government prescribes what history should be taught and that prescription is normally dominated by national history. Whether that creates a patriotic nation or not is another matter.

HISTORY IS AN INTELLECTUAL PURSUIT, AN ACTIVITY OF THE REASONING MIND

For many historians this is the fundamental reason for studying history. History is a search for the truth through the continual re-evaluation of the past in the context of changing attitudes and information.

SOCIETIES NEED TO KNOW AND UNDERSTAND THEIR PAST

Imagine, following an illness, you woke up one day in a hospital with no idea of who you were and where you had come from, all memory of your personal identity eliminated by a virus. How could you relate to yourself? You would have to seriously set about the task of reconstructing your past in order to have some sense of your identity. Societies need a similar sense of identity, without an awareness of the past, societies are not able to cope with the present and plan for the future.

HISTORY HELPS US TO UNDERSTAND THE PRESENT

Looking at how things were in the past can explain the situations we are now in. The development of a county's road system, from footpaths through bridal paths through cart tracks to main roads and highways can explain the often apparently arbitrary route of roads. Analysing these developments may also be helpful in planning for the future.

HISTORY EXPLAINS WHY THINGS HAPPEN

A major part of a historian's work is to understand not only what happened and how it happened but why it happened. This most fundamental historical question is beloved of examiners. The causes of the First World War are perhaps the most written about historical subject of all time, not in books and learned journals but in examination papers. This 'why' question is in historians' words, 'the complexity of causation'.

HISTORY TEACHES US ABOUT HUMAN BEHAVIOUR

History is about humans and their relationships with other humans. It takes us beyond our own experience and enables us to look at patterns of behaviour of our common past. It is this 'pastness' which differentiates history from the human sciences. Our understanding of Wolfe's strategy before Quebec is put by historians into a time frame which is complete and we can study his behaviour in a finite way that other disciplines are unable to do.

UNDERSTANDING THE HISTORY OF OTHER COUNTRIES MAKES US MORE TOLERANT

If we understand the history of nations and continents other than our own, we will become more understanding. Learning how other countries have internally developed or struggled to develop, how they have related to themselves and their neighbouring countries, striven for ideals or have been exploited, will make us more tolerant of them and their cultural identity.

HISTORY PROVIDES A PLEASURABLE LEISURE TIME ACTIVITY

Many people are fascinated by history. Serious television series dealing with historical events attract huge audiences. The American television series about the Civil War, a serious piece of historical scholarship using only original source material, attracted many viewers and the video tapes of the series still sell well. Many people avidly read biographies of eminent (and not so eminent) historical figures for the pleasure of coming to an understanding of the past and the people who lived in it.

General U. S. Grant

WHY SCHOOL HISTORY IS NOT REAL HISTORY

Real history is created by historians. Historians, within certain limits, choose their field of interest and research. They then select from all the material available to them the information they consider significant. They interpret that material and they then write their history. The selection, interpretation and writing are creative acts. In this lies the fundamental difference between school history and real history. When you study history at school you are not involved in a creative act. I will return to this idea in a moment.

Up till the 1970s school history was limited to the stories of kings and queens and 'great' men and some women, what they did to whom and why they did it and above all, when they did it. School history was also ethnocentric: schools in America taught American history, schools in Peru taught Peruvian history and so on, and mostly school history was a view of the past as interpreted by the dominant socio-economic group. For students in Western Europe, school history was largely Euro-centric.

In the last two decades of the 20th century school history changed dramatically. As the world became a global village and societies became much more multi-cultural the biases and prejudices of traditional school history became increasingly obvious and academically unacceptable. Educators and professional historians wanted school history to reflect the process of history not a selection of filtered facts. They wanted history to be seen as a search for truth, as a discipline with integrity and objectivity. So school history moved from being a process in which selected facts were presented for subsequent regurgitation in exams, to a subject where the specific skills of historians were practised and developed. The aim was to develop an awareness of the accuracy of factual information about the past and an ability to analyse that information to further understand the past. Students were encouraged to look at historical events from different viewpoints, to analyse them for reliability, usefulness and appropriateness to the task in hand, to look at causes, consequences and for change and continuity.

In some ways then this 'new' school history emulates real history. It demands real analysis, a real search for truth. But as I stated above: it is not real history. And it is not real history for three reasons.

REASON ONE:

School history is packaged. It must be packaged. It is part of a school curriculum, and at the end of the course there is an examination. The examination must be something that the examiner can assess. Therefore school students cannot choose the area of interest, the subject matter, of their school history. It is chosen for them. It may be chosen for sound educational reasons: to give insight into the present state of the country or region in which students live or to help them have a sense of their own past, but it is chosen for them, not by them.

REASON TWO:

School students have no hand in selecting the primary sources they have to analyse to write their history. It is probably unlikely that they handled any genuine primary material at all. They probably handled facsimiles. But above all they were not involved in that fundamentally important step of selection. That is done for them, probably by a teacher.

REASON THREE:

Their interpretation of the material was pre-empted. The teacher or the examiner knew in advance what school students were expected to think and write after they have examined the given sources. A student's task in a school history assignment is to predict what the teacher or examiner wants and deliver accordingly.

School history can never be real history. What it can and should be is a rigorous intellectual exercise: a search for truth much more demanding than the straightforward empiricism of natural science.

Kirti Joshi, History and ToK teacher Munich International School

TAKE UP THE CHALLENGE: BE AN HISTORIAN

Study the Sources 1-4 that follow. Determine what similarities and discrepancies there are in the descriptions of the Coronation of Charlemagne and also what inferences are made about the events described. What possible reasons might there be for the variations?

THE CORONATION OF CHARLEMAGNE

Charlemagne (742-814) was King of the Franks. In 800 he was crowned Emperor of the West. Or was he? Customarily Charlemagne wore his crown on Christmas Day and Easter Day. He would not wear it when receiving Communion.

Source One: From the biography of Pope Leo III written by clergymen for the Papal Court. Charlemagne was crowned in 800 AD and this account was written shortly after Leo's death in 816 AD.

After these things, the day of the birth of our Lord Jesus Christ having come, all were again gathered in the aforesaid basilica of the Blessed Peter the Apostle. And the gracious and venerable pontiff with his own hands crowned him (Charles) with a very precious crown. Then all the faithful people of Rome, seeing the deference that he gave and the love that he bore for the holy Roman Church and her Vicar, by the will of God and of the blessed Peter, the keeper of the keys of the kingdom of heaven cried with one accord in a loud voice: 'To Charles, the most pious Augustus, crowned by God, the great and peace-giving Emperor, life and victory'. While he was invoking diverse saints before the holy confession of the blessed Peter the Apostle, it was proclaimed three times and he was constituted by all to be Emperor of the Romans. Then the most holy pontiff anointed his most excellent son to be king, upon the very day of the birth of our Lord Jesus Christ; and when Mass finished, then the most serene lord Emperor offered gifts.

Source Two: From the Frankish Royal Annals, compiled by annalists connected to Charlemagne's court. Written soon after the coronation.

> *On the most holy day of the Lord's birth, when the king at Mass before the confession of St. Peter rose up from prayer, Pope Leo placed on his head a crown; and he was proclaimed by the whole populace of Rome: 'To Charles, Augustus, crowned by God the great and peaceful emperor of the Romans, life and victory!' And after these praises he was adored by the Pope in the manner of ancient princes, and, the title of Patricius being dropped, he was called emperor and Augustus.*

Source Three: From a monastic chronicle which normally reflected very closely the opinion of the court. Written about 803, perhaps three years after source two.

> *And because the name of the emperor had now ceased to exist in the mind of the Greeks and because they had a woman as an emperor, it was seen both by the apostolic Leo himself and all the fathers who were present in the council (i.e. the council held to decide the fate of Leo III and before which he took his purification oath) and the rest of the people, that they ought to name as Emperor Charles himself, king of the Franks, who now held Rome itself, where the Ceasars were always accustomed to have their residence, and the rest of the places which they held in Italy, Gaul and Germany. For Almighty God conceded all these places into his hands, and therefore it seemed to them to be just, that he - with the aid of God and with all the Christian people asking - should not be lacking that title. King Charles did not wish to deny them their request, and with all humility, subjecting himself to God and to petition of the priests and all the Christian people, he received the title of emperor through the coronation of the lord Pope Leo on the day of the birth of the Lord. And the first thing that he did was to recall the Holy Roman Church from the discord which existed there to peace and order.*

Source Four: From the official biography of Charlemagne, written by the court scholar Einhard, a great admirer of Charlemagne, a few years after his death.

> *His last voyage to Rome was a result of another cause. The Romans having caused Pope Leo many injuries - torn out his eyes and blinded him - were moved to ask the aid of the king. Therefore coming to Rome in order to put to order that which was causing too much disturbance in the order of the Church, he passed the whole winter there. It was at this time he accepted the title of emperor and Augustus. But at first he was much opposed that he affirmed that, even though it was an important feast day, he would not have entered the church that day had he known of the plan of the pope. He bore with great patience the envy of the Roman emperors, who were so indignant at the title he had taken and by his magnanimity by which he was so much superior to them, he conquered their anger by sending to them many legates and by calling them 'brothers' in his letters.*

HISTORY: SOME ASSERTIONS

History makes men wise.

Francis Bacon, (1561-1626) Philosopher and Statesman

History is bunk.

Henry Ford, (1863-1957) Industrialist

The history of the world is but the biography of great men.

Thomas Carlyle, (1795-1881) Man of letters

When one is too curious about the practice of past centuries, one ordinarily remains very ignorant about the practices of this one.

René Descartes, (1596-1650) Philosopher and Mathematician

The present is what exists, and all that is not present does not exist. The past does not exist.

Jean Paul Sartre, (1905-1980) Philosopher and Writer

Happy is the country that has no history.

16th century English proverb

History; which is, indeed, little more than the register of the crimes, follies, and misfortunes of mankind.

Edward Gibbon, (1737-94) Historian

The historian, essentially, wants more documents than he can really use; the dramatist only wants more liberties than he can take.

Henry James, (1843-1916) Novelist

It has been said that though God cannot alter the past, historians can; it is perhaps because they can be useful to Him in this respect that He tolerates their existence.

Samuel Butler, (1835-1902) Writer

In a very real sense the study of history is concerned with a subject matter more objective and independent than that of the natural sciences. Just because historical matter is in the past, is gone, irrecoverable and inaccessible, its objective reality is guaranteed, it is beyond being altered for any purpose whatsoever.

G.R. Elton, 20th century Historian

Does History repeat itself, the first time as tragedy, the second time as farce? No, that's too grand, too considered a process. History just burps, and we taste again the raw-onion sandwich it swallowed centuries ago.

Julian Barnes, 20th century Novelist

Now
you have read Chapter 7.4 ...

consider or undertake the following:

1. Take a straightforward historical 'fact', one of which you are convinced and apply to it Plato's three tests for justified true belief. Discuss with your group the relevance of justified true belief for historians seeking to reconstruct the past accurately.

2. Write a paragraph, as brief as possible, explaining the difference between natural science knowledge, human science knowledge and historical knowledge. Discuss your writing with others in your group and obtain some consensus as to the difference between the three areas of knowledge.

3. As a group, plan the writing of a history of the first Monday of this school year, as it was at your school. The historical problem, of course, is sources. List all the sources you could use.

4. Look through the assertions on history and discuss those you find particularly insightful. Do you think Henry Ford really thought history was bunk?

5. Read again the *Uses of History* on page 210. Rate the reasons given for the study of history in order of their significance for you. Do you think history should be a compulsory school subject?

6. Why should each generation want to reconstruct the past? Does the past change?

7. Having read *Why School History is not Real History* (page 212) do you feel your history studies are worth while?

Want to know more?

You may find the following books helpful.

Carr E. H. *What is History ?* Penguin 1990

Marwick A. *The Nature of History* Macmillan 1997

SECTION TWO
AREAS OF KNOWLEDGE

THE ARTS

7.5

CHAPTER CONTENTS

- The Arts as an Area of Knowledge
- Literature
- The Visual Arts
- Music
- Aesthetics

Before *you read Chapter 7.5 ...*

discuss or undertake the following:

1. List all the subjects you consider as *the arts*. Attempt to determine what they have in common.

2. What do you think is taught in the art classes in your school?

3. What is taught in your literature classes?

4. Listen to a piece of popular music that you like. Attempt to describe to your group why you like it. Is there any way you could claim that the music brings you knowledge?

5. Describe an object you consider beautiful. What is it that makes it beautiful?

6. What do you believe determines which pictures get hung in art galleries?

7.5 THE ARTS

The arts comprise a huge range of human creative activity. They include painting, sculpture, ceramics, architecture, music, dance, film, and all the many genres of literature: all those artistic activities which appeal to the human intellect and spirit.

Schools and colleges often organise their teaching of music and art and drama through a Department of Fine Arts. Literature is usually taught through English or modern language departments.

ARE THE ARTS A UNIQUE AREA OF KNOWLEDGE?

When you study science at school you learn scientific 'facts'. You do not become scientists yourselves, although you may imitate the scientific method in your experiments, replicating what real scientists already know. To some extent you do the same thing when you study the arts. You read novels and discuss their structure. You look at copies of paintings and sculptures by famous artists and discuss texture and balance. You listen to recordings of symphonies and concertos, alert for rhythm and tone. Structure, texture, balance, rhythm, tone are some of the 'facts' of the arts. Facts which your teachers will introduce to you, and to the next class, and the next.

But in your arts classes you also do something very different from what you do in your science classes. You become an artist yourself in a way that you do not become a scientist in your science classes. When you study 'the arts', especially the visual arts, much of your time will go into creating works of art. You will paint, weave, sculpt and photograph with the intention of creating a finished piece of art. When you study music you will interpret scores and even compose pieces yourself. To a lesser extent when you study literature, especially if there is a creative writing component to your course, you may be expected to write poems or short stories. In each of these cases you are assuming the role of the artist. In doing so you are creating something unique and original in a way that you never do when you study science or mathematics or history. And in your creation lies the answer to the question 'Are the arts a unique area of knowledge?' When your fellow students or your teachers or any one else at all studies your picture, listens to your music or reads your poem, does that experience give them an understanding, an insight, an awareness, which they previously did not have?

Your picture, your painting, your story, if it is to have any significance as a work of art, must in some way explore the experience of being human. It will have given some form to the reality of your human-ness as you perceive it. It will also organise that reality of your human-ness in such a way that you can transmit it and others can receive it.

Both science and art organise reality. The 'reality' of science is the natural world organised rationally through our sense perception. The 'reality' of art is the reality of our inner experience as humans organised in such a way that we can communicate it to others.

Tolstoy, a serious artist himself, defined art's way-of-knowing:

> To evoke in oneself a feeling one has experienced, and having evoked it in oneself, then, by means of movements, lines, colours, sounds or forms, expressed in words, so to transmit that feeling that others may experience the same feeling – that is the activity of art. Art is a human activity, consisting in this, that one man consciously, by means of certain external signs, hands on to others feelings he has lived through, and that other people are infected by these feelings, and also experience them.

To reduce art as a way-of-knowing to a diagram is inviting scorn from philosophers, but for those of you who are uncertain what Tolstoy is saying, here it is, reduced to its basics.

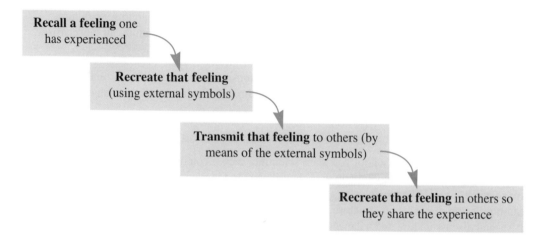

Recall a feeling one has experienced

Recreate that feeling (using external symbols)

Transmit that feeling to others (by means of the external symbols)

Recreate that feeling in others so they share the experience

There is, above the desk at which I am now sitting, a watercolour painting of the somewhat run down main street of a small town in New England which I used to visit. The artist who created the picture obviously enjoyed the town and felt very comfortable there. The painting depicts the town in the Fall. The leaves on the trees are a watery yellow. There are puddles on the road and there is a deserted slightly down-at-heel feeling about the place. The physical reality, the elusive atmosphere, the affection the artist has for the town, the artist's feeling for the place, have, in Tolstoy's words, been evoked. That feeling has been recreated with the brush strokes of water colour on paper (the external symbols) and that feeling of the artist is transmitted to me every time I look up and consciously focus on the picture. I am able to share the inner experience of the artist, her human response to that town on that Fall day.

COUNT LEO TOLSTOY 1828-1910
Tolstoy was a Russian land owner and writer whose works include *War and Peace* (considered by many the greatest novel ever written), *Anna Karenina* and *Death of Ivan Ulich*. He spent the last years of his life in voluntary poverty, living as a peasant, having given his estate to his family and disposed of all his possessions, In 1901 he was excommunicated by the Russian Orthodox Church because of his hostility to their practices. His description of art, quoted is taken from his work *What is Art?* published in 1898.

THE QUALITY OF CREATION

We can all create, but what distinguishes successful artists from the rest of us is the quality of their creation, the human 'truth' of their feelings and their ability to manipulate symbols to transmit that truth. Great artists, Rembrandt, Shakespeare, Beethoven are great because their ability to evoke and transmit 'feelings' to illuminate our human-ness is exceptional, absolutely unique. The works of these, and many other artists, convey profound knowledge and truth. This knowledge and truth arises from their exceptional intellects, their ability to understand the human experience in a more profound way than we lesser mortals and their ability to recreate that understanding with their chosen symbols, be it paint, words or music.

The truth great art generates, an understanding of our human-ness, transcends the sensibility of individuals. Hamlet's dilemma has been 'truth' for the last four hundred years and will continue to be truth for the next four hundred. At a lower level than 'great' art the sensibility of the viewer may be important. Examination of the quality of artistic representation, what makes a work of art good, is the subject matter of a branch of philosophy called aesthetics, which we shall return to briefly at the end of this chapter.

LOVE AND DEATH[1]

What distinguishes (great works of art) is largely the capacity to express some new concrete variation of an old universal theme. About two thirds of the poems in the Oxford Book of English Verse *deal with the timeless themes of love and death, and yet each one is a unique creation. The artist pours his knowledge into works of art. He knows - he does not merely feel - but he knows by sympathetic identification and imaginative insight. He knows as the perspicacious lover knows about the nature of love, by 'proving it upon his pulses' He knows by feeling at one with the object, as Keats felt at one with the sparrow. He knows the reality that he suffers when the outer object is drawn into his own being, into the mysterious depths of subjectivity. He knows not bare facts or abstract laws but vivid values - he knows things appreciatively, in their immediacy and concreteness. He knows with the totality of his body: with sense, mood, instinct, and intelligence, both conscious and subconscious. He knows by descending to the roots of being, which no idea can encompass - to the obscure spring of man's creative intuition - the source of dreams and of art alike.*

There, in the deep recesses of his mind, he is in touch with the instinctively common part of man's nature - with the values that are not peculiar to him as an artist not to one man or a few, but are basic in the emotional experiences and secret longings of most human beings. If it were not so, art could not serve as the language of all humanity - a way of communicating across all the barriers of place and time. The cave paintings by men of the reindeer age - the paintings at Lascaux and Altamira - would not speak so eloquently to us today; nor would the art of the whole world be a 'museum without walls' where any man can find incomparable treasures. The work of all ages and countries - Gothic counterpoint, Egyptian sculpture, Chinese landscape, Mayan temple, Russian ballet, English drama, and American novel - bear alike the spiritual imprint of humanity. In the realm of art, far more than in morals, politics, or religion, the whole world is kin.

INDIVIDUALITY

The arts, as an area of knowledge , depend on individual achievement and creativity. If Shakespeare had not lived there would be no *Hamlet* and no exquisite lines like these:

> *But, look, the morn, in russet mantle clad,*
> *Walks o'er the dew of yon high eastern hill.*

---

1. From *The Meaning of Art* Herbert Read 1972

This is one significant reason why the arts, as an area of knowledge, are quite different from the sciences. If Newton had not discovered the Laws of Gravity some other scientist would have, sooner rather than later. If Shakespeare had not written *Hamlet* it would never have been written. Artistic creation is unique and individual. Knowledge created by the arts transcends the individual creator and enables us to share the human experience in a unique way. Art expands and deepens our awareness of the wonder of being alive and being human.

THE DIFFERENCE BETWEEN 'HUMAN BEHAVIOUR' IN THE ARTS AND THE SOCIAL SCIENCES

The social sciences aim to be objective in their study of human society and the individuals who create it. Social scientists explore the behaviour of their fellow humans so they can understand and explain it rationally and predict likely patterns of behaviour in the future. The quality of their knowledge depends on the accuracy of their observations and the quality of their inductive and deductive logic.

Artists also explore human behaviour but are not at all concerned with objectivity. Arthur Miller's *Death of a Salesman* explores the so-called American Dream but it does so in a subjective and judgmental way. The quality of the art, of Miller's play, depends on his ability to understand and interpret the society he is describing and his ability to structure his play in such a way as to share his understanding with the audience.

AREA OF KNOWLEDGE OR AREA OF EXPERIENCE?

Because the arts as an area of knowledge depend on creativity and individual insights, it has been suggested that it is an area of *experience* rather than an area of *knowledge*. Within Tolstoy's definition there does seem to be a case to be made that knowledge is generated and transmitted, although the 'knowledge' is the knowledge of individual experience. Whether you call the arts an *area of knowledge* or an *area of experience* depends on your understanding of what knowledge is and what it is to know.

The profound knowledge within the arts, the evocation of feelings, is not knowledge-by-description, the justified true belief of Plato. In fact Plato was hostile to art in general. For him it was a rival to the pursuit of truth and had the potential to corrupt. And it is not difficult to have some sympathy for the pragmatic Plato. The 'truth' of the arts is often difficult to put into words, because the truth of the arts frequently transcends words. Students often have immense difficulty explaining the thoughts and feelings in a poem even though they respond emotionally to it. It is impossible to explain adequately in words the knowledge created by Beethoven's 6th Symphony. My New England water colour communicates with me in a way I have attempted to explain, but my description of the picture is a poor substitute for the picture itself.

The knowledge of art is knowledge acquired by introspection, belief and acquaintance Above all it is knowledge acquired by our ability to understand our fellow humans' emotions, our ability to *empathise*. Empathy is to the artist what empiricism is to the scientist. Maja is certainly empathetic and has the potential for creating artistic knowledge. Whether she does so or not depends on her intellectual ability to interpret the world about her and her ability to manipulate the 'external symbols' that artists use.

LITERATURE AS AN AREA OF KNOWLEDGE

'Literature' is one of those bewitching words that can mean many things. In the context of 'the arts', certainly in the context of the arts as an area of knowledge, it means: poetry, drama, novels and short stories, works of art created with language by individual poets, playwrights and novelists.

Tolstoy himself, was a great novelist and his definition of art certainly seems appropriate for literature.

It is an accurate description of the poem *Snake* by D. H. Lawrence. Read it yourself and then consider what knowledge is created by Lawrence and then transmitted to you, the reader.

A snake came to my water-trough
On a hot, hot day, and I in pyjamas for the heat,
To drink there.
In the deep, strange-scented shade of the great dark carob-tree
I came down the steps with my pitcher
And must wait, must stand and wait, for there he was at the trough before me.

He reached down from a fissure in the earth-wall in the gloom
And trailed his yellow-brown slackness soft-bellied down, over the
edge of the stone trough
And rested his throat upon the stone bottom,
And where water had dripped from the tap, in a small clearness,
He sipped with his straight mouth,
Softly drank through his straight gums, into his slack long body,
Silently.

Someone was before me at the water-trough,
And I, like a second comer, waiting.

He lifted his head from his drinking, as cattle do,
And looked at me vaguely, as drinking cattle do,
And flickered his two-forked tongue from his lips, and mused a moment,
And stopped and drank a little more,
Being earth-brown, earth-golden from the burning bowels of the earth
On the day of Sicilian July, with Etna smoking.

The voice of my education said to me
He must be killed,
For in Sicily the black, black snakes are innocent, the gold are
venomous.
And voices in me said, If you were a man
You would take a stick and break him now, and finish him off.

But must I confess how I liked him,
How glad I was he had come like a guest in quiet, to drink at my
water-trough
And depart peaceful, pacified and thankless,
In the burning bowels of this earth?

Was it cowardice, that I dared not kill him?
Was it perversity, that I longed to talk to him?
Was it humility, to feel so honoured?
I felt so honoured.
And yet those voices:

If you were not afraid, you would kill him!

And truly I was afraid, I was most afraid,
But even so, honoured still more
That he should seek my hospitality
 From out the dark door of the secret earth.
He drank enough
And lifted his head, dreamily, as one who has drunken,
And flickered his tongue like a forked night on the air, so black,
Seeming to lick his lips,
And looked around like a god, unseeing, into the air,
And slowly turned his head,
And slowly, very slowly, as if thrice a dream,
Proceeded to draw his slow length curving round
And climb again the broken bank of my wall-face.

And as he put his head into that dreadful hole,
And as he slowly drew up, snake easing his shoulders, and entered
farther,
A sort of horror, a sort of protest against his withdrawing into that
horrid black hole,
Deliberately going into the blackness, and slowly drawing himself after,
Overcame me now his back was turned.

I looked round, I put down my pitcher,
I picked up a clumsy log
And threw it at the water-trough with a clatter.

I think it did not hit him,
But suddenly that part of him that was left behind convulsed in
undignified haste,
Writhed like lightning, and was gone
Into the black hole, the earth-lipped fissure in the wall-front,
At which, in the intense still noon, I stared with fascination.

And immediately I regretted it.
I thought how paltry, how vulgar, what a mean act!
I despised myself and the voices of my accursed human education.

And I thought of the albatross,
And I wished he would come back, my snake.

For he seemed to me again like a king,
Like a king in exile, uncrowned in the underworld,
Now due to be crowned again.

And so, I missed my chance with one of the lords
Of life.
And I have something to expiate;
A pettiness.

Lawrence has evoked and transmitted the feeling of great privilege he experienced on that hot, hot day in Sicily. He transmits that feeling using a poetic form, and transmits it in such a way that the reader of the poem, or anyone who hears it read, shares that experience. The knowledge created by the poem is certainly profound knowledge: having become familiar with this poem never again will I see wild creatures unaware of my existence, without a sense of privilege, of sharing the natural world with other living creatures. The 'art' of the poem is twofold. Firstly it is the poet's perception of the moment - the heat and the snake have aroused his feelings, his emotions in a unique and personal way. Secondly he is able to recreate those emotions artistically - poetically- by manipulating words in such a way that they evoke those same emotions in the reader or listener.

Lawrence manipulates those words with great skill and care. The techniques he uses, the 'external symbols' of Tolstoy's description: the juxtaposition of ideas, the creation of images, the use of the sounds of the phrases, the patterning of the words on the paper are essential in helping him to communicate the emotion he feels. But these techniques are not the area of knowledge. When you study literature you study these techniques (amongst other things) in order to understand how writers achieve their communication; how the external symbols they use reinforce the feelings or emotions that the writer is evoking. The relationship between the symbols and the 'feeling', the 'medium' and the 'message' as it is sometimes called, determines the quality of the poem. Lawrence's supreme poetic skill is in his selection and arrangement of the words in order to communicate his emotions. But it is the emotions that are the foundations of this area of knowledge.

Perhaps you are thinking, well, Tolstoy's description of art may be applicable to that restricted poem with its clear and obvious 'message' but is it applicable to more extended literary pieces, novels, for instance? How can the novel *Huckleberry Finn* possibly recall a 'feeling' that Mark Twain had experienced? The answer to that question is simple. *Huckleberry Finn* recalls not one feeling but a multitude of feelings that Mark Twain had about, amongst other things, the pains and pleasures of childhood, hypocrisy and pretence, and the values of the people who lived on and along the Mississippi River in the mid nineteenth century. His 'external symbols' - the extended prose narrative, the choice of Huck, a 14 year old, as narrator, the selection of events - determine the effectiveness of the recreation and transmission of Mark Twain's feelings. That *Huckleberry Finn* has been read and enjoyed for over a century, and continues to be read in the 21st century is proof of the quality of the 'medium' of the novel as well as its 'message.'

A problem some people find in reading literature is that of accepting the message that is transmitted. If you do not share Lawrence's sense of privilege at sharing a moment of his life with a snake, or, if you do not believe in the pains and pleasures of childhood that Twain recreates, you have to suspend your disbelief in order to appreciate other aspects of the writing. But if you are not able to accept the truth of literature then it has failed as literature. Literature 'exemplifies and displays truths rather than argues for them'. Mark Twain doesn't openly list the pains and pleasures of childhood. His feeling, his truth, comes from the convincing way in which he presents Huck and his values, displays the truth rather than explains it. If Huck is not convincing then the reader will not accept the truth on which his portrayal is based.

This 'convincingness' leads to another problem some people have with literature: how can you be convinced by something you know doesn't exist? Huck is a character in a book. He is not a real person. He is an imaginary person, a product of Mark Twain's imagination, they argue. You can only be convinced by him if you are prepared to be imaginative too. Literature demands the reader uses imagination. Imaginative involvement in literature can take us into a whole range of awareness that is not otherwise easily accessible or might even be dangerous. We can suffer with Huck in his relationship with his father. We can savour the splendour of the river. We can comprehend the bitterness and the folly of family feuds. Our imaginative involvement is caused by the skill of the writer in creating, through external symbols, the situation in which we willingly suspend our disbelief.

This imaginative projection can be seen clearly in drama or film. We know when we watch a play that before us are actors pretending to be people other than themselves but we totally accept that pretence. When a production of *Othello* was touring in the old 'wild west' a member of the audience shot dead the actor who was playing Iago. As a child I had to be taken out of the cinema because I cried so loudly when Bambi's mother died that I unsettled the rest of the audience. Literature, and the other arts, not only demand our imaginative involvement, they nurture the imagination, an immensely advantageous side effect for this area of knowledge.

IMAGINATION

Imagination is the power of the mind to create images of things which are not present and to relate to images of things that are not real. Our imagination enables us to be at the water trough with Lawrence, to 'see' the snake sipping water and to fear for Huck in the presence of his drunken father. In these examples imagination could be described as creative thought. When we are creatively thinking – imagining – in this way, when we are drifting down the Mississippi with Huck, we are not deluding ourselves. We know our imaginary experience is not real.

When we read literature our imagination is brought into action by the feelings and external symbols of the writer creating images in our minds. We 'see' the waves ripple on the surface of the water and we 'see' the paddle boat, belching smoke, steaming up the centre of the river. When writers present us with events or people that we cannot accept, that our imaginations can't process, either our imagination, or the writer, has failed.

THE VISUAL ARTS AS AN AREA OF KNOWLEDGE

CLASSIFYING THE VISUAL ARTS.

Classifying the arts, like classifying many other things, is frustrating and challenging. If we classify the visual arts as those artistic human endeavours that depend for their achievement on being seen doesn't this mean the *performing arts* (ballet, dance, drama, mime, film, etc.) are visual arts? Certainly the performing arts depend enormously for their effect on their visual impact, as every movie goer knows. Directors of stage presentations of all kinds take great care to ensure the visual impact of their productions reinforces the 'feelings', intellectual and emotional, of the artist whose work they are presenting. The *graphic arts* (in a narrow sense the design and production of typographic work and its accompanying pictures and diagrams) can also be classified as including several of the visual arts, specifically painting, etching, engraving and drawing in general.

For our purposes, (understanding the arts as an area of knowledge), classifying the visual arts is not really important. Let us simply define the visual arts as those arts which, conventionally, high schools, and art colleges and universities teach: painting, sculpture, ceramics, photography and architecture, and apply Tolstoy's definition of art to these activities.

OSCAR WILDE: ALL ART IS QUITE USELESS

An individual who has to make things for the use of others, and with reference to their wants and their wishes, does not work with interest, and consequently cannot put into his work what is best in him. Upon the other hand, whenever a community or a powerful section of a community, or a government of any kind, attempts to dictate to the artist what he is to do, Art either entirely vanishes, or becomes stereotyped, or degenerates into a low, ignoble form of craft. A work of art is a unique result of a unique temperament. Its beauty comes from the fact that the author is what he is. It has nothing to do with the fact that other people want what they want. Indeed, the moment that an artist takes notice of what other people want, and tries to supply the demand, he ceases to be an artist, and becomes a dull or an amusing craftsman, an honest or dishonest tradesman. He has no further claim to be considered as an artist. Art is the most intense mode of individualism the world has ever known. I am inclined to say that it is the only real mode of individualism, since, alone, without any reference to his neighbours, without any interference the artist can fashion beautiful things; and if he does not do it solely for his own pleasure, he is not an artist at all .... . All art is quite useless.

Oscar Wilde *Art Without a Public* 1888

ART AND NON-ART

It is necessary to differentiate between a work of art, a painting or a photograph say, from human creations that *resemble* works of art. When I am in Corsica on holiday and I photograph a view of the village in which I am spending a relaxed and enjoyable evening. I take the photograph knowing it will evoke in me memories, 'feelings' if you use Tolstoy's words, of that relaxed and enjoyable evening. This photograph will not evoke these feelings in anyone else. Therefore, by our definition, it is not a work of art. If, however, I am an accomplished photographer and with great skill, with careful attention to light, shape, form, texture, tone and image selection, deliberately recreate with my camera the relaxed and enjoyable ambience of the village, and, if that photograph transmits that feeling in such a way that anyone looking at it would feel that ambience, then I have made a work of art.

GREAT BUILDINGS AS ART

My Corsican 'art' photograph may be trivial art and the knowledge it transmits may be insignificant. But much visual art is neither insignificant nor trivial. The great palaces of the world, The Imperial Palaces of the Forbidden City in Beijing, the Topkapi Palace in Istanbul, the Palace of Versailles (pictured) in France, evoke a definite feeling about the power and status of the dynastic families that commissioned and owned them and the feelings the architects had when they designed them. By the use of external symbols - stone, glass, wood, space, trees - the architects of these palaces transmit the 'truth' of the wealth and opulence and power of the great ruling families. In the same way 'the glory of God' is transmitted through the architecture of the great mosques, temples and cathedrals throughout the world.

These palaces and great religious buildings create a problem identical to that encountered in literature, the problem of the 'convincingness' of the feeling of the original artist. If you have contempt for the power of the ruling families of China and Istanbul and France, and if you are

227

utterly unconvinced of the glory of God how can the physical artistic quality of the buildings that make these statements mean anything? For you they have no truth. But for many republicans and atheists, palaces and religious buildings do have truth. Tourists flock in their millions to these places each year. Why do they do this if the buildings contradict their values? The answer is as straightforward here as it was with literature. One can appreciate the 'feeling' for what it means to the artist, without necessarily accepting that this feeling has validity for you. And one can appreciate the supreme manipulation of 'external symbols' without accepting the values that they represent. The architects of the palaces have created, through their art, their feeling of power or glory. If their art is successful they have communicated that feeling. We do not have to agree with their feeling to appreciate the 'truth' of their art. We can admire the 'external symbols' easily, the design and shape of the buildings, the craftsmanship by which art is constructed. But we also visit the Imperial Palace to sense the glory and power of the Chinese Emperors, however much we may regard them as despotic tyrants.

What I have written applies to the other visual arts, even though these may lack the grandeur of great architecture. A Persian miniature can convey the excitement of a hunt, a French impressionist the delight of a garden two dimensionally, as a cathedral displays the glory of God three dimensionally.

LANGUAGE AND VISUAL ART

All the visual arts have one great advantage over literature, an advantage they share with music: they are free from the bewitchment of language. The knowledge generated by the visual arts is wordless. It lacks the precision and the confusion, the ambiguity, that words so often create. The mediaeval architects' feeling for the glory of God expressed and transmitted through great cathedrals transcends any attempt to put this feeling into words. Words, as symbols, we already know, create a barrier to our knowing. Visual art, in a metaphorical sense, creates its own language. The external symbols used by artists, the paint, the canvas, the marble, the bricks and mortar, become the language, and on the skill of the artist in manipulating this language depends, partially, the success of the art. 'Partially' is important here. If the knowledge is not worth transmitting no amount of artistic skill in the manipulation of the external symbols will make it so.

ABSTRACT ART

Abstract art which developed in the 1940s and 1950s is as much *art* in Tolstoy's definition as the more conventional art of the cathedral architects and the French impressionist. By eliminating recognisable figures and objects, artists are free to express their feelings with abstract lines, colours and shapes. Wassily Kandinsky (1866-1944), a pioneer abstract painter produced in his paintings 'the choir of colours which nature has so painfully thrust into my soul'. Painting was for him 'an exact replica of an inner emotion'. You can see one of his paintings in colour plate 1. To what extent are you aware of the 'inner emotion' of the painting?

MUSIC AS AN AREA OF KNOWLEDGE

Music is the simplest of the arts to relate to our interpretation of Tolstoy's way-of-knowing. Anyone who has attended an American major league baseball game knows what knowledge is transmitted through music. Just before the game begins, the guest singer walks to the diamond, the spectators rise and with hands on their hearts join together to sing *The Star Spangled Banner*. Everyone in the stadium is for that moment part of a confident, united nation: 'the land of the free and the home of the brave'. Patriotism, pride in one's country, fills the ballpark. You can feel the stars and stripes rising above the stadium, spreading the message of freedom and self-confidence.

The Star Spangled Banner makes its statement with absolute clarity: its external symbols, the musical sounds, evoke the composer's feeling of patriotism and recreate that feeling within those baseball fans. The musical message in this case is far from subtle but it is certainly effective; effective in a style that no language can be. The power of music is a way-of-knowing. A power it shares with the visual arts, quite disinct from knowledge transmitted through language.

This power is, for some people, difficult to understand. It is not unusual for people to feel they 'don't understand and appreciate' music because they cannot relate their response to music to anything specific. Perhaps one reason such people find it is difficult to understand is because the feelings that are created uniquely by music are feelings that cannot be expressed in language, feelings for which words are inadequate. Some music, music for instance which captures the sound of a train in motion or the violence of a thunder storm, is easily understood. It simply imitates the sound of the train or the storm within a musical framework. But worthwhile music transmits a profounder knowledge: it is this music that some people find difficult to understand.

BEETHOVEN ON MUSIC

Beethoven was convinced of the power of music as an area of knowledge. 'Music', he said, 'is a higher revelation than all wisdom and philosophy.' He claimed it was 'an entrance into the higher world of knowledge which comprehends mankind but which mankind cannot comprehend.' He stated also that it was 'the mediator between the intellectual and the sensuous life'.

Music expresses mood and atmosphere - serenity, exuberance, anticipation, triumph, sadness, fury and much else - in a way language cannot. Movie makers claim that music is responsible for 80% of the emotional impact of their work. More important than these definable moods and atmospheres is the power of music to express feelings which can only be expressed, and transmitted, through music itself. Feelings for which there are no words. Listen to, and become familiar with, a Beethoven symphony. It is impossible to turn into words, into 'justified true belief' what you 'know' through the music. And neither is that knowledge constant. A Beethoven symphony does not transmit one feeling, to use Tolstoy's word again, but many feelings and these feelings change each time you hear the music. Great music is alive: it creates indefinable feelings that change as you become increasingly familiar with it and feelings of which you never tire. Learn from Beethoven when you are fifteen and you will still be learning from him when you are fifty, or even one hundred and fifty. Great music, like all great art, is timeless.

Not all music, not all art, is great and timeless. Popular music, as it is called, the music of the charts, is hypnotic, entertaining and temporary. Why is it temporary? Why are our cupboards full of CDs that we once played incessantly and now forget we own? Is this music temporary because its message, its 'feeling' is insubstantial or superficial, or is it temporary because its external symbol, its sound, is quick to captivate and quick to jade? Alan Bloom, a distinguished American political philosopher has this to say about rock music in particular:

> *(it) has one appeal only, a barbaric appeal, to sexual desire not love, not eros, but sexual desire undeveloped and untutored. It acknowledges the first emanations of children's emerging sensuality and addresses them seriously, eliciting them and legitimating them, not as little sprouts that must be carefully tended in order to grow into gorgeous flowers, but as the real thing. Rock gives children, on a silver platter, with all the public authority*

of the entertainment industry, everything their parents used to tell them they had to wait for until they grew up and would understand later.

.... these are the three great lyrical themes (of rock music): sex, hate and a smarmy, hypocritical version of brotherly love ..... . A glance at the videos that project images on the wall of Plato's cave since MTV took it over suffices to prove this .... Nothing noble, sublime, profound, delicate, tasteful or even decent can find a place in such a tableaux. There is room only for the intense, changing, crude and immediate .....

If it does nothing else this tirade confirms the power of music. Professor Bloom feels as passionately about rock music as many baseball fans do about *The Star Spangled Banner* and opera lovers feel about the overture to Mozart's *Marriage of Figaro*.

AESTHETICS

Aesthetics (or esthetics as it is alternatively spelled) is the branch of philosophy which explores the nature of art. Philosophers of aesthetics discuss, amongst other things, the possibility or otherwise of establishing universal cross cultural standards in judging art, and the concept of 'beauty'. They ask themselves such questions as:

Can we determine the merit of a work of art?

Are there criteria we can apply to a work of art so we can objectively judge it? Can we rise above saying 'Well, I like it, so as far as I'm concerned it's good art.'

It is worth attempting to answer these questions in terms of what we already know about the arts as an area of knowledge. As an area of knowledge, the arts are based on two ideas, the 'feeling' of the artists and the 'external symbols' they use to recreate and transmit those feelings.

WHAT IS A MASTERPIECE?
1. A masterpiece moulds a series of deep and complex emotions into a single idea expressive of the artist's own epoch yet with a relationship to the past.
2. A masterpiece must have a human element.
3. A masterpiece must be devoted to the truth.
4. A masterpiece must represent a dramatic situation.
5. A masterpiece must illustrate great themes.

6.   In the presence of the masterpiece we must stand in awe at the complete supremacy of the artist's art.

7.   A masterpiece will be written in the 'language' of the day.

Adapted from Kenneth Clark: What is a Masterpiece?

JUDGING THE EXTERNAL SYMBOLS

When you judge the merit of a work of art, your judgement, it is argued by some philosophers, should be based on its effectiveness as an object in its own right, as art for art's sake.

TECHNIQUE

At its simplest you can judge the object, whether it be a sonnet or a painting or a Grecian urn by the quality of the technique used in its structure. Is the urn finely made? Is the perspective of the painting as it should be? Are the brush strokes intrusive? Are the details of the engraving perfectly executed? Has the novelist structured his narration in such a way to achieve maximum entertainment for the reader? These, as the word 'technique' suggests, are technical questions rather than artistic questions. They determine a 'necessary' condition for art not a 'sufficient' condition. Another necessary condition associated with technique is that the medium is handled in the best possible way and is entirely suited to the purpose of the art. Artists need to be completely in control of the techniques and the media they use, but to produce great art, this control is a necessary, rather than sufficient, condition.

ART OR CRAFT

Mastery of technique and absolute control of the media are also aspects of craft, as distinct from art. There is a fundamental difference between art and craft, although the two words are often used side by side. Art is an entirely original activity: artists create what no one has created before. Artists may use the skills of the craftsman. The craft of the foundry worker may be used to forge three dimensional bronze sculptures but the artistic quality of the finished sculpture is entirely dependent on the artist, not the craftsman. Craft is directly useful and many craft workers have considerable skill, but they are not artists unless they create original works, works reflecting their own emotions and aesthetic sensibility.

INTEGRITY AND UNITY

Another criterion for judging art for art's sake is the 'integrity and unity' of the work. Both of these ideas are a little difficult to understand. A work has 'integrity if one senses the artist is sincere about the feelings being expressed. Is Shakespeare's exploration of Hamlet's tortured mind really convincing? Does the hero of Thomas Mann's *Death in Venice* convince us with his obsession or is Mann merely titillating our imagination? Is some contemporary art merely a hoax, produced by confidence tricksters pandering to the public's insatiable desire for novelty?

The unity of a piece of art is its completeness, the sum of its parts: the technique and the medium and the 'feeling' united in a unique, original, complete creation.

IMPACT

Another criterion is the impact of the piece. Is there a special way in which it reflects the feeling of the artist, which makes a special, powerful impression? Great works of art certainly do this.

Understanding these criteria depends on knowledge-by-acquaintance, the 'kennen' knowledge of German, the knowledge of the connoisseur. Judging art in this way takes us away from aesthetics to the realm of art criticism. Art critics are steeped in knowledge-by-acquaintance. Our papers, journals and magazines are steeped in their writing. They make their readers aware of the techniques, the integrity, the unity, the impact of art, the external symbols. Critics also explore the 'feeling' of the artist but they do so at their own risk: artists chip away at the borders of intellectual and emotional knowledge, critics stay within known territory. When Picasso was told his portrait of Gertrude Stein did not look like her, he replied, "Don't worry, it will". Ibsen's women did not behave like 19th heroines. They do behave like 20th century heroines.

JUDGING THE 'FEELING'

Aesthetics explores many problems but one of the most difficult ones is the nature of the aesthetic experience, the defining of the 'feeling' that is expressed in literature, music and the fine arts and the relationship of this experience to 'truth'. A work of art is a way of organising reality, the internal reality of the artist. If art is to have truth, then this internal reality of the artist is the truth of art. The 'artist', Joseph Conrad writes, 'speaks to our capacity for delight and wonder, to the sense of mystery surrounding our lives: to our sense of pity and beauty and pain'.

What could be more truthful?

ARTISTS ON ART

Oh, doubtless a mediocre man copying nature will never produce a work of art, because he really looks without seeing, and though he may have noted each detail minutely, the result will be flat and without character. But the profession of artist is not meant for the mediocre, and to them the best counsels will never succeed in giving talent. The artist, on the contrary sees; that is to say, his eye, grafted on his heart, reads deeply into the bosom of nature.

Auguste Rodin (1840-1917) Sculptor

To be shaken out of the ruts of ordinary perception, to be shown for a few timeless hours the outer and the inner world, not as they appear to an animal obsessed with words and notions, but as they are apprehended, directly and unconditionally, by Mind at large - this is an experience of inestimable value to everyone.

Aldous Huxley (1894-1963) Novelist and Essayist

Art can amplify man's short time on earth by enabling him to receive from another the whole range of someone else's experience with all their problems, colours and flavours ... the only substitute for experience we have not personally lived through is art or literature. Art can sometimes shorten the dangerous twisted road, man's history.

Alexander Solzhenitsyn (1918-) Writer

When the world ceases to be the scene of our personal hopes and wishes, when we face it as free beings, admiring, asking and observing, then we enter the realm of art and science. If what is seen .... is communicated through forms whose connections are not accessible to the conscious mind, but are recognised intuitively as meaningful, then we are engaged in art.

Albert Einstein (1879-1955) Writer (and scientist)

Plate I: Abstract, Vassily Kandinsky (see page 228)

Plate II: Abstract

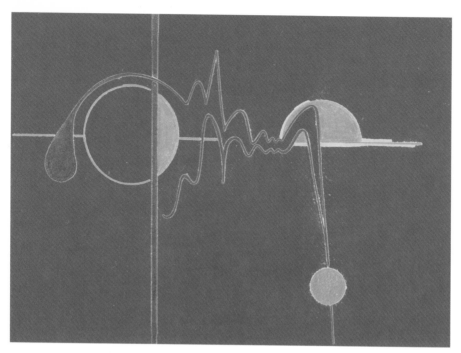

Plate III: Abstract

Plate IV

Plate V

Plate VI

Plate VII

Plate VIII

Works of art are of an infinite solitariness, and nothing is less likely to bring us near to them than criticism. Only love can apprehend and hold them, and can be just towards them.

Rainer Maria Rilke (1875-1926) Poet

Human life is a sad show, undoubtedly: ugly, heavy and complex. Art has no other end, for people of feeling, than to conjure away the burden and the bitterness.

Gustave Flaubert (1821-80) Novelist

When power leads men towards arrogance, poetry reminds him of his limitations. When power narrows the areas of man's concerns, poetry reminds him of the richness and diversity of his existence. When power corrupts, poetry cleanses. For art establishes the basic human truths which must serve as the touchstone of our judgement.

John F. Kennedy (1917-63) Speech writer (and US president)

Shakespeare would have grasped wave functions, Donne would have understood complementarity and relative time. They would have been excited. What richness! They would have plundered this new science for their imagery. And they would have educated their audiences, too. But you 'arts' people, you're not only ignorant of these magnificent things, you're rather proud of knowing nothing.

Ian McEwan (1948-) Novelist

 Now *you have read Chapter 7.5 ...*

consider or undertake the following:

1. Read the comments of artists on art (page 232) and relate them to ideas outlined in Chapter 7.5. Which of these comments do you find most in tune with your own thinking about the arts as an area of knowledge?

2. Re-read the section 'Are the arts a unique area of knowledge ? (page 219 on) and decide to what extent the area of knowledge described matches your own experience.

3. Are we all equally competent judges of the arts? Many people claim that judgements in art are so subjective that personal opinion is all that matters. To what extent is the content of Chapter 7.5 in conflict with this idea?

4. There is no discussion in Chapter 7.5 of the idea that artistic knowledge is culturally bound. Are you able to appreciate and enjoy art, music and literature from other cultures? Think of the answer to this question in terms of your own experience and the art work reproduced in the colour plates.

5. Read D H Lawrence's poem *Snake* (page 223). Is it a masterpiece within the terms of Clark's definition (page 230)?

6. Does Oscar Wilde really think art is quite useless (page 227) or is he bewitching us with words?

7. Apply the principles if Tolstoy's art as an area of knowledge to the pictures reproduced on the colour plates. Determine the feeling or experience that is being evoked and how that feeling is transmitted through the external symbols of the painting. How successful are these pieces of art in terms of your awareness of art as an area of knowledge?

Want to know more?

You may find the following books helpful.

Berger John *Ways of Seeing* BBC and Penguin 1972

Read Herbert *The Meaning of Art* Faber and Faber 1972

Fleming William *Art and Ideas* (8th edition) Harcourt Brace 1990

SECTION TWO
AREAS OF KNOWLEDGE

ETHICS

7.6

Before

you read Chapter 7.6 ...

discuss or undertake the following:

1. Most schools insist that students line up in an orderly way when they use the school cafeteria. Why do they do this? Is it a sensible rule? Is it simply practical or is there a moral reason why they do this?

2. One of the most frequently heard cries in schools is 'It's not fair'. What examples of what you consider 'unfairness' have you encountered in the recent past. Why were these examples 'unfair'? Students often seem obsessed with the idea that things should be 'fair'. Why do you think this? Do you think that as people get older they are more accepting of unfairness?

3. It is frequently reported that 60% of the gross national product of the world's poorest countries goes to the rich countries in interest payments. Is this fair?

4. List five virtues that you, personally, would be proud to be described as having.

5. Would you report a fellow student who was selling drugs at school? What principles underpin your decision?

6. How convinced are you that 'god' is a morally positive force? Why?

7. What historical, literary or contemporary figures do you associate with good? Why? What personal values do you reveal in your choice?

Aristotle - as imagined
by Raphael

7.6   KNOWING RIGHT AND WRONG

Maja, you may recall, 'knows' it is wrong to steal and wrong to kill people. We all probably agree with Maja that stealing, and killing people, are wrong.

How do we know it is wrong to steal and kill? Maja knows through her conscience and her 'moral belief', as you probably do too. But where do her conscience and her moral beliefs come from? How does she know if her actions and thoughts are good or bad, desirable or undesirable, right or wrong? How can she be sure that stealing and killing people are wrong? In what way can she justify her 'knowing' these actions are wrong? And if she can't justify her 'knowing', other than by the rather vague idea of 'conscience' or 'belief' why shouldn't people be allowed to steal and kill as they wish? If her conscience told her that stealing was fine so long as she didn't get caught and that killing could be justified if it made her happy, would stealing and killing be right?

ETHICS

The branch of philosophy in which you can find answers to these and other similar questions is called *Ethics*. (It is also called *Moral Philosophy* but let us stay with *Ethics*.)

Ethics is a word you are probably familiar with. Some schools have an 'Ethical Code', a set of rules to regulate and control the way the members of the school behave. 'Ethical Code' is sometimes just a euphemism for 'School Rules' but some schools' 'Ethical Codes' do more than simply state the rules which must be followed: they lay down principles on which the rules are based. You are also probably familiar with the word *ethics* in connection with medical practice. 'Medical ethics' are the ethical principles on which doctors base their 'non-medical' judgement on how their patients should be treated.

These ethical principles in schools or medical practices underpin the aims of the services that created them. The main aim of schools is to educate. If the ethical code of a school requires that students do not chew gum in class, it is presumably because the creators of the code believed that chewing gum is bad for the concentration of the learner and the teacher, that somehow chewing interferes with the process of education. This could certainly be interpreted as an ethical issue: the school authorities have a duty to ensure that learning and teaching is as effective as it can be. If the school does not do this it is failing in its responsibility, clearly an ethical issue. Therefore no chewing.

The main aim of doctors is to prevent and cure illness and disease. Doctors' ethical code is underpinned by this aim. Medical ethics guarantee the confidentiality of the doctor's consulting room. This confidentiality encourages the patient to be open and honest, which in turn helps the doctor to diagnose and treat the patient, to prevent and cure illness and disease.

If a set of principles, an ethical code, is useful for defining standards for schools or the medical professions then, it could be argued, a set of clearly stated moral principles would be useful for the conduct of our everyday life. We live and work among people, so why not a code of ethics to guide us through our relationship with ourselves and others? To guarantee we treat each other ethically?

WHEN ARE WE CONSIDERED TO BE MAKING AN ETHICAL DECISION?

Not all our actions and behaviour need to be based on ethical decisions or principles. For instance, if you ask the way to the movie theatre and are told to turn left at the next traffic light, there is no ethical basis involved in your behaviour; you just want to get somewhere. Similarly if you decide to go on vacation in Alaska because you want to avoid crowded beaches, that decision, based on that reason, involves no ethical decision.

For your action to be considered an ethical action it must have the following four characteristics.

1. **You must believe your action is right and be prepared to justify it as such**.
Some apparently 'wrong' behaviour, blowing up the manufacturers of land mines with their own products, for instance, might be argued as ethically right, and believed to be ethically right for good reason, by those who did it.

2. **The interests of someone other than yourself must be involved**
If you were shipwrecked alone a desert island you could do nothing that was ethically wrong because no-one else's interests are involved. Similarly, actions carried out purely for your own self advancement do not count as ethical behaviour. Working hard to pass an examination, is not in itself ethically good, simply self gratifying. If though, you are working hard to please your grandmother, then that could be ethically good.

3. **You must act of your own free will**
If your classmate is selling marijuana at school and you believe her threat that she, or her 'friend' would kill you if you informed the school administration of her activities, your silence would not be considered as unethical. (Although you might think it was).

4. **Your action must be deliberate**.
If you pick up notes from the desk of the student sitting next to you with the intention of depriving her of the notes then your action is unethical. If you accidentally pick them up because you thought they were yours, you still deprive her of the notes, but your action is not deliberate and therefore not to be judged in ethical terms. If your collection of the notes was due to your careless or casual behaviour though, that could have ethical implications.

Most of us are brought up to follow certain ethical rules, to behave in ways which are considered by the society we live in, to be acceptable. Here are some examples of moral rules that different groups of people have followed at some time or another.

> Never take a human life.
> Never cause needless pain or suffering.
> Do not gamble.
> Do not drink alcoholic drinks.
> Do not eat pork.
> Do not steal.
> Never tell a lie.

Each of these rules covers only a certain type of activity. Each rule also tells you what to do but doesn't tell you why you should do it.

What we need, to know right from wrong, is a set of ethical principles, which form the basis for these rules. With such a set of ethical principles we could decide, we could know what is right and wrong, what is good or evil. But where could such a set of ethical principles come from? And what kind of knowledge would they be? Empirical? *A priori*? Logical? Faith based? From the earliest recorded times philosophers and religious thinkers have developed such sets of ethical principles, which are now called *Theories of Conduct*. These Theories of Conduct, for our purposes of understanding how we know ethically, can be divided into four groups:

1. Religious Theories.
2. The Self Interest Theory.
3. The Universal Law Theory.
4. The Utilitarian Theory.

RELIGIOUS THEORIES

Maja, we know, believes there is a god. She 'knows' that when she dies she is going to heaven. She knows this through her faith. She is absolutely convinced there is a benign god who will give her life after death in heaven. She might also be convinced that god has also given her a conscience and a sense of morality, a sense of what is right and wrong, good or evil. Her belief that killing people is wrong is probably based on her belief in god.

DIVINE REVELATION

As you can read in Chapter 4 *Faith*, the major religions of the world have ethical codes or moral laws which set standards of behaviour for their members. These codes are usually revealed through divine revelation; that is directly from god through a 'prophet'. The Ten Commandments were revealed to the tribes of Israel through the prophet Moses. The Sharia, the Islamic code of religious law, is based on the teachings of the Koran and the sayings of the prophet Mohammed. The basic principles on which Christians base their moral behaviour are found in the four gospels of the New Testament. These gospels, describing the life and teachings of Jesus of Nazareth, were written by his followers or 'disciples', who lived and worked with him.

THE TEN COMMANDMENTS

Thou shalt have no other gods before me.

Thou shalt not make unto thee any graven image, or any likeness of anything that is in heaven above, or that is in the earth beneath, or that is in the water under the earth: Thou shalt not bow down thyself to them: for I, the Lord thy God, am a jealous God, visiting the iniquity of the fathers upon the children unto the third and fourth generation of them that hate me; And showing mercy unto them that love me, and keep my commandments.

Thou shalt not take the name of the lord God in vain; for the Lord will not hold him guiltless that taketh his name in vain.

Remember the Sabbath day, to keep it holy. Six days shalt thou labour, and do all thy work. But the seventh day is the Sabbath day of the Lord thy God: in it thou shalt not do any work, thou, not thy son, nor thy daughter, thy manservant, nor thy maid servant, nor thy cattle, nor thy stranger that is within thy gates: For in six days the Lord made heaven and earth, the sea, and all that in them is, and rested the seventh day: wherefore the Lord blessed the Sabbath day and hallowed it.

Honour thy father and thy mother: that thy days may be long upon the land which the Lord thy God giveth thee.

Thou shalt not kill.

Thou shalt not commit adultery.

Thou shalt not steal.

Thou shalt not bear false witness against thy neighbour.

Thou shalt not covet thy neighbour's house. Thou shalt not covet thy neighbour's wife, nor his manservant, nor his maidservant, nor his ox, nor his ass, nor anything that is thy neighbour's.

Some ethical codes based on religion, like the Ten Commandments above, are stated as a set of rules, as a list of *dos* and *don'ts*. Other religious ethical codes are based on the sayings and lives of prophets or holy men and women. For someone who has a strong belief in god, knowing right from wrong is easy. Right is following the rules of god and the prophets. Wrong is when you stray from these rules. If through prophets god is telling you killing is wrong, then killing is wrong. If the prophets tell you to pray three times a day and you pray three times a day, then you are behaving in a right way.

PROBLEMS WITH RELIGIOUS THEORIES OF CONDUCT

Many philosophers (and other people) have difficulties accepting religious ethical codes as guides to ethical behaviour. These problems focus round three questions.

1. Does god command what is ethically right or does god's command make it ethically right?
2. Who can decide, and how can they decide, what the actual ethical code is?
3. Does god actually exist?

Let us look at each of these questions.

QUESTION ONE:
Does god command what is ethically right or does god's command make it ethically right?

This is a question that has intrigued philosophers since Plato first discussed it in *Euthyphro*, one of his earliest Socratic dialogues. Consider the implications for ethics in the first part of the question: does god command what is ethically right? If god commands his followers to follow what is ethically right then what god commands must be independent of god. God has merely identified ethical values that already exist somewhere in the universe and brought them to the attention of followers. God may be the source of the information we have about these values but god has not made them; god has simply brought them to the attention of the followers and told them to adhere to them. One could, therefore, describe these ethical values without involving god at all. God is simply the messenger, not the message.

Now consider the implications of the second part of the question: does god's command make it ethically right? The 'it' there refers to god's commands. It implies quite simply that, what god says is ethically right because god says so. In this case ethical behaviour comes from the arbitrary will of god and obedience to it is obedience to authority. We are taking this ethical code on trust and have no responsibility for it ourselves at all. This reduces all humanity to immature children, unable to decide ethical issues for themselves: just do as you are told, because god told you.

QUESTION TWO:
Who can decide, and how can they decide, what the actual ethical code is?

Any religious ethical code is much more than the simple list of rules it is often reduced to. Jewish religious leaders, for instance, and others who study Jewish religious law, interpret their divinely revealed code in different ways. One of the ten commandments states 'Thou shalt not kill', but are there any circumstances when killing is ethically justifiable? Are there no circumstances in which war, and therefore killing, is justified to end suffering? The 'sacred texts' of the world's religions are handed down to prophets and can, and often are, interpreted in different ways. Some Christians, for instance, believe the creation story in the Bible is literally true, while others regard it as a metaphor compatible with the scientific theory of evolution. Muslims believe that in certain circumstances a 'holy war' is justified to defend their faith, although it is not always clear what these certain circumstances are.

QUESTION THREE:
Does god actually exist?

The controversial question of the existence, or otherwise, of god, has absorbed philosophers and others, for over two thousand years. Philosophers attempting to come to some understanding of the controversy examine the arguments that have been given for and against the existence of god and discuss the implications of these arguments. Some of the more frequently discussed arguments are given in the box below. None of the arguments for the existence of god would pass the tests of justified true belief as defined by Plato. This does not mean that god does not exist, merely that there is no rational evidence for that belief.

For our purposes here, attempting to understand how we know right from wrong, where our shared ethical code comes from, divine revelation leaves much to be desired. Maja's faith led her to her belief in god, but it is not a faith we all share, or are expected to share.

The search for a religious foundation for our ethical code has taken us up an interesting side road. This is not only because any religion based ethical code has no universally acceptable rational basis but also because many people who have no faith at all, no belief in god, clearly show they ethically distinguish right and wrong and act in accordance with that distinction.

DOES GOD EXIST?

For many people god gives meaning and purpose to life. For them god is the source of all good and the creator of the entire universe and all things within it. God, they argue, is deeply concerned about the condition of humanity in general and with the behaviour of individuals. God, they assert, cannot be 'known', perceived or understood, in the way we know other things such as science or mathematics or art. God cannot be seen or heard and there is absolutely no physical proof of god's existence. Knowledge of this existence is, therefore, entirely different from any other kind of knowledge, as you can read in Chapter 4. There are three main 'Arguments' for the existence of god, the *Design* Argument, the *First Cause* Argument and the *Existence* Argument.

THE DESIGN ARGUMENT

This is the most frequently used argument for the existence of god. The universe, it is claimed, is such a wonderful integrated system that it must be designed, it must be master minded, it couldn't just have happened. The design, for instance, of DNA is so complex and so efficient that only a supreme being, god, could have created it. Advocates of the Design Argument claim that everywhere we look in the natural world there is evidence of god's existence. The theoretical physicist, Stephen Hawking[1], is presumably a supporter of this argument as he writes: *If we found the answer to that* (why it is that we and the universe exist) *it would be the ultimate triumph of human reason - for then we would know the mind of God.*

THE FIRST CAUSE ARGUMENT

This argument, as its name suggests, is based on the idea that everything is caused by something that existed, or happened, previously. The cause of this book was to provide a text for a particular course. The course was caused by teachers believing you should be taught certain things. This in turn was caused ... and so on. Everything, it is argued, has a cause: the world exists in the universe through a chain of events which caused it to be created. If we follow the causes back, it is argued, we must eventually find a cause, a first cause that has no cause. That first cause is god.

THE EXISTENCE ARGUMENT

The Existence Argument is the most difficult of the arguments to understand and also the most difficult to accept. Descartes used this argument in his *Fifth Meditation*, although Anselm (1033-1109 AD) was the first religious thinker to develop the idea as part of his search for 'necessary reasons' for the existence of god. Everyone, Descartes argued, has the idea of a perfect being, and this perfect being, must, by definition, be perfect. To be perfect it must exist as existence is part of perfection. Therefore this model of perfection, god, must exist.

---

1. *A Brief History of Time* 1988

THE SELF-INTEREST THEORY

ABOVE ALL, LOOK AFTER YOURSELF

The self-interest theory asserts that the ethical goal of each of us should be the promotion of our own self-interests. These interests include the acquisition of all those things we most desire: wealth, health, security, love, freedom to choose, status, influence, our own version of the good life. We must define and promote our own welfare; make ourselves as happy and fulfilled as we possibly can.

ARISTOTLE, VIRTUE AND HAPPINESS

The most celebrated account of the self-interest theory is to be found in the lecture notes of Aristotle. In these incomplete and condensed notes, Aristotle asserts that the difference between humans and all other living forms is that humans are rational, reasoning beings. The concepts of right and wrong, of virtue and vice are an intrinsic part of human rationality. Aristotle also maintained that, as part of our human rationality, we strive to lead a successful life. We all seek what he calls *eudaimonia*. (Classical scholars say *eudaimonia* is a difficult word to translate. Sometimes it is translated as happiness but it seems to mean more than that, something *like being content with life in a fulfilled and virtuous way*.) Good humans, 'good' in an ethical sense, take pleasure in being virtuous and this virtuousness leads to *eudaimonia*. It is in our own self-interest to rationally cultivate virtues like generosity, bravery, temperance and loyalty because the long term practice of such virtues leads us into a state of *eudaimonia*.

Our concern for ourselves is, of course, a long term concern, our self-interest over our entire lifespan[2]. Our self-interest, for instance, would determine that we work hard when we are young to obtain good qualifications which in the long run will make us happy, fulfilled and, of course rich.

SELF-INTEREST NOT SELFISHNESS

But doesn't this seem rather in conflict with what we have been brought up to believe as our ethical duty? Doesn't it sound as if we are being advised to be selfish, to concentrate on working to our own advantage and being deficient in our consideration for others? Isn't this encouraging us to abandon our responsibilities and indulge ourselves and to exploit others' weaknesses?

Supporters of self-interest ethics argue strongly that self-interest is not selfishness. Concern for others is not only compatible with self-interest, it is basic to it. Concern for others is rational self-interest. To help others is to help oneself. If you lie and steal and treat others with contempt you will soon be rejected by the community in which you live. If you attempt to dominate those around you they will soon resent your company. If you borrow in the cafeteria queue today and don't pay back promptly you won't be able to borrow again tomorrow. Selfish actions backfire: you will be treated by others in the same way as you treat them and that will not be in your self-interest. If you rob banks to obtain money to 'do your own thing' sooner or later you will end up in prison and in the meantime spend a lot of emotional energy worrying about being caught. Being in prison or worrying about being put into in prison are not in your own long term self-interest. People in prison want to get out.

The ancient ethical self-interest theory gains support from twentieth century psychology. Psychologists tell us we can't love others unless we first love ourselves. What value is any affection if it springs from a person, in this case our self, we don't esteem. How lacking in self esteem Groucho Marx must have felt when he said 'I don't want to belong to any club that will accept me as member.'

---

2. *Nichomachean Ethics*

A PSYCHOLOGIST ON SELF-INTEREST

It is one's view of oneself that determines one's view of human nature and one's way of relating to other human beings. The respect and goodwill that persons of high self-esteem tend to feel towards other persons is profoundly egoistic; they feel, in effect, 'Other people are of value because they are the same species as myself'. This is the psychological basis of any emotion of sympathy and any feeling of species solidarity. But this causal relationship cannot be reversed. A person must first value him - or herself - and only then can he value others.

The self-interest ethical theory must, of course, apply to everyone. If I promote my own self-interest but also expect everyone else to promote my interests as well, then I really am selfish and I would soon find myself despised. Being despised would not be in my own self-interest. If we concentrate on promoting our own self-interest we should not only expect every one else to concentrate on promoting their self-interests but we should also approve of them so doing. Even if it is in conflict with our own interests.

Nathaniel Brandon *Honouring Self* quoted in Hospers: *An Introduction to Philosophical Analysis*

CONFLICTS OF SELF-INTEREST

What happens if your self-interest is in direct conflict with someone else's self-interest? Your self-interest, for instance means you must win the school's Othello Award for the best actor of the year. You have a rival whose self-interest also requires that she wins the award. A rational outcome of the conflict, in Aristotle's terms a virtuous outcome of the conflict, would be that you both accept the decision of the judges. A rational, virtuous person seeking his or her own interests wouldn't want to win the award if they didn't deserve it. In the long term your interests are only served by receiving awards you have merited. In practical terms you and your rival have agreed to compete on equal terms to the best of your abilities, displaying the virtue of temperance. Your self-interest is better served by compromise than by determinedly seeking the award.

CAPITALISM

Capitalism appears to show ethical self-interest working at its best. After you have left college with your MBA, you invest your hard-won expertise and your parents' hard-earned money in a new business which manufactures and markets regurgitable chewing gum. Your product sells in vast quantities. You become rich as you planned. You provide employment and profit for many other people and a new product for millions of high school students and others who want to be able to chew gum, swallow it and regurgitate it into their mouths when necessary or desirable. You don't really care about your employees and retailers or about the happiness of the chewers, but your enterprise has improved the lives of many people.

Doesn't that appear to be a perfect example of ethical self interest?

PROBLEMS WITH THE SELF-INTEREST THEORY

There are two fundamental problems with the self-interest theory of ethical conduct and you have probably spotted them for yourself already.

The first one is that some people, however much they may want to, are not able to look after their own self-interest. They may be sick or mentally handicapped or old or feeble. Shouldn't that be our concern?

The second problem is concerned with people who simply do not share the same search for fulfilment that most of us have. The theory rests on the assumption that all people seek the same kind of fulfilment in life. But people are different. Some people do not care if society holds them in contempt, they do not hesitate to steal and do not worry about being caught stealing and being sent to prison. Ethical self-interest simply doesn't work for them. They are not prepared to accept that everyone should be treated the same. What works for them works for them and if it doesn't work for you that's your problem.

THE UNIVERSAL LAW THEORY

'DO AS YOU WOULD BE DONE BY'

Universal Law theory asserts that ethical conduct should be based on the principle that you treat everybody as you wish to be treated yourself. If the way you treated people was universally accepted as a law you would happily accept that law to apply to yourself: you would 'do as you would be done by'. The most well known proponent of this theory is the eighteenth century philosopher Immanuel Kant[3], some of whose ideas we have already looked at in connection with *a priori* knowledge (page 178).

IMMANUEL KANT AND THE 'CATEGORICAL IMPERATIVE'

Kant, although himself a devout Christian, argued that there was an entirely rational explanation for ethical behaviour. He saw such behaviour as completely objective, transcending all cultures and applying to all rational human beings and having nothing whatsoever to do with any religious beliefs. He explains this 'supreme principle of morality' which he calls the 'categorical imperative' in his introductory book on the nature of morality. What follows is a very simplified account of his theories.

As physical human beings we are controlled by the physical laws of the universe, those laws which natural scientists explore and define. If we act out of instinct, adhering to these physical laws, even if the instinct is positive as it is when we love, this act is not rational. Such instinctive, non-rational action is neither good nor bad, neither right nor wrong.

Kant agreed with Aristotle that we are also controlled by moral laws which our reason imposes on us. We are, because we are capable of reason, aware of our ethical responsibilities, our moral duties to each other and to ourselves. These ethical responsibilities come from our ability as humans to reason, to be rational. When we act, aware of our duty, with rational intention, in a good way, doing what our reason rather than our instinct, tells us to do, then that action is ethically good. The rational guidance we give ourselves to act out of duty is the 'categorical imperative'.

An imperative is a command, an instruction that something must be done. Categorical here means absolute. A categorical imperative therefore is something that, because we are rational, absolutely must be done. The rational guidance we give ourselves when we act according to the categorical imperative can be summed up in two laws, the Universal Law and the Law of Respecting Others.

THE UNIVERSAL LAW

The Universal Law requires that we act in such a way that our actions could become a universal rule of human conduct. Consider for a moment what this implies: before we, as reasoning beings, decide to do anything about which we are ethically uncertain we should consider what would happen if everyone did what we are about to do. If we are about to lie, steal or kill consider what the world would be like if everyone lied, stole or killed. And, if you do not want others in the world to lie, steal and kill, don't do those things yourself.

---

3. *Foundations of the Metaphysics of Morals* 1795.

If you contemplate any action, say copying your older sister's course work from two years ago, for which she got an A, and submitting it as your own, don't do it unless you are prepared to accept that all students, everywhere, are allowed to do the same thing and pass other people's work off as their own. (You might quibble here and say that your older sister's work is not 'other people's work', but that argument won't hold up. Your sister is definitely another person as far as work is concerned.) If you are prepared to decide that cheating of this kind should become a universal law, then go ahead and copy your sister's work. But before you do so consider the implications. What would be the effect on society in general and education in particular if copying was universally acceptable?

THE LAW OF RESPECTING OTHERS

The second part of Kant's categorical imperative is more specific about how you should treat other people. People, Kant rules, should be respected as rational beings with goals of their own. No-one should use other people simply to attain their own goals.

If I was your English teacher I should not treat you merely as a member of a group I have to teach in order to receive my monthly pay check. I must treat you as a human being, understand your reasons for coming to class, appreciate your aspirations as a fellow human being and respect you as an individual. Equally you must treat me not simply as a resource to get high grades but as a human being in my own right too.

The Law of Respecting Others, if universally applied, insists we respect all the humans we meet in the same way as we respect ourselves and, of course, expect to be treated by others.

Just one problem ... which has already been hinted at: the Universal Law seems to permit obviously unethical acts if the decision is made to accept them as universal laws. 'Let everyone cheat in exams' could be accepted as a moral law by everyone, even though it is obviously quite unethical. But Kant covers this criticism by his Law of Respecting Others. To let everyone cheat is failing to respect them and their legitimate aspirations and goals. It is failing to set a worthwhile standard which is worthy of respect.

THE UTILITARIAN THEORY

THE GREATEST HAPPINESS OF THE GREATEST NUMBER

Both the Self-Interest Theory and the Universal Law Theory focus on the well being of the individual as the basis for ethical theory. The Utilitarian Theory shifts the focus to the well being of everybody. The word *utilitarian* means *useful* and the doctrine of Utilitarianism means that actions are right if they are useful, or for the benefit, of the majority. The nineteenth century Scottish philosopher, social reformer and co-founder of the theory, John Stuart Mill (1806-73, pictured) described the basic doctrine in his book *Utilitarianism*[4].

> *The happiness which forms the utilitarian standard of what is right conduct is not the agent's own happiness, but that of all concerned .... As the means of making the nearest approach to this ideal, utility would enjoin, first, that laws and social arrangements should place the happiness, or, the interest, of every individual, as nearly as possible in harmony with the interest of the whole; and secondly, that education and opinion ... establish in the mind of every individual an indissoluble association between his own happiness and the good of the whole.*

---

4. *Utilitarianism* 1863

The Utilitarian Theory clearly states your happiness is only one happiness among many and that you should not aim at just promoting your own happiness but at promoting the happiness of everyone else too. In fact this theory suggests that if you could do something which will make many people happy but will make you unhappy, then you should do it, because the happiness of the greatest number is the goal of the utilitarian. If happiness is good, then it is good no matter who has it.

You should, as a utilitarian calculate the happiness and unhappiness created by what you are about to do, counting happiness as plus and unhappiness as a minus, and then do what will produce the greatest plus figure. Imagine you are one of those people who find it impossible to be punctual for anything. Your consistent late arrival in class makes your teacher annoyed. Her annoyance unsettles the otherwise positive learning atmosphere of the class and affects the happiness or otherwise of all your classmates. Your punctual arrival, on the other hand, relaxes the teacher and thus the class is relaxed and learning takes place in a pleasant atmosphere. There doesn't seem to be much doubt here that your unhappiness at being punctual is more than balanced by your colleagues' happiness when you get there on time. Therefore your moral responsibility is to get there on time. (There may be other arguments why you should get there on time, too, but perhaps you can sort them out with your counsellor.)

The Utilitarian Theory sounds simple but of course it isn't always as simple to practise as it might seem. How can you measure happiness? Jeremy Bentham, an early utilitarian, believed that happiness was simply a blissful state of mind. He even went so far as to calculate the intensity of pleasure for different actions. If all we are expecting from a moral theory is that it maximises happiness then we should all start taking Prozac and smile our way through the rest of our lives.

John Stuart Mill found Bentham's calculation idea rather unsatisfactory. He suggested that there were higher pleasures and lower pleasures, with higher pleasures being more intellectual than lower pleasures. He claimed he would, for instance, rather be an unhappy Socrates than a happy fool, which sounds as if he is justifying his own value system.

Problems of measuring happiness apart, there are other practical problems. We can't always predict what the outcomes of our actions will be; therefore even attempting to assess the greatest happiness is difficult. If parents are extremely permissive and let children do what they want, both the children and the parents might be happy. But later, when everyone treats the children like the spoiled brats they are, they will be extremely unhappy. And should you give up going to college to pay your grandmother's hospital expenses? Is your education likely to produce more happiness than your grandmother's medical treatment?

Utilitarianism, it is often argued, is a public, not a personal ethical code. It seems more applicable to governments or organisations that have more power and influence than private citizens.

247

So much for conventional Theories of Conduct. Here are three other ideas, from distinguished scholars, that you might like to consider before you decide for yourself what ethics is all about:

1. Ethics as a law of human nature.
2. A contemporary view that, metaphorically we will all sink if we don't co-operate.
3. And finally, that ethics is a scientifically based Theory of Conduct.

1.   IS ETHICS A LAW OF HUMAN NATURE?

Are ethics instinctive? C.S. Lewis[5] certainly thought so and puts forth his argument strongly. Here is what he has to say.

Everyone has heard people quarrelling. Sometimes it sounds funny and sometimes it sounds merely unpleasant; but however it sounds, I believe we can learn something very important from listening to the kinds of things they say. They say things like this:

> How'd you like it if they did the same to you?
> That's my seat, I was there first.
> Leave him alone. He isn't doing any harm.
> Why should you shove in first?
> Give me a bit of your orange. I gave you a bit of mine.
> Come, on, you promised.

People say things like that every day, educated people as well as uneducated, and children as well as grown-ups. Now what interests me about all these remarks is that the person who makes them is not merely saying that the other person's behaviour does not happen to please. He or she is appealing to some kind of standard of behaviour which the other person is expected to know about. And the other person very seldom replies 'To hell with your standard'. Nearly always they try to make out that what has been done does not really go against the standard, or that there is some special excuse. They pretend there is some special reason in this particular case why the person who took the seat first should not keep it, or that things were quite different when the first piece of orange was given or that something has turned up which means the promise need not be kept. It looks, in fact, as if both parties had in mind some kind of Law or Rule, of fair play or decent behaviour or morality or whatever you like to call it, about which they really agreed. And they have. If they had not, they might, of course, fight like animals but they could not quarrel in the human sense of the word. Quarrelling means trying to show that the other man is wrong. And there would be no sense in trying to do that unless you had some sense of agreement as to what Right and Wrong are; just as there would be no sense in saying that a footballer had committed a foul unless there was some agreement about the rules of football. Now this Law or Rule about Right and Wrong used to be called the Law of Nature. Nowadays, when we talk of 'laws of nature' we usually mean things like gravitation, or heredity, or the laws of chemistry. But when the older thinkers called the Law of Right and Wrong 'the Law of Nature', they really meant the Law of Human Nature. The idea was that, just as all bodies are governed by the law of gravitation and organisms by biological laws, so the humans also had their law - with this great difference, that a body could not choose whether it obeyed the law of gravitation or not, but a man could choose either to obey the Law of Human Nature or to disobey it.

---

5. In his book *Clue to the Meaning of the Universe.*

We may put this in another way. Every person is at some moment subjected to several sets of laws but there is only one of these that he or she is free to obey. As a body we are subject to gravitation and cannot disobey it; if left unsupported in mid-air, we have no more choice about falling than a stone has. As an organism, we are subjected to various biological laws which we cannot disobey any more than an animal can. That is we cannot disobey those laws which we share with other things; but the law which is peculiar to our human nature, the law we do not share with animals or vegetables or inorganic things, is the one we can disobey if we choose. This law was called the Law of Nature because people thought that everyone knew it by nature and did not need to be taught it. They did not mean, of course, that you might not find an odd individual here and there who did not know it, just as you find a few people who are colour blind or have no ear for a tune. But, taking the race as a whole, they thought the human idea of decent behaviour was obvious to everyone. And I believe they were right. If they were not then all things said about the war were nonsense. What was the sense; in saying the enemy was in the wrong unless Right is a real thing which the Nazis at bottom knew as well as we did and ought to have practised? If they had no notion of what we mean by right, then, though we might still have had to fight them, we could no more have blamed them for the colour of their hair. I know that some people say the idea of a Law of Nature or decent behaviour known to all men is unsound, because different civilisations and different ages have had quite different moralities. But this is not true. There have been differences between their moralities, but these have never amounted to anything like a total difference. If you take the trouble to compare the moral teaching of say, the ancient Egyptians, Babylonians, Hindus, Chinese, Greeks, and Romans, what really will strike you will be how very like they are to each other and to our own. Some of the evidence for this I have put together in the appendix of another book called *The Abolition of Man*; but for our present purposes I need only ask the reader to think what a totally different morality would mean. Think of a country where people were admired for running away in battle, or where a man felt proud of double crossing all the people who had been kindest to him. You might just as well try to imagine a country where two and two make five. People have differed in regard to who they ought to be unselfish to - whether it was only their own family, or their fellow countrymen, or everyone. But they have always agreed that you ought not to put yourself first. Selfishness has never been admired. Men have differed as to whether you should have one wife or four. But they have always agreed that you must not simply have any women you liked.

But the most remarkable thing is this. Whenever you find a person who says he or she does not believe in a real Right or Wrong, you'll find the same person going back on this a moment later. They may break their promise to you, but if you try breaking one to them they will be complaining that it's not fair before you can call Jack Robinson. A nation may say treaties do not matter, but then, next minute, they spoil their case by saying that the particular treaty they want to break was an unfair one. But if treaties do not matter, and if there is no such thing as Right and Wrong - in other words if there is no Law of Nature - what is the difference between a fair treaty and an unfair one? Have they not let the cat out of the bag and shown that, whatever they say, they really know the Law of Nature just like everyone else.

2.   A CONTEMPORARY DEFINITION OF 'THE ETHICAL': CO-OPERATE OR SINK

Contemporary philosophers generally agree that there are no objective moral truths although they do concern themselves with practical ethical problems such as euthanasia, abortion and genetic modification. Moral philosophy, or ethics, is a complicated arena of argument and counter argument, in which philosophers strive to define both what ethics is, and where it comes from.

Here, as almost the last word, is a statement from Mary Warnock,[6] a distinguished practical English moral philosopher.

> The ethical then arises when someone begins to see that he must postpone his immediate wishes for the sake of the good. And 'the good' here embraces both his own goodness, and the goodness of the society of which he is a member. It arises, to lapse into metaphor, when people begin to see that, first their own society, then human beings at large are all in the same boat, and it is a precarious boat that will sink if there is no co-operation among those who are on board. Thus arises a willingness to be generous, to share, and to restrain one's natural wishes when their fulfilment would damage the rest of the boat-load. In a precarious situation, people must assert and share certain values, or perish. It is this realisation it seems to me, which lies at the root of the ethical. This is what opens up the possibility of altruism, as each person thinks for himself, about his own relation to the rest.

3.   A SCIENTIFICALLY BASED THEORY OF CONDUCT?

The contemporary American scientist and philosopher Edward. O. Wilson[7] argues that all forms of knowledge have a fundamental unity. This unity, '*Consilience*', is created by a way-of-knowing, empiricism, which he argues is common to all the disciplines. Ethics is no exception to this rule. Ethics has an empirical underpinning.

In the recent past, he argues, much research has been undertaken into the way the human brain works, into how humans respond mentally, both instinctively and rationally. If we harness the information resulting from this research to what we know about the behaviour of early human settlements, we should be able to understand the origins of our universal ethical code.

Our moral decision making system is part of our evolutionary genetic development. In the earliest hunter-gatherer and agricultural societies, tribes evolved a pragmatic pattern of behaviour which enabled them to survive. A pattern of behaviour they must follow for their own mutual good.

THE BIOLOGICAL BASIS OF ETHICS

The absolute rock bottom of this morality, Wilson argues, is simply the relationship between working together and 'going-it-alone' (although he doesn't use these words). The members of the earliest tribal communities realised that co-operating gave a greater chance of survival, and a more satisfying life, than going-it-alone. The selfish genes of the intelligent individuals therefore guided them to co-operation. It has been proved that certain human behavioural traits are genetically passed on and Wilson suggests that co-operation is one of these traits. Certain people are innately more co-operative than others and these people, obviously, tend to live longer than those who are not co-operative. Because they live longer they produce more offspring. Over thousands of generations these co-operative genes have become dominant. Through genetic evolution humans

---

6. *An Intelligent Person's Guide to Ethics* Duckworth 1998.
7. *The Biological Basis of Morality.* The Atlantic Monthly 1998.

have developed co-operative traits which have encouraged them to act in certain ways. These ways of behaving have been incorporated into their culture as things they 'ought' to do. Their instinct for survival produced a 'theory of conduct' which the tribe perpetuated.

AND RELIGION?

As societies became more settled, as labour was divided up, hierarchies developed and leaders, chiefs and priests, took control of the organisation of the communities. They formalised these 'co-operative' rules to stabilise the society and their place in its hierarchy. Gods began to appear to ensure the continued advantage of the ruling group. For this reason communities develop rites of passage ceremonies, which often become religious ceremonies, to induct the young into the community.

Wilson states quite clearly that he might be wrong.

Saltaire is a Victorian era model village in West Yorkshire, England. The town was built by Titus Salt for the workers in his cotton mill. It is noted for the high quality of its amenities. At a time when most working people lived in squalor, Salt's workers had decent family houses, a school, library etc.. Opinion is divided as to whether Titus was a philanthopist or just an astute businessman.

Saltaire is on the World Heritage List.

Now *you have read Chapter 7.6 …*

consider or undertake the following:

1. Look again at the four characteristics of an ethical, as distinct from a non-ethical, action (page 238). Using this list as a guideline what ethical actions have you taken in the recent past?

2. Which, if any, of the four Theories of Conduct described seem acceptable to you?

3. Read The Law of Human Nature (page 248). Why is it, do you think, that the Law of Human nature doesn't feature prominently in philosophical theories of conduct? How convincing is C. S. Lewis's argument to you?

4. In your opinion is there a common human understanding of morality which transcends regional and national communities? Do people throughout the world share a common set of moral values?

6. How convinced are you by Wilson's *Consilience* theory (page 250)? How justified is he in calling it an 'empirical' theory?

5. From the Introduction to *The Book of Virtues* by William Bennett, 1993.

This book is intended to aid in the time-honored task of the moral education of the young. Moral education – the training of heart and mind towards the good – involves many things. It involves rules and precepts – the dos and don'ts of life with others – as well as explicit instruction, exhortation, and training. Moral education must provide training in good habits. Aristotle wrote that good habits formed at youth make all the difference. And moral education must affirm the central importance of moral example. For children to take morality seriously they must be in the presence of adults who take morality seriously. And with their own eyes they must see adults take morality seriously. Along with precept, habit, and example, there is also need for what we might call moral literacy .... The purpose of this book is to show parents, teachers, students, and children what the virtues look like ....

The ten virtues explored and illustrated in Bennett's book are: Self-Discipline, Compassion, Responsibility, Friendship, Work, Courage, Perseverance, Honesty, Loyalty & Faith.

Are 'precepts, habits and example' the best way to teach children ethics ? Are the ten virtues explored by Bennet virtues would you like your children to have?

6.

Read this paragraph and attempt to answer the question at the end.

Jim finds himself in the central square of a small South American town. Tied up against the wall are a row of Indians, most terrified, a few defiant, in front of them several armed men in uniform. A heavy man in a sweat stained khaki shirt turns out to be the captain in charge, and after a good deal of questioning of Jim which establishes he got there by accident while on a botanical expedition, explains that the Indians are a random group who, after recent acts of protest against the government, are just about to be killed to remind other possible protesters of the advantages of not protesting. However, since Jim is an honoured visitor from another land, the captain is happy to offer him a guest's privilege of killing one of the Indians himself. If Jim accepts, then, as a special mark of the occasion, the other Indians will be let off. Of course, if Jim refuses, then there is no special occasion, and Pedro here will do what he was about to do when Jim arrived and kill them all. Jim, with some desperate recollection of schoolboy fiction, wonders whether if he got hold of a gun, he could hold the captain, Pedro and the rest of the soldiers to threat, but it is quite clear from the set-up that nothing of that kind is going to work: any attempt at that sort of thing will mean that all the Indians will be killed, and himself. The men against the wall, and the other villagers, understand the situation, and are obviously begging him to accept. What should he do?

From *A Critique of Utilitarianism*, in J. J. C. Smart and Bernard Williams, *Utilitarianism for and against* (Cambridge University Press: Cambridge 1973.)

Want to know more?

You may find the following books helpful

Peter Singer (Ed) *Oxford Readers: Ethics* Oxford University Press 1994.

Mary Warnock *An Intelligent Person's Guide to Ethics* George Duckworth & Co.1998.

SECTION THREE

AN INTERNATIONAL AREA OF KNOWLEDGE?

8

CHAPTER CONTENTS

Before *you read Chapter 8 ...*

consider possible responses to these:

1. Are Maja's ways-of-knowing the ways-of-knowing of people all over the world or do people from different cultures have different ways-of-knowing?

2. Is there such a thing as 'international knowledge'? If there is, what is it? If there isn't, why not?

3. Are there any human values which are shared by people everywhere or are values culturally bound?

4. Is there any art of any sort, (painting, drama, music etc.) which you find you cannot appreciate at all?

5. Is it possible to really understand any culture other than the one you were brought up in?

6. What way(s)-of-knowing or areas of knowledge are involved in learning a language?

8.0 AN INTERNATIONAL AREA OF KNOWLEDGE?

The second half of the twentieth century saw the spread of 'international' schools and colleges throughout the world. Most of these institutions were international in the sense that they provided an education for the children of expatriate families. Businesses and governments and aid organisations needed representatives and workers in many countries. The families of these employees needed to be educated: international schools were invented. As these 'international' schools expanded and flourished, each catering for a diverse group of students from all over the world, speaking a variety of mother tongues, an awareness grew that the knowledge transmitted in these schools and colleges should be international too, that there should be an 'international' program of learning. Specifically it was hoped that this international program would prepare the learners for 'global citizenship' in the twenty-first century. Implicit in this idealism was the concept of either an international way-of-knowing or an international area of knowledge.

INTERNATIONAL EDUCATION

'International' as in 'international education' is one of those words which bewitches the intelligence. *The mission of international education* it has been stated[1], *is to respond to the intellectual and emotional needs of the children of the world, bearing in mind the intellectual and cultural mobility not only of the individual, but most of all, of thought.* A rather more pragmatic definition of international education is the education which students receive in a school or college in which they mix with those *from other cultures and in which teachers set an example of being international by their open mindedness and interest in other cultures, and encourage students to consider issues from a variety of cultural perspectives.*

An 'international school' need not necessarily offer an international education of either kind described above. According to the Council of International Schools, the regulatory and advisory body of several hundred international schools throughout the world, a school qualifies as international if it has any of the following:

1. a curriculum in which the culture and educational system of two or more countries is represented;

2. a curriculum of one country, but located in another country, and actively pursuing cultural exchange with its host country;

3. a student body of diverse nationalities and educational aims and curricular offerings which promote and support the purposes of the Council. Most 'international schools' have, in practice, arisen from the needs of expatriate communities.

These school are 'market driven' and their international ideals, should they have any, are sacrificed to the ideals of financial survival. There are, however, a handful of international schools, those sponsored by the United Nations for instance, and the United World Colleges, which were founded for the express purpose of furthering international educational and co-operation.

---

1. R. Belle-Isle *Learning for a New Humanism* International Schools Journal No .1 1986

Seen from Maja's perspective, is the idea of an international way-of-knowing an acceptable idea? Are there any ways in which Maja could claim that her ways-of-knowing are, or are not, international? If Maja were not Maja from central Europe but Maijoo from Canton would her ways-of-knowing be any different?

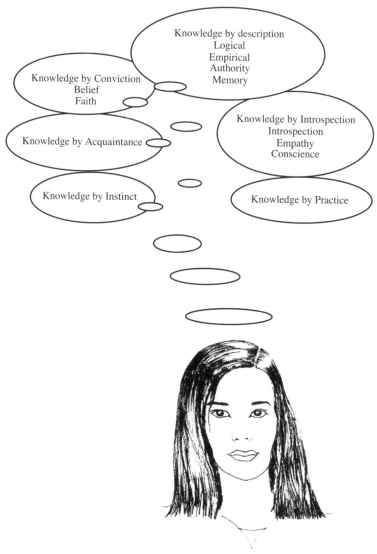

The answer to this last question seems obvious: No, of course they wouldn't. Maja's ways-of knowing are the ways-of-knowing that are shared by all humankind. She has knowledge by description, by conviction, by acquaintance, by introspection, by practice and by instinct. The kinds of knowledge Maijoo has are the same kinds of knowledge that Maja has. But clearly some of the actual knowledge, (as distinct from way-of-knowing) is knowledge which they both have in common. But there are also many things that Maja knows that Maijoo does not know and there are many things that Maijoo knows that Maja does not. What knowledge should be selected as 'international' knowledge? What knowledge will best prepare Maja and/or Maijoo for global citizenship? Maja's knowledge or Maijoo's knowledge? Or does neither set of knowledge qualify as international knowledge?

It seems beyond dispute to include as international knowledge that knowledge which Maja and Maijoo have in common. Natural science is the same in Canton as it is in Croatia. The research focus of the scientists may be different, but apples fall from trees and steam raises saucepan lids in exactly the same way in both places. Mathematical knowledge is also the same everywhere throughout the world: wherever you happen to be, in Alaska or Samoa, in Tokyo or New York, six lots of three children make eighteen children and the square root of sixteen is (±) four. Natural science and mathematics are both, intrinsically, international. Ways of measuring in natural science may vary, inches, for instance, might be replaced by centimetres. And ways of calculating in mathematics may also vary. Maijoo may be more comfortable with an abacus than with paper and pencil, but both Maijoo and Maja explore the same mathematical concepts.

JUSTIFIED TRUE BELIEF AS INTERNATIONAL KNOWLEDGE?

Natural science and mathematics are the areas of knowledge that Plato thoroughly approved of. Is Plato's Justified True Belief then the knowledge that is most clearly and indisputably 'international'? Central to Plato's idea is, of course, truth. Truth, with its three necessary characteristics of being public, independent and eternal is not in itself a way-of-knowing. But what is publicly, independently and eternally true is as publicly, independently and eternally true in Canton as in Croatia, or indeed in any part of the world whose name begins with C or any other letter of the Roman alphabet or any letter in any other alphabet. Is Plato's Justified True Belief then the test by which international knowledge should stand or fall?

The human sciences and history each have unique and distinct ways-of-knowing and both involve, to some extent, something that would have raised Plato's eyebrows, if not his ire: human values.

HUMAN VALUES

The human sciences, the study of human behaviour, are inevitably influenced by the *values* of the scholars who create the knowledge. Similarly History is determined to a considerable extent by the historian's selection of material, a selection influenced by the *values* of the selector.

Now, is it possible that Maijoo's values are fundamentally different from Maja's values? And furthermore that the values of social scientists and historians in Canton are fundamentally different from the values of social scientists and historians in Croatia? Are human values, those values that Plato was so wary of, different in different parts of the world? This last question seems to be one of the questions at the heart of the search for a definition of international knowledge. Can there be an agreed body of international knowledge if the body of knowledge is based, however slightly, on human values.

A CORE OF HUMAN VALUES

For me the answer is quite clear. There is a core of human values, not by all means all human values, but a core, that, and here I make a clear judgmental statement, ought to be held in common all over the world at the beginning of the twenty-first century. International knowledge can go beyond the hard platonic standards of Justified True Belief. It can, indeed it must, accept knowledge based on these core human values. And what are these core values, I can almost hear you asking. Where can I find these values that transcend all cultures and national boundaries and that we all ought to hold? You can probably instantly list a selection of the most obvious of these yourself:

- a respect for truth (we have already mentioned);

- respect for the rights of others;

- respect for the individual in society;

- mutual responsibility for one's fellow humans;

These core values are not always adhered to in our twenty-first century. But that does not mean they ought not to be. If you have any uncertainty about these values read the *United Nations Universal Declaration of Human Rights*. That Declaration, arguably one of humanity's greatest achievements has been validated by all the member nations of the United Nations. If the values which are implicit in that charter are the values which are implicit in the social scientists, historians and artists that create knowledge, then there is a basis for international knowledge in these areas-of-knowledge. The values that underpin that Declaration, values based on the belief that people are innately deserving, are the values of international knowledge, values which any global citizen ought to embrace.

THE UNITED NATIONS UNIVERSAL DECLARATION OF HUMAN RIGHTS

Whereas recognition of the inherent dignity and of the equal and inalienable rights of all members of the human family is the foundation of freedom, justice and peace in the world, Whereas disregard and contempt for human rights have resulted in barbarous acts which have outraged the conscience of mankind, and the advent of a world in which human beings shall enjoy freedom of speech and belief and freedom from fear and want has been proclaimed as the highest aspiration of the common people,

Whereas it is essential, if man is not to be compelled to have recourse as a last resort, to rebellion against tyranny and oppression, that human rights should be protected by the rule of law,

Whereas it is essential to promote the development of friendly relations between nations,

Whereas the peoples of the United Nations have in the Charter reaffirmed their faith in fundamental human rights, in the dignity and worth of the human person and in the equal rights of men and women and have determined to promote social progress and better standards of life in larger freedom,

Whereas member States have pledged themselves to achieve, in co-operation with the United Nations, the promotion of universal respect for and observance of human rights and fundamental freedoms,

Whereas a common understanding of these rights and freedoms is of the greatest importance for the full realisation of this pledge, now, therefore, the General Assembly proclaims the Universal Declaration of Human Rights as a common standard of achievement for all peoples and all nations, to the end that every individual and every organ of society, keeping this declaration constantly in mind, shall strive, by teaching and education to promote respect for these rights and freedoms and by progressive measures, national and international, to secure their universal and effective recognition, both among the peoples of Member States themselves and among peoples of territories under their jurisdiction.

Article 1.   All human beings are born free and equal in dignity and rights. They are endowed with reason and conscience and should act towards one another in a spirit of brotherhood.

Article 2.   Everyone is entitled to all the rights and freedoms set forth in the Declaration, without distinction of and kind, such as race, colour, sex, language, religion, political or other opinion, national or social origin, property, birth or other status.

Furthermore, no distinction shall be made on the basis of the political, jurisdictional or international status of the country or territory to which a person belongs, whether it be independent, trust, non-self-governing or under any other limitations of sovereignty.

Article 3.   Every one has the right to life, liberty and security of person.

Article 4.   No one shall be held in slavery or servitude; slavery and the slave trade shall be prohibited in all their forms.

Article 5.   No one shall be subjected to torture or to cruel, inhuman or degrading treatment or punishment.

Article 6.   Everyone has the right to recognition everywhere as a person before the law.

Article 7.   All are equal before the law and are entitled without any discrimination in violation of this Declaration and against any incitement to such discrimination.

Article 8.   Everyone has the right to an effective remedy by the competent national tribunals for acts violating the fundamental rights granted him by the constitution or by law.

Article 9.   No one shall be subjected to arbitrary arrest, detention or exile.

Article 10.   Everyone is entitled in full equality to a fair and public hearing by an independent and impartial tribunal, in the determination of his rights and obligations and of any criminal charge against him.

Article 11.   (1) Everyone charged with a penal offence has the right to be presumed innocent until proved guilty according to law in a public trial at which he has had all the guarantees necessary for his defence.
(2) No one shall be held guilty of any penal offence on account of any act or omission which did not constitute a penal offence, under national or international law, at the time when it was committed. Nor shall a heavier penalty be imposed than the one that was applicable at the time the penal offence was committed.

Article 12.   No one shall be subjected to arbitrary interference with his privacy, family, home or correspondence, or to attacks upon his honour and reputation. Everyone has the right to the protection of the law against such interference or attacks.

Article 13.   (1) Everyone has the right to freedom of movement and residence within the borders of each State.
(2) Everyone has the right to leave any country, including his own, and to return to his country.

Article 14.   (1) Everyone has the right to seek and to enjoy in other countries asylum from persecution.
(2) This right may not be invoked in the case of persecutions genuinely arising from non-political crimes or from acts contrary to the purposes and principles of the United Nations.

Article 15.   (1) Everyone has the right to a nationality.
(2) No one shall be arbitrarily deprived of his nationality nor denied the right to change his nationality.

Article 16.   (1) Men and women of full age, without any limitation due to race, nationality or religion, have the right to marry and to found a family. They are entitled to equal rights as to marriage, during marriage and at its dissolution.
(2) Marriage shall be entered into only with the free and full consent of the intending spouses.
(3) The family is the natural and fundamental group unit of society and is entitled to protection by society and the State.

Article 17.   (1) Everyone has the right to own property alone as well as in association with others.
(2) No one shall be arbitrarily deprived of his property.

Chapter 8: An Area of International Knowledge?

Article 18.   Everyone has the right to freedom of thought, conscience and religion; this right includes freedom to change his religion or belief, and freedom, either alone or in community with others and in public or private, to manifest his religion or belief in teaching practice, worship and observance.

Article 19.   Everyone has the right to freedom of opinion and expression; this right includes freedom to hold opinions without interference and to seek, receive and impart information and ideas through any media and regardless of frontiers.

Article 20.   (1) Everyone has the right to freedom of peaceful assembly and association.
(2) No one may be compelled to belong to an association.

Article 21.   (1) Everyone has the right to take part in the government of his country, directly or through freely chosen representatives.
(2) Everyone has the right of equal access to public service in his country.
(3) The will of the people shall be the basis of the authority of government; this will shall be expressed in periodic and genuine elections which shall be by universal and equal suffrage and shall be held by secret vote or by equivalent free voting procedures.

Article 22.   Everyone, as a member of society, has the right to social security and is entitled to realisation, through national effort and international cooperation and in accordance with the organisation and resources of each State, of the economic, social and cultural rights indispensable for his dignity and the free development of his personality.

Article 23.   (1) Everyone has the right to work, to free choice of employment, to just and favourable conditions of work and to protection against unemployment.
(2) Everyone, without any discrimination has the right to equal pay for equal work.
(3) Everyone has the right to just and favourable remuneration ensuring for himself and his family an existence worthy of human dignity, and supplemented, if necessary, by other means of social protection.
(4) Everyone has the right to join and to form trade unions for the protection of his interests.

Article 24.   ˋEveryone has the right to rest and leisure, including reasonable limitations on working hours and periodic holidays with pay.

Article 25.   (1) Everyone has the right to a standard of living adequate for the health and well-being of himself and of his family, including food, clothing, and housing and medical care and necessary social services, and the right to security in the event of unemployment, sickness, disability, widowhood, old age or other lack of livelihood in circumstances beyond his control.
(2) Motherhood and childhood are entitled to special care and assistance. All children, whether born in or out of wedlock, shall enjoy the same social protection.

Article 26.   (1) Everyone has the right to education. Education shall be free, at least in the elementary and fundamental stages. Elementary education shall be compulsory. Technical and professional education shall be made generally available and higher education shall be equally accessible to all on the basis of merit.
(2) Education shall be directed to the full development of the human personality and to the strengthening of the respect for human rights and fundamental freedoms. It shall promote understanding, tolerance and friendship among all nations, racial or religious groups, and shall further the activities of the United Nations for the maintenance of peace.
(3) Parents have a prior right to choose the kind of education that shall be given to their children.

Article 27.   (1) Everyone has the right to freely participate in the cultural life of the community to enjoy the arts and to share in scientific advancement and its benefits.

(2) Everyone has the right to the protection of the moral and material interests resulting from any scientific, literary or artistic production of which he is author.

Article 28. Everyone is entitled to a social and international order in which the rights and freedoms set forth in this Declaration can be fully realised.

Article 29. (1) Everyone has duties to the community in which alone the free and full development of his personality is possible.

(2) In the exercise of his rights and freedoms, everyone shall be subject only to such limitations as are determined by law solely for the purpose of securing due recognition and respect for the rights and freedoms of others and of meeting the just requirements of morality, public order and the general welfare in a democratic society.

(3) These rights and freedoms may in no case be exercised contrary to the purposes and principles of the United Nations.

Article 30. Nothing in this declaration may be interpreted as implying any State, group or person any right to engage in any activity or to perform any act aimed at the destruction of any of the rights and freedoms set forth therein.

Adopted by the UN General Assembly December 1948

INTERNATIONAL KNOWLEDGE: A DEFINITION

International knowledge then, if such a thing can be said to exist, has at least two components. Firstly it is that knowledge which transcends all national and regional barriers; the knowledge of science and mathematics. Secondly it is that knowledge which is underpinned by a core of human values which are accepted globally as desirable.

But there is nothing intrinsically 'international' about knowledge so defined. Most national educational systems would claim to be delivering this kind of knowledge. Teachers in England, encouraging their students to explore and understand the societal changes created by the Industrial Revolution in nineteenth century Britain could claim, with justification, that, according to the definition above, what they are transmitting is international knowledge. Teachers in Guatemala explaining the causes and effects of the Revolution there between 1944 and 1954 and teachers in China encouraging their students to understand the causes and effects of Mao Tse-Tung's Great Proletariat Revolution of 1965, could also claim they too are transmitting knowledge that is 'international' within this definition.

THE ARTS

The idea of a shared and universal core of human values is supported by the area of knowledge not yet mentioned in the context of international knowledge: the arts. Worthwhile art, whether it be visual, literary, or musical explores and explains universal human experiences, not only intellectually but also emotionally. Good art is international: galleries and museums and monuments throughout the world are testimony to this. Appreciative humans spend much time, energy and money to see the glories of Aztec gold, imperial Chinese architecture and to hear aboriginal music from Australia. The novels of Chinua Achebe are translated into many languages. The plays of Shakespeare are performed nightly in most capital cities of the world. These works of art explore, and at times extol, the values that the citizens of the world share; that is why they are esteemed. That is why they are gazed at, listened to and read.

INTERNATIONALISM

What those international schools are seeking, when they develop a program for global citizenship, is not 'international' knowledge' but 'internationalism'. Internationalism, in general terms, is the ideal of a 'community of common and universal interests among nations'. Internationalism then, in educational terms, should enable students to understand what these common and universal interests among nations really are. To do this an educational program must:

1. first introduce students to a range of human cultural diversity; then
2. teach them to evaluate this diversity and isolate the common and universal interests; and
3. encourage them to modify their own behaviour so that they become part of 'a community of common and universal interests among nations'.

What this means in practise is that, firstly, students should become aware of the diversity of human cultures, with their different practices, customs, languages, ways of living, sense of identity and values. A deliberate intercultural awareness must be taught: students need to be introduced to cultures other than their own. All cultural behaviour is underpinned by a system of values and beliefs. These values and beliefs are shaped by the historical, geographical, and economic circumstances of the culture and can therefore be understood through the areas of knowledge we have called human science and history, and the arts. These areas of knowledge, used to promote intercultural awareness, are the vehicle for internationalism. Thus internationalism would have the English, the Guatemalans and the Chinese looking at all three of their revolutions and examining the diverse range of cultural values that these revolutions demonstrate, evaluating them and 'isolating their common and universal human interests'.

WHAT IS A CULTURE?

A culture is a 'way of life': the customs, civilisation, achievement and of course values, of a particular group of people at a particular time. When we refer to ancient Egyptian culture we mean 'the way of life' of the ancient Egyptians. In a related way 'culture' is the way of life of a contemporary society which blends the traditional with the contemporary as in 'Scottish culture'.

Many international schools, rather ironically if they are promoting global citizenship, encourage students to 'celebrate' their own cultures by marking national days with assemblies and having national costume days and bring-your-own-food festivals. These fun activities in themselves do little to promote intercultural understanding but they do indicate the existence of cultures which need to be transcended to produce 'global citizens'. Perhaps more importantly they indicate that global citizens need not lose their own national identity.

It may help to understand the ideas of both internationalism and of intercultural awareness through the definitions of kinds of culture given by the anthropologist Margaret Mead. She divides cultures into three broad groups.

The *Traditional* Culture is closed, rooted in the past, static and controlled by elders.

The *Transitional* Culture arises and develops when traditional knowledge is inadequate. When it is available, knowledge from other systems is adopted and adapted as necessary.

The *Learning* Culture is an organisation in which voices of diversity are welcomed and respected. Agreements about the central ideas and values of the culture are formed by a pluralistic community and diversity is not a problem to be solved but to be appreciated for its own sake. Using these definitions, education for global citizenship will look at Traditional and Transitional cultures but will itself be a Learning Culture. This Learning Culture will synthesise and integrate the best of the values of many cultures and bring a precision to the often vague concepts of internationalism and global citizenship.

THE INTERNATIONAL BACCALAUREATE MISSION STATEMENT

The IBO curriculum programmes, The Primary Years Programme, The Middle Years Programme and The Diploma Programme are used in many international and non-international schools throughout the world. Here is their mission statement, the ideology that underpins all three programmes.

The International Baccalaureate Organization aims to develop inquiring, knowledgeable and caring young people who help to create a better and more peaceful world through intercultural understanding and respect.

To this end the IBO works with schools, governments and international organizations to develop challenging programmes of international education and rigorous assessment.

These programmes encourage students across the world to become active, compassionate and lifelong learners who understand that other people, with their differences, can also be right. ©IBO

Many of these culturally diverse values and beliefs will be different from the students' own values and beliefs. Some may arouse their respect and admiration and others may not. But internationalism demands a judgement, a standard. To accept all the values and beliefs of all cultures as equally worthwhile is expecting too much. Internationalism, to mean anything, must be prepared to make some value judgements. Much of what passes as international education is international relativism. International relativism accepts that there is no such thing as acceptable or unacceptable values and beliefs; there are values for one culture and values for another, and these values are relative to that culture. If one culture wants to sacrifice babies to appease the gods of the sea, well, that's their business. If another culture wants to circumcise pre-adolescent males or females, that's their business too. But internationalism demands a standard, an evaluation. And that is where we can return to the Universal Declaration of Human Rights, the document that brings together the idea of international knowledge and internationalism. That declaration sets the standard by which other cultures can be evaluated, the standard by which we can 'isolate the common and universal interests of cultures'.

Having evaluated these, potential global citizens can then move on to the third stage of internationalism's program, modifying their own behaviour, by comparing their own values, and the values of their culture, with values from other cultures. If they can allow themselves not only to understand the values of other cultures but also to modify themselves to share these values of others, they then can begin to become global citizens.

In practise what should this intercultural awareness mean? What knowledge will these global citizens have acquired? A comprehensive answer to these questions is impossible, but they will be aware, for instance, of the influence of cultural traditions on social behaviour. They will understand the reasons for political structures which are fundamentally different from their own. They will be interested in the achievements of artists totally unlike the achievements of artists in their own culture. They will be aware of the teachings and beliefs of the world's major religions and the moral codes which these religions promote. And they will be increasingly aware of their own values and any possible biases or prejudices they might have. The following extract from *The Marriage of East and West* gives an interesting perspective on this idea.

THE MARRIAGE OF EAST AND WEST

When the mind in meditation goes beyond images and concepts, beyond reason and will to the ultimate ground of its consciousness, it experiences in this timeless and spaceless unity of Being, and this is expressed in the 'great sayings' of the Upanishads: "I am Brahman", 'Thou Art That'. The Ultimate is expressed in the depths of the soul, in the substance or Centre of its consciousness, as its own Ground or Source, as its very Being or Self (Atman).

This experience of God is summed up in the word saccidananda. God, or Ultimate Reality, is experienced as absolute being (sac), known in pure consciousness (cit), communicating absolute bliss (ananda). This was the experience of the seers of the Upanishads as it has been that of Innumerable holy men in India ever since. It is an experience of transcendence, which gives an intuitive insight into Reality.

It is this knowledge which Western man has to learn to acquire. All alike have to discover this other dimension of human consciousness, this feminine intuitive awareness, in which the rational mind is no longer the master, but has to submit itself to a higher law of its own being and transcend its limitations. This is what the West has to learn from the East and the East has to relearn, if it is not to lose its own soul.

There are signs already that this new consciousness is beginning to dawn as the West comes into contact with the East. The age of scientific materialism, which dominated the nineteenth century, is passing and a new age of spiritual wisdom is coming to birth. Western science itself has prepared the way for this. The 'scientific' image of the world which prevailed from the time of Socrates as an objective reality extended in time and space, which could be observed objectively by a detached human observer, has collapsed under the impact of science itself. The Newtonian universe of solid bodies moving in absolute space has given way to the view of relativity and quantum physics. 'In modern Physics,' it has been said, 'the universe is experienced as a dynamic inseparable whole, which always includes the observer in an essential way. It is not only that science no longer recognises a world of separate bodies moving in an objective space and time, but rather a complicated web of relationships between the various parts of a united whole. It goes far beyond this and recognises that the human consciousness is essentially involved in the object which it observes.

'Natural Science,' says Heisenberg, does not simply describe and explain nature; it is part of the interplay between nature and ourselves. In other words, science does not give knowledge of reality as such, but of reality reflected through the human consciousness. This, as the author of *The Tao of Physics* observes, brings Western science very near to the traditional Eastern view of reality. There is no objective world outside us as opposed to a subjective world within. There is one Reality, which manifests itself objectively outside us and subjectively within, but which itself is beyond the distinction of subject and object, and is known when the human mind transcends both sense (by which we perceive the 'outside' world) and reason (by which we perceive the mental world of science and philosophy) and discovers the Reality itself, which is both being and consciousness in an indivisible unity.

From Bede Griffith: *The Marriage of East and West* 1985

LEARNING A LANGUAGE = LEARNING A CULTURE?

Within the context of internationalism and intercultural awareness, it is often claimed that knowledge of a foreign language 'promotes understanding, tolerance and respect for the culture identity, rights and values of others'. For this reason internationalists give priority to language learning.

There are certainly many sound reasons why languages should be learned but this one should be approached with some caution. 'Understanding, tolerance and respect' are not the inevitable consequences of having command of another language. Knowledge of a language may actually give a false sense of intercultural awareness as the following statement shows. This writer is describing the discomfort many Japanese feel about non-native speakers who are fluent in Japanese.

> .... *speaking Japanese, or any foreign language to an extent, with a non-native communication style can constitute the sociolinguistic equivalent of a bull in a china shop. For example, a group of non-Japanese went into a no-frills restaurant that was busy and asked that tables be put together for their party. The reply was that they do not do this, but women insisted on it in Japanese, which hardly any native speaker would do in that situation. Staff members acceded to the request, but the cross cultural damage was done.*[2]

Knowing the language is one thing. Knowing how to use it with 'cultural communication style' is another.

Many speakers do combine the two skills, but, just because a person can speak a language, one must not presume that same person has an understanding of the culture.

Certainly language fluency can promote a measure of understanding and appreciation of another culture, but it neither guarantees it nor is essential to it. Many people appreciate and understand cultures other than their own without speaking the language of the culture. The culture of ancient Greeks, for instance, is appreciated by many people who read about it in contemporary scholarly works, visit ancient Greek archaeological sites and enjoy the poetry of Homer, and the philosophy of Plato and Socrates in translation. Of course it could be said, and with force, that if these same people read the texts in the original their understanding and appreciation would be greater. But an understanding of a culture is not dependent on knowing the language of the culture.

Which is just as well for our potential global citizens. Accepting that there is a limit to how many languages one has time to learn, which languages should they learn? It is most unusual to maintain proficiency in more than two or three languages at a time, and most students are able, for practical reasons, to learn a maximum of two foreign languages. Unless one is omnilingual, knowing all languages, any intercultural awareness, if it is dependent on language, will be limited to three cultures. So which languages should be taught in an international school? Which cultures are to be selected as having their door opened through language?

---

2. S.McCarty *Language as a Window into Japanese Culture* in Webgeist 1997.

HOW MANY LANGUAGES ARE THERE AND HOW MANY CAN YOU LEARN?

The Cambridge Encyclopaedia of Language lists almost 1 000 living languages with more than 10 000 speakers. The standard scholarly work on the world's languages, Voegelin and Voegelin's Classification and Index of the World's Languages (1977) lists 20 000 languages or distinct dialects of a language and groups them into approximately 4 500 living languages. 138 of these languages are spoken by more than 100 000 people.

If these 138 were the only languages in the world, it is possible, just possible, to be omnilingual. The 19th century Englishman John Bowring was able to speak 100 languages and read another 100. One of the Vatican's 19th century librarians, Cardinal Guiseppe Mezzofanti, spoke 50 languages and understood a further 20.

OTHER REASONS FOR LEARNING A FOREIGN LANGUAGE

Many reasons have been forwarded for learning foreign languages and certainly much time and energy and money is invested in the teaching and learning of them. Much of this learning is for entirely practical reasons. A French diplomat posted to Tokyo needs to understand and speak Japanese in order to represent his country in Japan. A Russian family emigrating to the USA needs to learn English in order to obtain work and flourish economically.

Some language learning is more of an intellectual exercise: students in high schools across the world are taught a foreign language as part of the ideal of education. Learning a language, it is often claimed, disciplines the mind and is good intellectual training.

Other reasons for learning foreign languages have been given: in Europe for instance it is seen by some as a sign of responsible European citizenship to be able to communicate in several languages; it is essential for mutual understanding and co-operation between world nations; it prepares children for a changing society; it presents greater opportunities for work; it helps understanding and appreciation of one's mother tongue.

For English mother tongue speakers the first foreign language should be one that is immediately relevant: the language of the country in which they are living. But this is not for cultural but for practical reasons. The culture can come later, aided and abetted by the language, but not necessarily dependent on it. If the language of the country is already English then arguably the foreign language learned should be one of the great languages of the world, 'great' in the sense of usage: Chinese is spoken in one form or another by 1 000 million people, Hindi by 700 million.

If the language spoken is not English then there can be no choice. English is spoken by an estimated 1 400 million people throughout the world. If we can't all be omnilingual then in practice we can all have one language in common and in practice that language is English. Not everyone speaks only English of course, but English is the *lingua anglia* of the world, however much that may be resented by some. And, of course, English would be learned for the purpose of making global communication easy, not as a doorway to the culture of England or America or Australia or the Falkland Islands or wherever English is spoken as the mother-tongue. True internationalists are more likely to become aware of a variety of cultures through a common language than through attempting to learn the culture through the language.

LANGUAGE AS AN AREA OF KNOWLEDGE

Maja's mother is Croatian and her father is German. She speaks Serbo-Croat with her mother and German with her father. How does she know how to speak these languages? What kind of knowledge is her knowledge of these two languages? Well, they are not languages she has learned as a young adult or at school. They are languages with which she was acquainted from the moment she was born. Her parents made a deliberate decision to bring her up as bilingual, so she would be comfortable in any of the Serbo-Croat or German speaking areas of Europe. These two languages she learned by acquaintance as we all learn our mother tongue. Maja was lucky; she had a mother tongue and a father tongue.

Because her father's employment was likely to lead to his moving to an English speaking part of the world it was decided that Maja, at the age of five, even though the family lived in Germany, would be enrolled in an International School in which the language of instruction was English. So at five years old Maja began to learn English. She was given some formal instruction in English by the teachers at the school but the language she heard around her all day, the language of her school friends and classmates was English, so within three years, by the time she was eight years old, she could speak English pretty well, and by the time she was thirteen she could pass as a native English speaker. How had she learned to speak English? Again, mostly by acquaintance, with a little formal teaching from time to time. She hadn't really made any special effort to learn it, she was given the right opportunity at the right age and, almost effortlessly, as she had learned Serbo-Croat and German, she became acquainted with English. So, by the time she was thirteen she was genuinely trilingual, fluent and confident of her ability in all three languages.

Then came a problem. Having prepared for the move to an English speaking country her father was moved to Moscow. Maja, still speaking Serbo-Croat with her mother and German with her father, enrolled in an international school in Moscow in which the language of instruction was English. And because the policy of the school was that all students should learn the language of the country in which they lived, she had to learn Russian. The language of her classmates and teachers was English, except when she had Russian lessons. She joined the beginners' class in Russian, confident of her ability in languages and expecting soon to move up to a more advanced course. But learning Russian was difficult. There were all kinds of unfamiliar grammatical rules to understand, even the appearance of the language was different. She instinctively tried to use the patterns of Serbo-Croat, German or English but they didn't always work. She was forced to sit down daily, learn by heart vocabulary and language structures which were quite different from any she was used too. Learning Russian, unlike learning Serbo-Croat, German and English, was difficult.

Maja was no longer becoming acquainted with knowledge, she was having to analyse her previous knowledge of languages, in a way entirely new to her and apply that analysis to learning a new language, knowledge by extension perhaps it could be called, with a strong addition of knowledge by practice. Maja has moved from unconscious acquisition of a language, to conscious acquisition, from unconscious processing to conscious. She now has to think about every sound and mark she makes rather than just spontaneously making them. And because she is older she is more self-conscious of her failure, and more self-critical.

you have read Chapter 8 ...

consider or undertake the following:

1. If you were given the task of establishing a school for the express purpose of educating students to further international co-operation what would be its salient features?

2. Should international knowledge just include knowledge that is value free? Is Justified True Belief an acceptable standard for international knowledge?

3. Look again at the four examples of values we 'ought' to share (page 259). Do you agree we 'ought' to share these values? Are there any values which you think should have sprung to mind as quickly as these?

4. Do you accept that internationalism demands a standard? Should standards be imposed on people for their own good?

5. Read the *Universal Declaration of Human Rights* (page 260 on). Has it stood the test of time? Is there anything you would add to it or subtract from it?

6. How convincing do you find the argument (*The Marriage of East and West*, page 266) that a new age of spiritual wisdom is coming to birth? Is this likely to lead to a new intercultural awareness, a new international way of knowing?

7. Look very carefully at the IBO Mission Statement on page 265. What do you think they mean by 'international education'? Bearing in mind the UN Declaration of Human Rights can you accept that other people, with their differences, can also be right, even when they do not conform to those Rights?

8. Are you convinced we should all learn Chinese? What languages do you think it should be compulsory to learn in your school? Why?

SECTION THREE

ASSESSMENT

9

9.0   ASSESSMENT

The Theory of Knowledge course, and at its completion the submission of an essay and its presentation, are a compulsory part of your Diploma Programme. The Curriculum Guide[1] is clear:

> A student who fails to submit a ToK essay, or who fails to make a presentation, will be awarded N for ToK, will score no points, and will not be awarded a diploma.

The Guide then goes on to give detailed information about the contents and nature of the essay and the presentation.

You are required to write an essay on a title chosen from a list of ten prescribed by the IBO. This essay gives you an opportunity to show your awareness of theoretical ToK concepts and to demonstrate thinking skills. It is assessed by an external examiner. You must also make an oral presentation to your class. This presentation must be about a real practical knowledge issue that concerns you. Both you and your teacher will formally assess the presentation and this assessment, with your teachers mark, will be submitted to the IBO and will count towards your final grade. The essay is marked out of 40, the presentation out of 20.

THE ESSAY AND THE PRESENTATION

Both tasks are designed to give students a chance to show how far they have achieved the course objectives:

Having completed the ToK course students should be able to:

1. analyse critically knowledge claims, their underlying assumptions and their implications
2. generate questions, explanations, conjectures, hypotheses, alternative ideas and possible solutions in response to *knowledge issues* concerning areas of knowledge, ways of knowing and students' own experience as learners
3. demonstrate an understanding of different perspectives *on knowledge issues*
4. draw links and make effective comparisons between different approaches to *knowledge issues* that derive from areas of knowledge, ways of knowing, theoretical positions and cultural values
5. demonstrate an ability to give a personal, self-aware response to a *knowledge issue*
6. formulate and communicate ideas clearly with due regard to accuracy and academic honesty.

The italics are mine. The key phrase when planning, writing and presenting your work is *knowledge issues*. The phrase appears in four of the six objectives. More significantly it appears as a key phrase in the assessment criteria[2] which the examiners have in front of them when they mark the essays and presentations.

The title of the first essay criterion is *Understanding Knowledge Issues*. The second criterion, *Knower's Perspective* begins by asking *To what extent have the knowledge issues relevant to the prescribed title been connected to the student's own experience as a learner?* The title of the third Criterion is *Quality and analysis of knowledge issues*. The fourth criterion is concerned with the organisation and structure of the essay itself. The same emphasis on *knowledge issues* can be seen

---

1. *Theory of Knowledge* International Baccalaureate 2006.
2. ibid.

in the criteria used for assessing the presentation: the first is *Identification of knowledge issues*, the second *Treatment of knowledge issues*, the third is about your perspective on those issues and the fourth criterion poses the question, amongst others, *Did the presentation show how the positions taken on the knowledge issues would have implications in other areas?*

Knowledge issues are at the heart of the formal assessment. So what precisely are they?

KNOWLEDGE ISSUES

Knowledge issues open enquiry into ToK ideas and concepts and the certainties and uncertainties embedded in them. It is the 'open enquiry' which is the key to understanding 'knowledge issues', with 'open' as a verb and not an adjective. Knowledge issues explore the positive aspects of verification and justification of knowing and knowledge as well as the biases and limitations. The word 'issues' encourages a reflective and diverse awareness of knowers and knowing.

Here is an example of knowledge issues opening enquiry. Consider the question *Are the human sciences an improvement on what can be known about human behaviour by studying literature?* The knowledge issues are the nature of knowledge in the two areas of knowing, the human sciences and the arts, and an awareness of the ways of knowing of each area and whether one is an 'improvement' on the other. The wording invites discussion of the knowledge issues involved and an opportunity to discuss language as a way of knowing through an exploration of the implications of using the word 'improvement'.

A more complex example of defining knowledge issues would be in the following:

As an experienced ToK student, what criteria do you use to distinguish between knowledge, opinion and propaganda? The temptation here might well be to define opinion and propaganda negatively in contrast to knowledge but an exploration of the knowledge issues implicit in 'opinion' and 'propaganda' would certainly need to give an awareness of the positive aspects of these two concepts, particularly in the context of, say, scientific opinion and government propaganda in the implementation of scientific policies.

The guide is also clear what knowledge issues are not. Concepts and ideas that are exclusively from the point of view of a particular area of knowledge are not knowledge issues. An example of this is sense perception, which is of course a knowledge issue when it serves as an ambiguous way of knowing but it is not a knowledge issue if it is considered solely from the point of view of the psychology or the biology of perception.

THE ESSAY

CRITERIA
As you have already read above, the essay is assessed on four criteria, each criterion being awarded a maximum of ten points.

Full details of the criteria can be found in the Course Guide but here is a summary of them. Each criterion can receive a maximum of 10 marks.

CRITERION A UNDERSTANDING KNOWLEDGE ISSUES

This criterion is concerned with the extent the essay concentrates on the knowledge issues relevant to the title and the depth and breadth of you exploration of these issues. The questions the guide poses to the examiner are :

- Does the essay demonstrate understanding of knowledge issues that are relevant to the prescribed title?

- Does the essay demonstrate an awareness of the connections between knowledge issues, areas of knowledge and ways of knowing?

CRITERION B KNOWER'S PERSPECTIVE

- To what extent have the knowledge issues relevant to the prescribed title been connected to the student's own experience as a learner?

- Does the student show an awareness of his or her own perspective as a knower in relation to other perspectives, such as those that may arise, for example, from academic and philosophical traditions, culture or position in society (gender, age, and so on)?

- Do the examples chosen show an individual approach consciously taken by the student, rather than mere repetition of standard commonplace cases or the impersonal recounting of sources?

CRITERION C QUALITY OF ANALYSIS OF KNOWLEDGE ISSUES

- What is the quality of the inquiry into knowledge issues?
- Are the main points in the essay justified? Are the arguments coherent and compelling?
- Have counterclaims been considered?
- Are the implications and underlying assumptions of the essay's arguments identified?

CRITERION D ORGANISATION OF IDEAS

- Is the essay well organized and relevant to the prescribed title?
- Does the use of language assist the reader's understanding and avoid confusion? Are central terms explained or developed clearly in a way that assists comprehension?
- Note: This task is not a test of 'first language' linguistic skills. No account should be taken of minor errors unless they significantly impede communication.
- When factual information is used or presented, is it accurate and, when necessary, referenced? 'Factual information' includes generalizations.
- If sources have been used, have they been properly referenced in a way that allows them to be traced (Internet references must include the date on which they were accessed)?

Let's look at an essay and see how these criteria can be applied. Here is an essay which was prepared as a part of course work. The essay was written to a prescribed title but was not submitted for examination as it was part of a 'mock' process designed to make students critical of their work and because of this the essay received more teacher and peer assistance than the guidelines allow.

PRESCRIBED TITLE:

Some people say that religious beliefs can neither be justified nor refuted by reason. However, while sometimes this claim is used for rejecting religious beliefs, at other times it is used to conclude that those beliefs are established by faith. To what extent is faith a legitimate basis for knowledge claims, in religion and different Areas of Knowledge?

As a ToK student and a critical thinker, the wording of this question intrigues me. It consists of three statements and a question. The first statement (ignoring the doubtful authority of 'Some people') seems clear enough: *religious beliefs can neither be justified nor refuted by reason.* The second statement: *sometimes this claim is used for rejecting religious beliefs* follows rationally. The third statement *at other times it is used to conclude that these beliefs are established by faith,* does not. The *it* here presumably refers to the first statement, in which there is no mention of faith. The *it* statement claims that religious belief can neither be justified nor refuted by reason, not that religious belief can be justified by faith. (Perhaps I need faith to make the connection).

Logic apart, the wording of the question is intended to initiate a discussion of faith as a Way-of-Knowing. Faith intrigues me even more than the wording of the question. Let me define it (after consulting a variety of sources) *as a system of beliefs based on a personal, spiritual knowledge of divine truth and reality.* We see the results of faith all around us. Mosques and churches mark our landscape. Politicians make decisions based on their faith. Many schools are faith based. Faith based organisations provide front line relief services following disasters. Terrorists die for their faith, and when they die they are buried, as most of us are, in a faith based funeral ceremony. Faith is perhaps at this moment in world history, the most powerful way of knowing. How can something so personal, so non-rational be such an effective force?

I must confess (confess?) I do not have faith. I was brought up as a Christian but never really, even as a small child, believed in god or had faith in his powers. I state this with some misgiving. I see around me many people whose life is made easy by their faith. People whose faith is their reason for living. For them god is the source of all good and the creator of the entire universe and all things within it. God, they know, cannot be understood in the way we understand other things. Faith, for the faithful, needs no justification or explanation. Any attempt to understand it with reason is to misunderstand it as a way of knowing. My misgiving is that I do not have this conviction, and to some extent I envy those who do.

Where does the conviction, this faith, come from? What, in terms of the title question, is its *legitimate basis*? Many philosophers and theologians have attempted to justify their faith intellectually. Perhaps the most famous of Christians to have done this is Henry Newman, a 19th century cardinal of the Roman Catholic Church. Newman, it seems, was driven by increasing awareness of Darwin's Theory of Evolution into a situation in which he felt he had to make faith credible to the intellectual community of which he was part. His main argument is that authentic faith is understood by the whole person, created by self awareness. This self awareness is created by conscience and imagination. If you search your conscience, he claims, you will find god in your heart. And truth about god is 'discerned, rested in and appropriated as a reality by the religious imagination.' [3] I have a good imagination and I have searched and not found.

I found another example of the origins of faith while I was preparing to write this essay; it coincided with the release of the Narnia movie and the subsequent publicity that went with it because of its overt Christian message. As a child C. S. Lewis loved the countryside and also stories, myths and

---

3. In *What is Faith* Anthony Kenny OUP 1992.

legends and fairy tales. These things gave him immense happiness, which he called the Joy, a sense of goodness and contentment. As an adult he kept this Joy which was converted into faith with the aid of his academic colleague at Oxford, Tolkien. If you got such joy from landscape and myth, argued Tolkien, you should understand that all existence is myth and that the Christian myth of Jesus explained it all and brought it together. [4]

Both Newman's and Lewis's faith depend on the acceptance of ideas that are beyond the rational. To dismiss them as non-rational is to judge them by criteria that are not implicit in their nature. But they are also not emotional in the conventional meaning of the word. I can understand the emotion of human suffering, can empathise, for instance with the indignity and suffering of the people in Darfur and the joy of the Brazilian football team when they win the World Cup. Those human emotions I understand because of my human empathy. But faith it seems to me is quite different from empathy. I can empathise with Lewis's 'Joy' in the countryside and legends and myths, but the link with the Jesus myth is beyond my understanding. Faith, as the basis for knowledge in religion requires an understanding and awareness that cannot be defined in conventional ToK ways. Through meditation, revelation and Holy Scriptures faith is created in ways mysterious to both rational thinkers and those sensitive to human emotions. Faith as a way-of-knowing I acknowledge, but do not understand.

How far can it be a basis for knowledge in other Areas of Knowledge?

Natural scientists, with their empirical, logical discipline would, it seems, want little to do with faith as a way-of-knowing. But Stephen Hawking has famously claimed that if and when we understand the universe completely we would understand the mind of god. Hawking is here supporting the intelligent design theory. Contemporary astrophysicist Neil de Grasse Tyson dismisses the intelligent design theory as simply what you resort to when you can't explain the situation in any other way. There is no place for intelligent design in his thinking:

> I don't want the students who could make the next breakthrough in renewable energy
> resources or space travel to have been taught that anything they don't understand, and
> that nobody yet understands, is divinely constructed and therefore beyond their
> intellectual capacity. [5]

Faith might be a powerful motivator for individual scientists who have strong religious convictions, but one would not expect these religious convictions to underpin their empirical and logical discipline.

Mathematics too, it has been argued, has possibilities that go beyond its ruthless logic. Einstein asked *how can it be that mathematics, a product of human thought independent of experience, is so admirably adapted to the objects of reality?* [6] The implication being that math, created by the human mind (created by god?) matches reality (created by god?). Encouraging as it is to see a little soul in mathematicians, one would not want their work to be anything other than independent of faith.

In history and human sciences we come closer to having to understand the nature of faith. Much of human history is the product of faith; great religious movements have dominated human progress

---

4. Adam Gopnik in *The New Yorker* November 21 2005.
5. In *Natural History* Vol 114. no 9 November 2005 published by The Museum of Natural History NY.
6. Quoted in *Ways of Knowing* M. Woolman IBID Press 2000.

(or lack of it). Much human behaviour, the raw material of the human sciences, is, and always has been, affected by faith. Historians and human scientists must understand the nature of faith in order to understand the way their subjects have acted. Egyptologists cannot empathise with the people living in the Nile Delta 5000 years ago unless they understand the concept of faith. Economists in 21st century Japan cannot understand the nature of oil prices unless they are aware of the faith of the people living in the countries from which much oil is exported. But faith is not a way-of-knowing they should bring to their disciplines. If a group of academic historians claimed that god informed them of the politics of the court of Rameses II, I would not be convinced of their scholarship.

That leaves us with the arts and ethics, two areas where faith, as a way-of-knowing, has a more obvious role.

The arts explore the human situation in imaginative, emotional ways. Great painting, great prose, great poetry, uplifts the spirit and gives unique insights. Music gives us profound experiences that we cannot describe in words. Great emotion, the externalisation and communication of the personal faith of the composer, can be heard in such works as Bach's St Mathew Passion, described in *The Oxford Companion to Music* as *emotionally and devotionally the greatest work of its kind ever written*. Obviously faith is a fundamental way of knowing to artists who create such works as the St. Mathew Passion.

The major religions of the world all have ethical codes. Both Jewish and Islamic codes were revealed by divine revelation: the Ten Commandments came to Moses from god, the Sharia, the Islamic code, is based on the word of god as revealed to Mohammed. To accept these codes one must have faith. Faith, as a way-of-knowing, is a fundamental to the ethics of millions of people throughout the world.

So is faith a legitimate basis for knowledge claims, in religion and different Areas of Knowledge?

As a ToK student I am aware of faith as a Way of Knowing and I find it challenging to understand. But there are many people for whom faith is vitally important as a way-of-knowing, bringing meaning and joy to their lives. That faith is beyond my understanding. And that, the faithful might say, is exactly what it is, for the 'love of Christ passeth all knowledge'.[7] To a rationalist like me as a way-of-knowing faith has little to offer, to many others it is clearly, the only important thing on offer.

1603 words.

Now let's look at this essay in the light of the assessment criteria. Consider carefully whether you agree with the assessment comments.

---

7. In *The Bible* Ephesians Ch 3 v 19. Date uncertain.

CRITERION A. UNDERSTANDING KNOWLEDGE ISSUES

This criterion is concerned with the extent the essay concentrates on the knowledge issues relevant to the title and the depth and breadth of your exploration of these issues.

1.   *Does the essay concentrate on knowledge issues relevant to the title?*
To some considerable extent: it defines faith in paragraph 2 and then discusses a key knowledge issue (how can something so non-rational be so effective?) in paragraph 3 before going on in paragraphs 4 and 5 to attempt to further understand the knowledge issue by looking at explanations of the basis of faith.

2.   *Does the essay respond to the question, in all its parts, and stay focussed on the question?*
Clearly it does. The question is *To what extent is faith a legitimate basis for knowledge claims, in religion and different areas of knowledge?* The main thrust of the argument is about faith as a way-of-knowing in religion but the essay also examines the knowledge issue of faith as a basis for knowledge in 'different areas of knowledge' in natural science, mathematics, history and the human sciences and in art and ethics.

3.   *Does the essay show 'depth and breadth of understanding'?* (indicated by awareness of differences within ways-of-knowing and between areas of knowledge and making comparisons between them.)
This particular prescribed title specifically asked for comparison with 'different Areas of Knowledge' and therefore it was easy to cover the depth and breadth of Ways-of-Knowing and Areas of Knowledge. Some titles would not give such an obvious invitation and the criteria would be applied with this in mind. But as a ToK essay writer always look for opportunities to discuss Ways-of-Knowing and Areas of Knowledge within the context of your chosen title.

> ### TO GET HIGH MARKS ON CRITERION A
> Define the knowledge issues
>
> Stay with the question
>
> Show connections with Ways-of-Knowing and Areas of Knowledge

CRITERION B. KNOWER'S PERSPECTIVE

This criterion assesses your personal response, how much you demonstrate your awareness of, and involvement in, the knowledge issues implied in the prescribed title.

1.   *Does this essay connect the knowledge issues to the student's own experience and learning?*
Well, clearly it does. The student's voice and opinions and dilemmas are very evident.

2.   *Does the essay show an awareness of the writer's own cultural and societal position?*
Yes but with a limit. The writer seems culturally bound. There is little discussion of faith, and the knowledge issues connected with it, outside of her own culture. A way of showing your awareness of your own cultural heritage is to put it into perspective with others. Here there is no in-depth mention of non-Christian faith.

3.   *Do the examples show an individual approach rather than impersonal recounting ?*
A reserved 'yes' again. She relates to the Newman and C.S.Lewis examples but the Hawking reference is a bit of a cliché as are the Egyptology and the Bach references. But these are more than counterbalanced by her frank third paragraph and her conclusion.

> **TO GET HIGH MARKS ON CRITERION B**
> Make connections with your own experience and learning
>
> Show an awareness of your own cultural and social perspective
>
> Choose interesting and original and personal examples

CRITERION C. QUALITY OF ANALYSIS OF KNOWLEDGE ISSUES

This criterion concerns itself with the intellectual quality of the essay: how well and how coherent is the writer's thinking about the knowledge issues.

1. *Are the main points in the 'Faith' essay justified?*
This means justified in the terms of the essay, not justified in general terms. You may not agree that her lack of faith (paragraph 3) is justified, but she does justify her lack of faith and her envy of those who have it. She also describes the justification that Newman and Lewis present in a sympathetic way. I find her arguments coherent and compelling but it could be argued that she is unable to make the step to accept the non-rational understanding that is basic to faith as a way-of-knowing and this makes it difficult to assess this criterion.

2. *Does she consider counterclaims?*
Yes, but not with conviction. She is aware of the strength of Faith as a way-of-knowing but the reader senses she is rather dismissive of it.

3. *Are the implications and assumptions of the argument identified?*
Yes. She is quite clearly aware of the non-rational nature of faith as a knowledge issue.

> **TO GET HIGH MARKS ON CRITERION C**
> Make sure your main points are justified
>
> Consider counter claims
>
> Identify the implications and assumptions of your main argument

CRITERION D ORGANISATION OF IDEAS

This is the easiest criterion to understand: it assesses how carefully the essay is written.

1. *Is the essay well organised and relevant to the title?*
Yes, it is. The argument and logic can be clearly seen and the subject matter is always focussed on the title.

2. *Is the language used clear and where necessary are terms explained in ways that can be understood?*
Yes, the essay defines both 'faith' (paragraph 2) and what she considers 'legitimate basis' (paragraph 4) in support of her argument. At no point does the language interfere with the meaning.

3. *Is factual information accurate and referenced?*
The only factual information concerns the origin of the Newman and Lewis 'facts'. Without actually reading the texts referred to you can't be sure that this is a true summary of what they say, but it seems a reasonable assumption that they are accurate. There seem to be no other claims made that require reference acknowledgement.

4. *Are the references traceable?*
They would seem to be so although the place of publication is omitted in all references.

You now know enough about the foundations of knowledge to appreciate the most carefully argued case is weak if its foundations are not sure. Details of referencing procedures are given in the ToK Guide. Basically you are advised to

a.   If in doubt give an authorities' source for the claim
b.   Reference only the works you have consulted
c   Refer to books by author, title, date and place of publication
d.   Refer to websites by the Publisher or URL (http //…) and the date you accessed the page.

5. *Is the essay the right length?*
Your essays must be between 1200 and 1600 words. If your essay fails to conform to his word limit the most you can score on this criterion is 4. The writer of this essay would possibly get away with the extra three words but why risk it?

TO GET HIGH MARKS ON CRITERION D

Plan your essay carefully so its organisation is quite apparent

Write clearly and explain terms which might not be obvious

Ensure factual information is accurate and referenced

Ensure your references are traceable

Write between 1200 and 1600 words

And remember the shorter the essay the less you say

TWO MORE ESSAYS FOR YOU TO ASSESS

To give you an opportunity to examine these criteria again here are two more essays written to prescribed titles. Identify the knowledge issues in them and assess them against the criteria given.

ESSAY 1

If someone says, 'I know this music' how can the claim be evaluated? Compare your answer with the evaluation of claims in Areas of Knowledge other than the arts.

Music is important in my life. I listen to music whenever I can. I can sight read music and play two instruments. I hope to study music at college next year. So I jumped at this question, thinking 'I know lots of music'. And then when I sat down to write this essay I realised that I didn't consciously evaluate any music I played and listened to. I played and listened and I just liked some music more than other music. Despite the importance of music in my life I have never really worked out what I mean when I say 'I know this music'. I just know it.

*So what **do** I mean when I say I 'know' a piece of music? On a very superficial level I mean I simply recognise it. I hear some music playing in an elevator or a store and I have heard it before and I know the melody and the words. And I say to my companion of the moment, 'Oh listen, they're playing Enya's new album'. I know the music: I can recognise* *the melody, I can put a name to it and I can relate to it. (Which isn't such a simple achievement really because most of Enya's albums all sound pretty much the same.) And that claim to 'know' can be evaluated easily. I can check if it is Enya's new album, I can name it (*Amarantine*) and I can describe the mood it helps create (relaxed).*

This trite answer is not worthy of someone who hopes to make a career in music and who has spent at least one hundred hours in the last two years trying to understand what it means to 'know' something and thousands of hours mastering two instruments. For a serious musician claiming to know a piece of so called 'classical' music is a serious business. I have been taught[8] that music can be analysed using six criteria or concepts: melody, harmony, rhythm, texture, form and aesthetic. The first five of these concepts are embedded in the structure of the piece, the composition, the instrumentation, the orchestration. I am tempted to describe these concepts in detail, to take a piece of music I know and love, Ravel's Pavane Pour Une Infant Defunte *for instance, and discuss it in terms of harmony and rhythm etc. I would be then describing it in terms of musical vocabulary and hopefully impressing you with my skill at 'knowing' the piece. But that would not be an evaluation of the claim 'I know that music' that would be proof that I could put forward a reasoned argument, based on intellectual concepts, that I was familiar with the technicalities of the piece. What I really need to concentrate on is the last of the six criteria listed by Dr Seers, music's* aesthetic. *What the aesthetic is about is the thoughts (if there are any) and the feelings communicated by the composer, the emotion(s) the composer has created and transmitted with his or her music. The first five criteria are about how he creates the emotions; aesthetic about understanding and sharing the emotions transmitted by the music. 'Knowing' 'music' is not only about reason, it is also about emotion. It is combining knowledge of the technical elements with an appreciation of the aesthetic and emotional communication intended by the composer.*

Plato had a lot to say about music and none of it suggested he thought it should be evaluated other than by emotion. Music he claimed was the soul's primitive and primary expression. It is not only not reasonable, it is hostile to reason. Even when words are added they are subordinate to, and determined by, the music and the passions it expresses.[9] Music then, put simply, should be evaluated in terms of its emotional impact. Romantic guitar music inspires and reinforces the emotion of the lover, church music exalts the soul of the spiritual, symphonies give aural delight and emotional satisfaction to the concert goer. How can these things be evaluated? With great difficulty *is the* answer. *Emotions can't be measured or even easily assessed. When I listen to Ravel's* Pavane *I hear the emotions that Ravel was transmitting: the sadness, the serenity, the re-assurance despite the sense of loss. How can my claim to know this music, to hear these emotions, be evaluated? Perhaps the only answer possible is that because that is the consensus of the people who know the music and share my emotional experience.*

I also enjoy popular music; in fact I play in a group. I 'know' rock and heavy metal music. And how do I evaluate that? In much the same way I suggest, although I haven't ever made the connection before: through its aesthetic, although the aesthetic is different and restricted. Rock music, young people's music, my generation's music, is raucous, loud, its heavy rhythms pound on the door of the establishment, it communicates anarchy and sexual license - fuck, fuck, fuck it screams at us, rebel, rebel, rebel. And how can this

---

8. By my music teacher Ross Seers.
9. In *The Closing of the American Mind* Allan Bloom. Simon & Schuster 1987.

claim be evaluated? With great difficulty. But look at the popularity of rock and heavy metal with my generation and see how it is progressively abandoned by its fans as they 'mature' and have children of their own. Look at, and listen to the videos on MTV.

In contrast to evaluating the claim I know this music *evaluating the claim* I know this math *seems relatively easy. In statistics, for example I know about averages, about the mean, the median and the mode. I can explain to you what these three terms mean and I can demonstrate to you with examples how to calculate the three kinds of average. It is a simple completely rational process. But that is rather like my proving I know a piece of music by playing it to you. My claim to really know this math must, I suppose, be based on an understanding of the axioms on which the number system is based and then an awareness of the deductive logical processes I use to arrive at the averages, whether it be mean, median or mode. If I could do all that I would then have evaluated the claim in terms which explain the 'I know'. Is that claim as rational as it seems? The* a priori *nature of the axioms might hint at the possibility of a glitch in the logic, but that is really nitpicking. Yes, the evaluation of my claim to know math is dependent on the nature of math itself, reason.*

Evaluating the claim I know this natural science *is not quite so straightforward. It seems that at their most simple scientific facts are arrived at by observation. Data obtained by this observation is then rationally processed by deductive and possibly inductive logic. But the collection and the processing are determined by the imaginative mind of the scientist: what data is collected? How is it collected? What logical tests are involved in the processing of the information? There must be emotional involvement of some degree, far removed as it is from the unbridled emotion of the musical composer. So when I say I know about DNA how can my claim be evaluated? Like playing the piece of music, by calculating for you three different averages, I could simply write an essay explaining, with lots of double helix diagrams, the nature of DNA. But the real claim for a scientist would involve explaining the empirical process that Watson and Crick undertook as they imaginatively wrestled out the DNA secrets. My explanation of the process would describe their reasoning but also their creativity that comes close to emotion. Watson and Crick had to imaginatively project.* What if..? *They had to postulate. Is this so different from Bach's 'What if I ... want to convey my sense of awe ...?'*

To evaluate the claim I know this human science *gives us a further problem. Watson and Crick were working with the hard constant facts of physical reality. Human scientists: economists, psychologist, sociologists work with the inconstant facts of human behaviour, much of which, including the writing of music, is emotional. How can they be sure that any of their findings have 'truth' and how can I evaluate their claims? Their task often is to attempt to measure, to quantify, human responses. A sociologist might attempt to discover why some people go to orchestral concerts and some don't. What the findings might be would depend on the method of his or her research and of course on the sample of people who were the object of the research. Evaluating the claim* I know why people go to orchestral concerts *is fraught with uncertainties. Evaluating the claim* I know this music *is about evaluating the sharing of an emotional experience. Evaluating the claim* I know his math *is about reason. Evaluating the claim* I know why people go to concerts *requires much more subtlety, the blend of emotion and reason, the challenge of producing statistics that mean something, is overwhelming.*

The question in the title of this essay is challenging because it is not about the claim to know something, it is about the evaluation of the claim to know something. How do we know we know? The question is not whether I know something, but how do I know that those who create knowledge, the composers, the university mathematicians, those academics researching into natural and humans scientists, know something. My answer, using the tools of the ToK diagram has been to try to place their practice on a reason-emotion continuum. One thing I do know, emotionally, is that is very difficult to do that. I will go and play my trumpet.

1616 words

ESSAY 2

Sometimes we hear reasoned arguments that oppose a view to which we are emotionally committed, sometimes we hear a passionate plea for a view we have good reason to reject. Bearing this in mind discuss the importance of reason and emotion in distinguishing between belief and knowledge.

The second part of the question seems fairly straightforward. We have to come to some conclusion as to the meaning in this ToK context of belief and knowledge, and then to look at how reason and emotion relate to these two concepts. The obvious conclusion is that reason is going to produce knowledge and belief is based on emotion.

Let's follow that through and see where we get. First we must come to some conclusion about the meaning of those two words knowledge and belief, both of them at the heart of ToK. Immediately of course, we get into problems because we have to use language to define these concepts, and language, as a Way of Knowing can be a little opaque.

Knowledge *seems the simpler of the concepts to define: accept the definition of knowledge as* that which I know with absolute certainty and can convince everybody else of that certainty. *This is not a dictionary or encyclopaedic definition but one I have worked towards in ToK. Knowledge then is hard line: it is the empirical facts of natural science (e.g. the fact that in our solar system the planets orbit our Sun) and the numerical facts of mathematics (a linear equation is one of the form $ax+b=0$ where a and b are numbers and the unknown quantity is x), and the created facts of human science (the price of shares is determined by the supply) and those incontestable facts of history (the date the atomic bomb was dropped on Hiroshima). This knowledge for our purposes is indisputable.*

Belief, *ToK belief, is not quite so simple to define. Of course I can believe anything I want to believe: that I will live for ever, that I will win the lottery, that I will score all eight goals in next Saturday's hockey match. But such beliefs are a little unreasonable. And there we have a form of the word* reason *that we have in the title of the essay. There are levels of belief. Those three beliefs listed above are all unreasonable. I will not live for ever, I will not win the lottery and I will not score all eight goals next time I play hockey. Nobody believes them and neither do I. In ToK terms one must talk of reasonable beliefs, things that could be, but are not, indisputable. I can, and do, believe with reasonable conviction that the short novel* One Day in the Life of Ivan Denisovich *helped in some small way, to bring about the downfall of the Berlin Wall. But my belief is not indisputable. Others could argue that is was possible the novel actually delayed the downfall of the Berlin wall because it encouraged the Soviet government to clamp down further on what they saw as dissidents. But I still believe the novel did help bring about the downfall of the Berlin Wall.*

Is that belief based on emotion? In other words am I convincing myself that knowledge, as defined above, is based on reason and belief springs from emotion? I think not. I think there is a fair amount of reason in my claim but not enough to claim with certainty that it is knowledge. There seem to be many things like this that we can believe without being absolutely certain and it seems reasonable that these beliefs provide acceptable working knowledge, even if that knowledge is not the knowledge of my definition.

Such reasonable beliefs can be calmly argued but the opening statement of the question demands a response to stronger emotions: emotional commitment *and* passionate plea.

My mother works in the World Health Organisation (WHO) and up until a year ago we lived in Geneva, where the WHO has its headquarters and where I attended an International School. I could not help but be aware of the vast amount of money it costs to have WHO HQ in Geneva. The main administrative building is palatial, the cost of rented accommodation for the hundreds of non-Swiss (and Swiss) who work there is astronomical, and Geneva is one of the most expensive cities in the world in which to live. Much of the money spent by WHO, it seemed obvious to me, went into the deep pockets of the Swiss landlords who owned the houses and apartments rented by WHO employees like my mother. The longer I lived in Geneva the more passionately I believed that the vast amounts of money going into maintaining the WHO HQ there were wasted money. Why didn't they just have a small place there, if even that was necessary, and split the organisation up around the world, with some modest offices in Moshi, some in Baku and some in Lima and other places like that. The cost of running the offices would be nothing compared to the immense expenses of the Geneva complex. And that would spread the money out to where it would be really appreciated and the health officials would actually be working where they were most needed, where the health problems of the world are most severe. The more I thought about this the more emotionally (and rationally?) committed I became to the idea. One can become emotionally committed to a rational idea. But whenever I brought up the idea with my mother or her colleagues, I was told, calmly and patiently, that my idea was not sound reasoning: WHO HQ was in Geneva for good reasons; the Geneva Canton government made special tax concessions, Geneva was centrally placed for world communication, people worked well there because the working and living conditions were good, Geneva was secure and comfortable, having all the branches of the organisation working under one roof encouraged efficiency, etc. etc.. The arguments were sound and rational. But I am unconvinced. My emotional commitment, my belief that WHO HQ should fragment and operate directly from the developing world has much greater force for me than any reasoned arguments given by my mother and her colleagues.

My belief that WHO HQ should fragment, and my mother's response to my belief, is an illustration of both sides of the opening statement in the title of this essay. I heard the reasoned argument of my mother in response to my emotional commitment and she heard my passionate plea to fragment and had good reason to reject it. And which of us had knowledge (as defined above) and which of us had belief, the reasonable belief?

I am forced as I write to answer the question to consider my definition of knowledge within the context of the WHO HQ issue as I see it. It is too stringent a definition. Indisputable knowledge in the working world is too severe a standard to be practical. There is a space where knowledge and belief overlap.

Should we be prepared to accept that knowledge and belief overlap in the academic Areas of Knowledge of the TOK course? Are there standards of 'knowing' that should apply to academic disciplines that are too demanding for the workaday world? In the Areas of Knowledge are reason and emotion synonymous with knowledge and belief as the title question implies?

For mathematics there seems to be a clear answer. Accepting their axiomatic basis and applying the rigour of deductive logic math is indisputable despite the odd quirks like Russell's Paradox which gives my ToK teacher such pleasure. Math knowledge is rational and hard line.

In the natural sciences there is similar rationality. It is, on the whole, reliable, precise, objective testable and self correcting. If belief is important it is because scientists put their beliefs up for empirical testing and logical analysis. Beliefs, logical or otherwise may be the cause of research but the research itself must be free of belief. My mother is dedicated to the relief of Aids Victims. She is emotionally involved in finding and implementing care and drugs which will cure or relieve sufferers from this disease. Her work is rational and she would argue it must be. She can't promote programmes which she believes will help Aids victims; she promotes programmes which she, as a scientist, knows will help Aids victims. Her emotional beliefs underpin her motivation; her reason underpins the actions she takes.

The overlapping of reason and emotion, of knowledge and belief, is most clearly seen in the arts. Solzhenitsyn did not claim to be rational when he wrote One Day in The Life of Ivan Denisovich. *Ivan was a character he created out of his imaginative, emotional mind. But Ivan represents a truth: a rational and emotional truth, a depiction of the human spirit under siege but not broken. Solzhenitsyn gave a passionate plea to the world to understand what was happening in the USSR and to those living there, to understand what was happening and to reject it. The four strands of belief and knowledge, emotion and reason are inextricably tangled in this novel. To disentangle them is an interesting mental exercise but doesn't add to the effect of the novel when I read it.*

My conclusion is not that reason produces knowledge and emotion produces belief. In practice (math and science apart) knowledge and belief are so closely intertwined we can't separate them. Our emotions must be involved in our rational decision making: my mother works to relieve suffering because, emotionally, she knows what rationally she wants to do. I want to fragment the WHO HQ because I rationally know what emotionally I believe is important.

1572 words

THE PRESENTATION

In the presentation students explore, before their class, knowledge issues raised by a real life situation which is of interest to them. This interest can be local, national or global. Presentations can be individual or group (maximum 5 students) and in a form chosen by the presenters (lectures, skits, games, interviews etc.) and can use videos, PowerPoint, recordings etc.. The only forbidden method of presentation is an essay read aloud. Each presentation, an integral part of the course, should be regarded as a ToK learning experience for the class as a whole. For this reason teachers can assist students in the choice of the topic and advise them on the method of presentation. Topics may not be repeated in the same teaching group.

The time allowed for each presentation is 10 minutes per person (with a maximum of 30 minutes for group presentations). After the presentation, time should be allocated for class discussion of the knowledge issues. Each presentation has two distinct stages. The first introduces the real life situation and specifies one or more knowledge issues arising from that situation. The second stage explores the nature of those knowledge issue(s) and the presenter's response to them.

PRESENTATION PLANNING DOCUMENT

Each student must complete and submit a single sided A4 Presentation Planning Document (PPD). This PPD must (a) summarise the thinking behind the presentation (b) state the specific knowledge issue(s) explored and (c) outline, in bullet points, the intended treatment of them. This completed PPD is given to the teacher, not the class, immediately before the presentation.

PRESENTATION MARKING FORM

On the reverse of the PPD is a Presentation Marking Form (PMF). Following the presentation students award themselves marks and briefly justify their marks. The teacher awards marks independently. If the teacher's mark is different from the student mark those entered in the teacher mark section of the form are those used in the award of the final grade.

THE PRESENTATION ASSESSMENT CRITERIA

Listed here are the four criteria and the questions, and following each, the question(s) posed to the assessor. Each criterion receives a maximum of 5 marks.

A   Identification of knowledge issue
- *Did the presentation identify a relevant knowledge issue involved, implicit or embedded in a real-life situation?*

B   Treatment of knowledge issues
- *Did the presentation show a good understanding of knowledge issues, in the context of the real-life situation?*

C   Knower's perspective
- *Did the presentation, particularly in the use of arguments and examples, show an individual approach and demonstrate the significance of the topic?*

D   Connections
- *Did the presentation give a balanced account of how the topic could be approached from different perspectives?*
- *Did the presentation show how the positions taken on the knowledge issues would have implications in related areas?*
- *In awarding the higher achievement levels, the emphasis should be more on the quality of the consideration of connections than on the quantity of connections mentioned.*

THREE EXAMPLES

Obviously I can't give examples of a complete oral presentation but I can suggest the kind of subjects suitable for a presentation. (The IBO *Theory of Knowledge* gives further examples of topics for presentation and suggestions as to how they might be treated in the Presentation.)

1.   A local example

Clearly local situations suitable for presentation subjects depend on where you are situated and what is happening in your local community, perhaps even your school. Look in your local newspaper and you will certainly find information about local controversies that lend themselves to interesting presentations: controversies about waste disposal, road bypasses and alterations to roads, dog control, air pollution, hospital closure or expansion, new office block design, the construction of a tramway system, planning permission for supermarkets and so on.

Example One: Local real life situation/contemporary problem: Expanding the school car park

One school I visited recently was considering moving and expanding its car park and the proposals for the new car park, and the considerable expense involved and the loss of playing fields, were the subject of considerable debate by the board of the school, the parents, the administration and faculties and the students.

- Knowledge Issues: How can we know that a new and expanded and costly school car park is really necessary and in the best long term interests of the school? How can we be sure that this is the best use of the land?

- Format: Students interview key players in the decision making process, selecting those with conflicting views and critically analyse their opinions and reproduce them in the form of a skit, or, possibly video real interviews. Alternatives to the proposed car park are examined. The views are then examined in the light of the school mission statement .

- Knowers' (students') point of view: the car park will solve problems in the short term but will not be in the long term interest of the school because of the increased air pollution and the loss of sports facilities.

2.   A national example

Topics for Presentation will depend on the country in which you live and the circumstances of that country at the time you make your presentation. Look in the national press, especially the weekly journals, and you will find lots of inspiration for Presentations. Some that are current topics as I write this in Europe are the arrival of avian flu, the architectural remodelling of St Petersburg's historic centre, the award of a prestigious prize to a controversial film about the rape of women in the Balkans Conflict, and the cause of the rioting in Clichy-sous-Bois last autumn. All of these topics have the potential to make a good Presentation and the knowledge issues are not difficult to define. Pick one you have a real interest in.

Example Two: National real life situation/contemporary problem: The arrival of Avian flu in France.

- Knowledge Issues: How can we assess the risk posed by avian flu and how can we know how best to deal with the arrival of avian flu?

- Format: Start with a video clip of the precautions taken to disinfect the farm where the flu was discovered, followed by the French president stating there is no danger. Then follow this with a PowerPoint presentation summarising newspaper arguments discussing the problem posed and the conflict amongst scientists about the most effective methods to combat the threat posed by the virus.

- Knowers' (students') point of view: Politicians seem to want to minimise the problem and potential danger and the scientists seem uncertain as to whether the vaccination programme will improve things or make them worse. How can we give credibility to either perspective.

3. A global example

Now's your chance to think big. Flick through any 'serious' journal or newspaper and you will be inundated with ideas for a presentation: China's internet censorship, Africa's AIDS crisis, the cocaine trade, illegal immigration, the banning of extreme Muslim groups advocating terrorism, smoking in public places, drug use among athletes as well as the perennials of global warming, genetic modification of crops and the truth of the creation story as it is told in the Bible. Define the knowledge issues and you have a presentation.

Example Three: Global real life situation/contemporary problem: What is the most effective way to make poverty history in sub-Saharan Africa.?

- Knowledge Issues: How can the developed countries of the world ensure their aid is effective in relieving poverty in sub-Saharan Africa?
- Format: OHPs of graphs of amounts of funding for Africa and role-play of western politicians making their speeches. Brief video of the Live Aid Concert, followed by pictures of starvation and poverty with OHP. Role-play of African politician opening a big new World Bank funded hospital. Role-play of farmer aided by micro funding of small local projects.
- Knowers' (students') point of view: Should we take part in a trip to Tanzania with the subsequent fundraising or should we send the price of the airfares to a micro project? Is there any point in sending aid when it seems to have little effect.

Obviously how successful these presentations are will depend on the quality of the research the students undertake and the way they present their findings, but the potential is there if each of the Knowledge Issues are defined. If the presentation is conscientiously undertaken they will score well on A and B **Identification** and **Treatment of the Knowledge Issues** and have plenty of opportunity to argue their own ideas in C **The Knowers Perspective**. There is also plenty of scope for the presenters to consider the questions in D **Connections**. What bulleted details will appear on the PPD will depend on the details of the Presentation. The Knowledge Issues and the Knowers' point of view are clearly stated in the examples above but the 'Format' section will require detail.

TO GET HIGH MARKS FOR YOUR PRESENTATION

Select a real life situation that concerns you and has knowledge issues implicit in it.

Clearly identify the knowledge issues.

Make your understanding of the the knowledge issues clear.

Demonstrate your own awareness of the issues through personal arguments and examples.

Present the issues from more than one perspective.

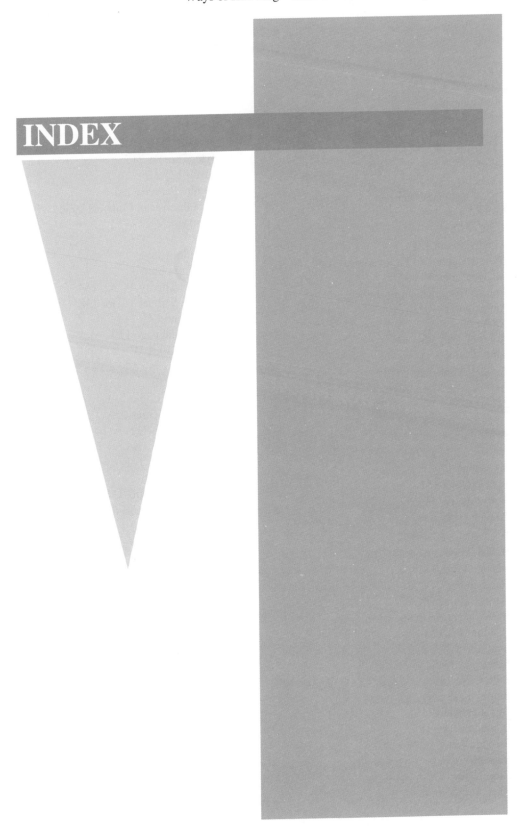

INDEX

Index

Index